The Theory, Practice, and Potential of Regional Development

Canadian regional development today involves multiple actors operating within nested scales from local to national and even international levels. Recent approaches to making sense of this complexity have drawn on concepts such as multi-level governance, relational assets, integration, innovation, and learning regions. These new regionalist concepts have become increasingly global in their formation and application, yet there has been little critical analysis of Canadian regional development policies and programs or the theories and concepts upon which many contemporary regional development strategies are implicitly based.

This volume offers the results of five years of cutting-edge empirical and theoretical analysis of changes in Canadian regional development and the potential of new approaches for improving the well-being of Canadian communities and regions, with an emphasis on rural regions. It situates the Canadian approach within comparative experiences and debates, offering the opportunity for broader lessons to be learnt.

This book will be of interest to policy-makers and practitioners across Canada, and in other jurisdictions where lessons from the Canadian experience may be applicable. At the same time, the volume contributes to and updates regional development theories and concepts that are taught in our universities and colleges, and upon which future research and analysis will build.

Kelly Vodden is Associate Vice-President (Grenfell) Research and Graduate Studies and Professor (Research) with the Environmental Policy Institute at Grenfell Campus, Memorial University, Corner Brook, Canada.

David J.A. Douglas is a Professor Emeritus at the University of Guelph, Canada, and has extensive experience in rural development across most Canadian regions, the EU, and other contexts (e.g., Indonesia, Iran, Ukraine, Pakistan).

Sean Markey is a Professor, and registered professional planner, with the School of Resource and Environmental Management at Simon Fraser University, Canada.

Sarah Minnes is a Research Associate and registered planner, with the School of Environment and Sustainability, University of Saskatchewan, Saskatoon, Canada.

Bill Reimer is a Professor Emeritus at Concordia University in Montréal, Canada. From 1997 to 2008, he directed a Canadian research project on the New Rural Economy which included 13 universities, 35 partners, and 32 rural communities from all parts of Canada.

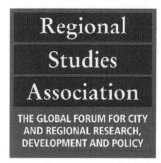

Regions and Cities

Series Editor in Chief
Joan Fitzgerald, *Northeastern University, USA*

Editors
Ron Martin, *University of Cambridge, UK*
Maryann Feldman, *University of North Carolina, USA*
Gernot Grabher, *HafenCity University Hamburg, Germany*
Kieran P. Donaghy, *Cornell University, USA*

In today's globalized, knowledge-driven and networked world, regions and cities have assumed heightened significance as the interconnected nodes of economic, social, and cultural production, and as sites of new modes of economic and territorial governance and policy experimentation. This book series brings together incisive and critically engaged international and interdisciplinary research on this resurgence of regions and cities, and should be of interest to geographers, economists, sociologists, political scientists, and cultural scholars, as well as to policy-makers involved in regional and urban development.

For more information on the Regional Studies Association visit www.regionalstudies.org

There is a **30% discount** available to RSA members on books in the *Regions and Cities* series, and other subject related Taylor and Francis books and e-books including Routledge titles. To order just e-mail Emilia Falcone, Emilia.Falcone@tandf.co.uk, or phone on +44 (0) 20 3377 3369 and declare your RSA membership. You can also visit the series page at www. routledge.com/Regions-and-Cities/book-series/RSA and use the discount code: **RSA0901**

For more information about this series, please visit:
www.routledge.com/Regions-and-Cities/book-series/RSA

The Theory, Practice, and Potential of Regional Development

The Case of Canada

Edited by Kelly Vodden, David J.A. Douglas, Sean Markey, Sarah Minnes, and Bill Reimer

LONDON AND NEW YORK

First published 2019
by Routledge
2 Park Square, Milton Park, Abingdon, Oxon OX14 4RN

and by Routledge
52 Vanderbilt Avenue, New York, NY 10017

First issued in paperback 2020

Routledge is an imprint of the Taylor & Francis Group, an informa business

British Library Cataloguing-in-Publication Data
A catalogue record for this book is available from the British Library.

Library of Congress Cataloging-in-Publication Data
Names: Vodden, Kelly, 1970- editor.
Title: The theory, practice and potential of regional development : the case of Canada / edited by Kelly Vodden [and four others].
Description: Abingdon, Oxon ; New York, NY : Routledge, 2019. | Series: Regions and cities ; 136 | Includes bibliographical references and index.
Identifiers: LCCN 2018053492 |
ISBN 9780815365211 (hardback : alk. paper)
Subjects: LCSH: Regional planning–Canada. | Regionalism–Canada.
Classification: LCC HT395.C3 T43 2019 | DDC 307.1/20971–dc23
LC record available at https://lccn.loc.gov/2018053492

ISBN 13: 978-0-367-67141-9 (pbk)
ISBN 13: 978-0-8153-6521-1 (hbk)

Typeset in Bembo
by Integra Software Services Pvt. Ltd.

Contents

Illustrations

Figures

Maps

Tables

Case studies

Contributors

Joshua Barrett is a Senior Policy Analyst in the Department of Natural Resources within the government of Newfoundland and Labrador, St. John's, Canada. In this current role, he works to shape public policy related to industrial development. His research interests include economic geography, regional development, public policy, democracy, governance, and labour mobility. Joshua serves on the board of various organizations, including his role as a co-optee board member of the Regional Studies Association. Joshua holds a Bachelor of Arts in geography and political science, and a Master of Arts in geography from Memorial University of Newfoundland.

Luc Bisson is a lecturer at the Université du Québec à Rimouski (UQAR), Québec, Canada. Luc holds a doctorate (PhD) in regional development from UQAR, a master's degree (MA) in regional development, and a bachelor's degree in business administration (BAA) from the Université du Québec en Abitibi-Témiscamingue (UQAT). His main research field is governance. For 28 years, he has traveled internationally to conduct more than 150 interviews as part of this research. He has been a lecturer at UQAR in the Department of Geography, where he taught territorial dynamics, and he is now teaching in the Department of Management where he teaches entrepreneurship and social networking.

Sarah-Patricia Breen is a post-doctoral scholar with the Conservation of Change lab at the University of Saskatchewan, Saskatoon, Canada. Sarah holds a PhD in Resource and Environmental Management from Simon Fraser University, a master's in geography from Memorial University, and an BA (honours) in geography from Lakehead University. Her work experience includes the public and private sectors, as well as academia. Her research interests include water management, climate change adaptation, regional resilience, and all things rural. Sarah currently serves as president of the Canadian Rural Revitalization Foundation's board of directors.

Jen Daniels is owner/operator of Radicle Roots, a forest school program connecting kids with nature in St. John's, Canada. Additionally, she coordinates the NL Paint Recycle program with Product Care Association. Emerging from her MA (2014) research – where she investigated the connections between identity, territory, and place-based development in Indigenous communities in central Newfoundland – Jen continues to explore the history and contemporary politics of salmon conservation with Dr. Charles Mather, Memorial University Geography. Throughout her master's and undergraduate degrees at Memorial, she has been involved in projects related to rural and regional planning and natural resource governance.

David J.A. Douglas is a Professor Emeritus at the University of Guelph, Canada, and has extensive experience in rural development across most Canadian regions, the EU, and other contexts (e.g., Indonesia, Iran, Ukraine, Pakistan). As former director of a graduate school he taught community and economic development, regional development policy and planning, strategic planning and management, and planning and development theory. A facilitator, trainer, policy adviser, and researcher, he has authored/edited four books, 21 book chapters, several journal papers, and numerous technical reports. Recent teaching has been in Haida Gwaii, Canada. Current research and publishing encompass rural governance, regionalism and development, and community resilience.

Ryan Gibson is the Libro Professor of Regional Economic Development at the University of Guelph, Canada. Ryan's main research interests focus on rural development, governance, philanthropy and wealth, and public policy. Recent book publications include *Place Peripheral: Place-based Development in Rural, Island, and Remote Communities* (ISER Press, 2015) and *From Black Horses to White Steeds: Building Community Resilience* (Island Studies Press, 2017). Dr. Gibson is the current president of the Canadian Community Economic Development Network and former president of the Canadian Rural Revitalization Foundation.

Heather M. Hall is an Assistant Professor in Economic Development and Innovation in the School of Environment, Enterprise, and Development at the University of Waterloo, Canada. She holds a PhD in Geography from Queen's University, an MA in Planning from the University of Waterloo, and a BA in Geography from Laurentian University. Her research focuses on: innovation and entrepreneurship in rural and northern contexts; regional economic development planning, policy and practice; community readiness & community impacts related to natural resource development; and planning in slow-growth and declining communities.

Sean Markey is a Professor, and registered professional planner, with the School of Resource and Environmental Management at Simon Fraser University, Canada. His research concerns issues of local and regional economic development, rural and small-town development, community sustainability, and sustainable infrastructure. He has published widely in academic journals and is the co-author and editor of several books, including *Doing Community-based Research: Perspectives from the Field* (McGill-Queens University Press, 2016); *Scaling Up: The Convergence of Social Economy and Sustainability* (Athabasca University Press, 2016); and *Investing in Place: Economic Renewal in Northern British Columbia* (UBC Press 2012).

Sarah Minnes is an interdisciplinary PhD candidate at Memorial University of Newfoundland, St. John's, Canada. Her research spans a range of topics related to Canadian regional development, sustainable watersheds and drinking water systems, and overall rural resilience. She is a registered professional planner, and has worked for Municipalities Newfoundland and Labrador, the Region of York Forestry, the Ontario Ministry of Natural Resources, the Ontario Federation of Anglers and Hunters, the Rural Policy Learning Commons, and is a past board member of the Canadian Rural Revitalization Foundation.

Bill Reimer is a Professor Emeritus at Concordia University in Montréal, Canada. From 1997 to 2008, he directed a Canadian research project on the New Rural Economy which included 13 universities, 35 partners, and 32 rural communities from all parts of Canada (http://nre.concordia.ca). From 2014 to 2017, he was the director of the seven-year Rural Policy Learning Commons project (http://rplc-capr.ca) – an international partnership involving 30 partners and 60 participants across nine countries. Both of these networks include researchers, policy-makers, practitioners, and citizens. His publications deal with community capacity-building, social support networks, social capital, social cohesion, municipal finances, the economy and the household, rural immigration, and the informal economy. Details can be found via http://billreimer.ca.

Donald J. Savoie is Canada Research Chair in Public Administration and Governance (Tier 1), Université de Moncton, Canada. He has published over 45 books. He founded the Canadian Institute for Research on Regional Development, l'Université de Moncton in 1983, which was renamed the Donald J. Savoie Institute in 2015. He has won numerous awards, including: the 2016 Donner Prize, the 2015 Killam Prize in Social Sciences, the Order of New Brunswick (2011), the Trudeau Fellowships Prize (2004), the Vanier Gold Medal (1999). He was honoured by the Public Policy Forum at its twelfth annual testimonial awards (1999), made an Officer of the Order of Canada (1993), and elected Fellow of the Royal Society of Canada (1992). His articles have appeared in all the significant journals in political science and public policy.

Kelly Vodden is Associate Vice-President (Grenfell) Research and Graduate Studies and Professor (Research) with the Environmental Policy Institute at Grenfell Campus, Memorial University, Corner Brook, Canada. She also serves as an advisor to Municipalities of Newfoundland and Labrador, a board member with Indian Bay Ecosystem Corporation, member of the

Advisory Board to the Leslie Harris Centre, Memorial University, and a former board member with the Canadian Rural Revitalization Foundation. Kelly's research and publications relate to governance and sustainable community and regional development, with a focus on rural, coastal, often natural resource-dependent communities. For more information see http://ruralresilience.ca.

Preface

This is an important book and it arrives at an important time. The authors have done both students and practitioners of regional economic development a great service by providing an accessible, balanced, and insightful book on regional economic development from a broad all-encompassing perspective.

The authors go to the heart of the matter in their very first sentence: "Canadian communities and regions face a wide array of challenges, opportunities, and struggles in a changing social-ecological environment." To be sure, Canada has been confronting regional economic development challenges virtually from the day it was born. Consider the following: Canada is the second largest country in the world; its national political institutions are designed for a unitary state, it is a federation without an Upper House in its national political institutions with a clear mandate to speak to Canada's regional socioeconomic circumstances in shaping national policies; Canada is home to vastly different regional economies; the federal government's regional development efforts have waxed and waned over the years; Canadian provinces have embraced province building to a far greater extent than states in other federations have; and Canada's urban–rural divide has become increasingly apparent with Statistics Canada recently declaring that "Canada goes urban."[1]

The government of Canada has sought to "fix things" through its spending power, as Chapter 2 explains. We have seen, over the years, Ottawa trying "this and that" to see what may work. I know of no other policy field that is so littered with acronyms from ARDA, FRED, DREE, RDIA, DRIE, MSERD, ACOA, to WD – and the list goes on. It is worth reminding the reader what the Economic Council of Canada had to say about the federal government's approach to regional development:

> Doctors used to try to cure syphilis with mercury and emetics. We now know that mercury works but emetics do not and moreover that penicillin is best of all. We suspect that the regional disparity disease is presently being treated with both mercury and emetic-type remedies but we do not know which is which. Perhaps one day an economic penicillin will be found.[2]

While we are still searching for penicillin to solve Canada's regional development problem, Ottawa appears to have thrown in the towel in its efforts to alleviate regional disparities. Motivated by national unity concerns and partisan political considerations, the federal government now has regional development agencies in place for every postal code in the country so that communities from Toronto to Bouctouche can access Ottawa's regional development programs. In brief, Ottawa's approach to regional development is now to be all things to all regions and to all communities large and small, have and have-less.

The above aims to make the point that this book is both important and timely. Policy makers need rigorous and fresh thinking to address Canada's evolving regional development challenges and this book does just that. It is no exaggeration that governments know that there is a regional development problem, but they do not know how to address it. The main regional development challenge today, as this book explains, is how best to deal with declining rural areas.

The book makes a substantive contribution to the literature for several reasons. The editors were able to assemble an impressive team of contributors drawn from a variety of backgrounds. The contributors include leading academics, aspiring academics already showing promise, and practitioners. I have often argued that students of regional development all too often ignore practitioners or those on the ground trying to make things work. This book also covers the full gamut of issues confronting Canada's regions and communities and sheds new light on both age-old problems and new concepts.

The authors deal with what is old (past regional development efforts), what is new (new regionalism) what is borrowed (integrated policy and planning) and what is blue (challenges confronting rural Canada). Among other issues, they document how Canada's approach to regional development has lived through various fashions and fads, from the growth pole concept to identifying comparative advantages at the regional level. They also dissect what new regionalism has to offer for policy makers. The authors explore fully the rural dimension to Canada's regional challenges and offer a substantial contribution on how to address it. They then very competently tie everything together in the concluding chapter. whichoffers important lessons learned for both students of economic development and policy-makers.

Given Canada's current political and socioeconomic environment, this book has been crying out to be written for some time. The authors have responded with an important contribution that will likely be widely consulted and will meet the test of time.

Donald J. Savoie
Canada Research Chair in Public
Administration and Governance
Université de Moncton

Notes

1 Canada, "Canada goes urban", Statistics Canada, undated, www150.statcan.gc.ca/n1/pub/11-630-x/11-630-x2015004-eng.htm.
2 Canada, *Living Together* (Ottawa: Economic Council of Canada, 1977).

Acknowledgements

The authors wish to thank the interview participants from across Canada who generously donated their time and expertise to this research. Thank you also to those who have continuously given feedback for this project from 2011 to 2018. The Canadian Rural Revitalization Foundation (http://crrf.ca) has been foremost in providing venues and networks to facilitate such feedback and we are grateful to the Foundation for these valuable opportunities. We are also grateful to the organizations that assisted with our field work and knowledge mobilization activities in the case study regions, including among others Selkirk College (with special thanks to Dr. Terri Macdonald and the Columbia Basin Rural Development Institute), L'Université du Québec à Rimouski (in particular Dr. Bruno Jean), the Rural Secretariat (Office of Public Engagement, Government of Newfoundland and Labrador), and the Kittiwake Economic Development Corporation.

The authors and editors also wish to thank Amanda Weightman for her help in the analysis of the rural–urban theme interview data (Chapter 8) and contributions to Chapter 2. In addition, we would like to thank Ken Carter for his contributions to the data and input into the analysis presented in Chapter 9. Furthermore, the research team is very grateful to the incredible research assistants associated with this project who contributed to the preparation of important working papers, conducted field research, and/or conducted analysis for the project. These research assistants include: Matthew Brett, Lauren Edens, Craig Mackie, Stephen Parmiter, Janelle Skeard, and Kyle White. Thank you also to John Dagevos and Brennan Lowery for their valuable comments on the draft volume. Lastly, thank you to Dr. Donald Savoie for providing a preface for this volume and so many important insights and suggestions.

Finally, thank you to the Social Sciences and Humanities Research Council of Canada for the financial support that made this research possible and to the Harris Centre, Memorial University of Newfoundland for funding through their Applied Research Fund. Materials for this book have been based on working papers for the Canadian Regional Development: A Critical Review of Theory, Practice, and Potential project. All materials can be found on the project website: http://cdnregdev.ruralresilience.ca.

1 Introduction

Sarah Minnes and Kelly Vodden

1 Introduction

Canadian communities and regions face a wide array of challenges, opportunities, and struggles in a changing social-ecological environment. This is especially the case in natural-resource-dependent regions, spread across rural and northern Canada, which struggle with economic and political restructuring and the implications of neoliberal ideologies for service delivery and infrastructure provision, economic development, protection of natural and cultural wealth, and other key facets of development. Rural Canada is home to a significant part of the Canadian population, with 17% of Canadians residing in non-metropolitan areas[1] (Bollman, 2016). There are 5,162 municipalities, the most prevalent form of local government, in Canada (Statistics Canada, 2016). Of these, the 15 largest are home to 37% of Canada's population, most located along the country's southern border. Yet the vast majority of Canadian municipalities have relatively small populations and are located well beyond metropolitan areas. In 2016, 86% of Canadian municipalities had populations smaller than 5,000 and 66% were located in areas with moderate to no metropolitan influence (Statistics Canada, 2016). Finally, these communities and the environments that surround them make vital contributions to environmental stewardship and to economic and cultural life. Rural Canada is responsible for approximately 30% of Canada's Gross Domestic Product, and is home to residents and settlements that often hold strong senses of community and are intertwined with the natural environments of which they are part (Canadian Rural Revitalization Foundation, 2015).

In short, rural Canada matters. However, with forces such as climate change, rapid technological innovation, urbanization, and globalization, there is a need for new development approaches that can build on and further enhance resilience in rural communities while recognizing their place in wider, interconnected regional contexts that include both rural and small town and urban settlements. Increased interest in regional resilience has accompanied a rise in awareness of the uncertainty facing such regions, and has also come as a response to increased focus on regional growth (Yamamoto, 2011). In order to adapt successfully in a changing world, resilient regions require the ability to anticipate, prepare for, respond to, and recover from disturbance, while maintaining or improving their situation over time (Simmie & Martin, 2010; Wolfe, 2010). There is a growing awareness that addressing challenges and harnessing opportunities requires regional approaches, particularly for rural communities. Such approaches are particularly promising to address problems such as the loss or degradation of services and infrastructure (Roberts & Townsend, 2015), the identification and pursuit of collective economic opportunities, and/or opportunities to adapt to environmental change.

In Canada and across the globe, regional development has been discussed as a tool for improving sustainability and resilience, whether in the context of the shifting political economy in Europe and North America, among industrializing countries previously striving to reach the Millennium Development Goals, or among countries in the north and south working to achieve the Sustainable Development Goals (Briceño-Ruiz & Morales, 2017; Hanson, Puplampu & Shaw, 2018; Scott, 2009). In this volume we conceptualize regional development as a purposeful and systematic intervention through public policy(ies), programs, projects, and practices to influence the development trajectory within a relatively large but sub-national spatial context, toward a set of desired economic, social, cultural, physical, environmental, and political goals that enhance well-being and prosperity in communities and regions.

The region as a concept is a long-contested one, with regions often being nested within other regions, and regional boundaries being defined by multiple factors. For example, regions can be based on political boundaries, environmental features such as watersheds, or on socioeconomic factors such as where residents in the region work, recreate, and/or purchase goods and services. However contentious and even shifting, these regional definitions have significance for government policy and programming, investments, social relationships, and culture, among other considerations. They are also integral to personal and community identities and to development policy and practice (Douglas, 2006).

In Canada, uneven patterns of development, resource distribution, and political initiatives have resulted in regional distinctions across groups of provinces and/or territories—such as western, central, Atlantic, or northern regions. For example, the Atlantic provinces, and especially Newfoundland and Labrador, have had consistently high rates of unemployment and out-migration. Significant disparities also occur within provinces, creating sub-provincial regions that frequently garner attention due to their special circumstances. Since the majority of Canadians live in the southern part of the country near the United States border (Statistics Canada, 2008), regional disparities occur and distinctions are often made, for example, between northern and southern parts of the provinces. It is this sub-provincial regional scale that is our main focus in this volume.

Canada's economic history has been defined by dependence on natural resource staples, particularly in the rural "periphery". Raw materials from these regions have been combined with technology, markets, and finances that have supported the extraction and export of these natural resources, which remain under the control of powerful external actors, whether they be located in decision-making centres of each province, in the capital region of central Canada, or in global centres of industry and finance. Subsequently, Canada has faced challenges associated with the boom and bust of commodity-dependent resource economies and with limited industrial diversification, particularly in the regions from which natural resources are extracted. Known as the "staples trap", such resource dependence has also had consequences for levels of education, entrepreneurialism, and social stratification, among other characteristics often found in rural resource regions. These inherent challenges have been exacerbated by the erosion and loss of services over the past three decades due to trends such as urbanization, centralization, and downloading of senior government responsibilities onto local authorities (Markey, Halseth & Manson, 2008). As Savoie (1992) points out, however, these regions also tend to have unique strengths, such as higher quality of life and more robust informal economies. The development circumstances of today's rural resource regions and related rural–urban relationships are, therefore, complex and embedded in political economies that cross temporal and spatial scales.

Canada has a long history of using regional development as a tool to address inequities associated with this development trajectory and thereby build the country and all of its provinces and territories (Savoie, 2017). This is reflected in the nation's constitution, which commits the federal government to equalization and reduction of fiscal disparities. While regional development has been pivotal to Canada's history (see Chapter 2), the nature of it continues to change and is frequently called into question. We expect this to continue into the future.

Canadian regional development today involves multiple actors operating within nested scales at local, provincial/territorial, national, and even international levels. Policies, programs, institutional structures, practices, and organizational arrangements are also increasingly diverse and often reliant on the organizing abilities and actions of local actors rather than the centralized, institutionalized actors of the past. New regionalist approaches engaging with this emergent complexity, and apparent shifts in the locus of agency, draw on concepts such as multi-level collaborative governance, relational assets, integration, innovation, and learning regions. While these concepts have become global in their formation and application, there has been little critical analysis of Canadian regional development policies and programs or the theories and concepts upon which many contemporary regional development strategies are based. This lack of critical analysis provides one of the major motivations for this book.

This book contributes to our understanding of the recent era of regional development in Canada (see Chapter 2), through the lens of new regionalism theory. New regionalism highlights approaches for creating more regionally resilient futures supported by informed development policy that is, among other things, flexible, adaptive, and context-appropriate. At the same time, our work subjects the application of new regionalism to research-based critiques through an exploratory examination of its practice (and in many cases its absence) in a selection of Canadian contexts. This volume represents the results of more than five years of empirical and theoretical analysis of changes in Canadian regional development and the potentials of new approaches for improving the well-being of Canadian communities and regions.

The main questions of the research presented in this volume are:

1. How has Canadian regional development evolved over the past two and a half decades (since the creation of existing federal regional development agencies, as discussed in Chapter 2)?
2. To what extent have Canadian regional development systems incorporated the ideas of new regionalism in their policy and practice?
3. What can we learn from the Canadian contexts about the merits or flaws of new regionalism?
4. What innovations have been developed in Canadian regional development that can contribute to the broader body of regional development theory and practice nationally and internationally?
5. To what extent is regional development in Canada characterized by knowledge transfers and shared learning and what factors or mechanisms constrain and/or facilitate learning, knowledge flow, and collaboration within Canadian regional development networks?

By answering these questions, we aim to inform policy-makers and provide concrete contributions to regional development analysis across Canada, and in other jurisdictions where lessons from the Canadian experience may be applicable. At the same time, we aim to inform and update regional development theories and concepts that are taught in our universities and colleges, and upon which future research and analysis will build. The literature review provided in each chapter takes an international scope in regards to new regionalism and provides comparative coverage of theoretical debates and policy practice.

It should be noted that although Indigenous governance in relation to Canadian regional development is not extensively discussed in this book, it is acknowledged by the authors as an important area of research for further investigation. This is especially the case as new governance, land use, and resource management arrangements are established under the many land claims negotiations currently taking place between Indigenous peoples and the Canadian government. Each one represents a new approach to regional development as Indigenous peoples re-imagine and implement their visions of themselves, their environments, social organizations, and governance. Furthermore, through the recent Truth and Reconciliation Commission of Canada (2015) calls to action, governments, educational, religious, and civil society groups and citizens across Canada (including rural communities and regions) are exploring how to engage in reconciliation with Indigenous communities. Activities emerging from reconciliation will have implications for existing governance structures, processes, and partnerships across the country, particularly for settler communities in rural areas that share resources and services with their Indigenous neighbours.

2 Examining new regionalism within the Canadian context

New regionalism is a multi-faceted concept that emerged in the 1990s in response to the socioeconomic and political restructuring that took place throughout the 1980s. The former decade was a time that saw the ascendency of neoliberal concepts, policies, and practices along with increased attention to localized responses to national and global trends. These changes required a reconceptualization of the "old" regionalism (further explained in Chapter 3) (Lovering, 1999; Wheeler, 2002). New regionalism has been posited as incorporating various concepts, such as new urbanism, smart growth, and sustainable communities, with a focus on the regional scale (Gibbs & Jonas, 2001; Hettne, 2005; Savitch & Vogel, 2000). It is acknowledged as taking place in a fundamentally different and changing world (Savitch & Vogel, 2000), and as having characteristics such as being rooted in place, focusing on competitive advantage, being co-constructed (i.e., combining top-down and bottom-up involvement), and having a focus on open governance processes that foster trust, collaboration, and empowerment among a range of development actors (Wallis, 2002; Zirul et al., 2015).

The research team took a comprehensive approach to the conceptualization of new regionalism in relation to Canadian regional development (which is outlined further in Chapter 3). The project focused around five main themes of new regionalism identified in the literature. These themes included: i) collaborative, multi-level collaborative governance; ii) place-based development; iii) integrated vs. sectoral and single objective approaches; iv) rural–urban interactions and interdependence; and v) fostering knowledge flow, learning, and innovation (see Figure 1.1). A full description of new regionalism is provided in Chapter 3 and more detail about each of the five themes is presented in Chapters 5 to 9. We sought, therefore, to examine the extent to which power and decision-making are shared among different groups engaged in regional development policy and practice at all levels: a key ingredient of collaborative, multi-level collaborative governance (Chapter 5). We also aimed to see if policy-makers and practitioners on the front lines are now re-focusing on place itself as a starting point for development (Chapter 6). We explored the extent to which a wide variety of sectors and issues are integrated into regional development practices (Chapter 7), along with how rural–urban relationships are understood and the impact these relationships have on development (Chapter 8). Finally, we were also interested in the extent to and ways in which knowledge and innovation are part of the development process (Chapter 9).

3 The research sites and scale of analysis

In conducting the research presented in this volume, we identified Canadian case studies with particular potential to provide insight into the five themes

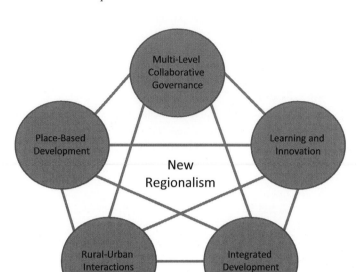

Figure 1.1 New regionalism framework

of new regionalism. Case study selection was based on literature reviews and the extensive experience of the research team. We conducted case studies in four provinces (British Columbia (BC), Ontario (ON), Québec (QC), and Newfoundland and Labrador (NL)), and in at least one sub-provincial region within each of these provinces. These include the case study regions of the Kootenay Development Region, BC; Eastern Ontario, ON; Rimouski, QC; Kittiwake, NL; and Northern Peninsula, NL.

We selected the sites through a combination of factors, including feasibility and strategic characteristics. The five case study sites were well-known by the principal researchers since their university affiliations and residences are located in the chosen provinces. In addition, they have a history of previous research conducted in the sub-regions chosen. This familiarity provided a foundation of knowledge from which to build. The provinces and sites also represent varied resource, political, social, and geographical locations in the country: from the maritime, fishing, and often isolated communities of NL, to the unique social, cultural, and political context of QC with its agriculture and forestry focus, the mixed economy of ON, and the forest, mining, and energy-dependent mountainous regions of BC. We provide a full description of our methods, including case study selection criteria in Chapter 4.

While these four provinces, their respective regions, and related research findings are the focus, we have also supplemented them with literature and insights from other Canadian regions, provinces, and territories to provide a more comprehensive Canada-wide perspective. For example, Chapter 5 sheds light on the governance approaches used for the Yukon Regional Round Table in the Yukon Territory. Furthermore, we have situated our research and findings in an international context, by drawing from and seeking to contribute to the global body of literature on new regionalism and through comparison of our findings with relevant international case studies, such as the explicit attention given to integration within Ireland's National Planning Framework, as shown by a case study example of Integrated Resource Development in Duhallow, Ireland (Chapter 7).

Much of the new regionalist literature has focused on city regions and global macro regions (e.g., South-East Asia, Central Europe) as units of analysis. These efforts include noteworthy interdisciplinary and international research to provide perspectives of new regionalism from the north and south (Briceño-Ruiz & Morales, 2017; Hanson, Puplampu & Shaw, 2018; Scott, 2009). Global in scope, these contributions focus on regionalism, regional relations, and institutions at multiple levels. However, the focus is largely on cross-border regions and coverage of the practice and implications of new regionalisms at the intra-national level is limited. This book provides the lens to analyze new regionalism at the local (sub-provincial) scale and the implications of such larger shifts for local communities. The focus of this book is on rural regions, thus making a novel contribution to new regionalism thinking, considering the largely urban–centric focus of studies informed by this framework to date (Savoie, 2017).

In addition to gaps in the new regionalism literature from a local, micro-regional scale, we provide a perspective from primarily rural regions while also examining and drawing attention to the important and changing relationships between urban and rural communities within these regions and between rural and metropolitan regions. As will be outlined in Chapter 3, regional development offers promise for increasing the resilience of rural and small-town communities. Given the ongoing importance of rural, remote, and small-town Canada to the nation's economy and identity, our research paid particular attention to rural regions and rural–urban relationships within regions.

4 Book outline

Following this introductory chapter, we provide in Chapter 2 an overview of the historical and current perspectives of regional development in Canada. Chapter 3 describes new regionalism and provides definitions of the concept, history, critiques, and more on the themes and conceptual framework of new regionalism as used in the research that has informed this book. Chapter 4 outlines the exploratory, mixed methods, case study approach used throughout the research project to examine the application of new regionalist perspectives, ideas in the Canadian context, and the critiques and responses associated with these methods. Chapters 5–9 describe in detail the literature and relevance to regional development behind each core theme explored in the research project: governance; place-based development; integrated development; rural–urban interactions and interdependencies; and learning, knowledge flows, and innovation.

The theme chapters discuss the evolution of each theme in the regional development literature, outline key debates and developments, and provide an analysis of the evolution of the theme (specifically in Canada). Research findings are presented with reflections about their relevance to the literature, policy, and development practice in rural Canada. We provide specific case examples within each theme chapter to illustrate the findings and provide material for reflections on the future directions.

In the last chapter (Chapter 10) we integrate the analysis of the five themes underpinning our conceptual framework (Figure 1.1) with the case study regions. This provides a comparison of overall findings regarding the presence of new regionalism and its applicability to the current Canadian context. We also provide overall lessons learned and the implications of the research for policy design and professional practice. We consider the book's contributions to academic concepts and emergent regional development theory, and discuss opportunities for future research initiatives. Supplementary materials to this book and a full database of related research activities, including full regional profiles, research reports, and further case studies, can be found on the project website: http://cdnregdev.ruralresilience.ca.

5 Findings in brief

Our findings suggest that select elements of the new regionalist paradigm can be seen in Canadian regional development in recent decades. We also identify, however, significant gaps between the expectations, theorization, and, in some cases, rhetoric of new regionalism and policies and practices at federal, provincial, and local levels as witnessed in rural regions of Canada. In short, empirical evidence of new regionalism is uneven and partial. We found instances of collaboration across and within levels of government together with other regional development actors, for example, but evidence of policy co-construction was limited (Chapter 5). While identity plays a critical role in fostering regional development processes, it remains largely emergent and/or is actively resisted within our research sites and therefore its power as a significant force for place-based regional development is suspended (Chapter 6). Further, integrated approaches were largely lacking, with a focus on innovation and infrastructure for economic growth rather than well-being and quality of life drawing from diverse rural and regional assets (Chapter 7).

In Chapter 8 we outline issues related to urban-centric regional politics and the need for increased attention to rural–urban relationships. Some attention has been paid to diversifying rural–urban relationships; however, the focus is primarily on city regions (which is consistent with trends globally). This raises questions about the nature of these relationships and the future of rural communities that may be seen as subservient to or in service of urban growth centres, and is particularly troublesome for communities that lie outside of rural–urban commuting zones. Further, institutional and economic relationships are emphasized while interdependencies related to the natural environment and shared identities receive limited recognition despite their importance. At the same time, examples of innovation and mobilization illustrate the potential for regional partnerships and the value of supportive rural development policies with a focus on the regional scale (Chapter 9).

As previously outlined, we conclude that there is a demonstrated gap between regional development theory and the theory in use in Canada. Incremental and uneven changes are occurring across the country's diverse and changing regional development landscape that variously align with new regionalist approaches and claims. A foundation for regional governance within a collaborative, multi-level collaborative governance framework exists in many jurisdictions, for example. However, this foundation is fraught with cracks of various sizes caused by funding cutbacks and attitudinal, structural, and policy barriers that may make it difficult to build upon without significant attention and support. This includes the need for stronger, more robust regional planning, co-constructed, partnership-driven models of rural and regional development policy, and enhanced training and capacity building efforts and other supports for existing local development groups and other actors to encourage and support participation in such efforts. Our approach and findings further highlight that regional development includes not only the narrow pillar of economic development upon which mainstream models have sought to build viable regions. Rather, it arises from a broad foundation of the social, economic, cultural, and environmental aspirations and practices that draw strategically from the suite of place-based assets that exist in rural regions and across the country.

Implications for policy, research, and practice outlined in Chapter 10 include a need to better understand and realize the diverse roles that various actors have to play in addressing the disparities, challenges, and opportunities related to regional development in the world's second largest country. Greater attention is also needed to rural–urban relationships, which should aim to foster recognition and healthy relations of interdependence in a climate that is all too frequently characterized by "us vs. them" attitudes and urban-centric ideas and discourse. Finally, our findings suggest a need to further encourage but also actively engage in regional development learning and knowledge sharing in Canada, an important aim to which this book seeks to contribute.

Note

1 Non-metropolitan (also called rural and small-town) refers to "areas outside Census Metropolitan Areas (CMAs) and outside Census Agglomerations (CAs). Census Metropolitan Areas (CMAs) have a total population of 100,000+ and Census Agglomerations (CAs) have a population of 10,000–99,999. Both include neighbouring municipalities where 50+% of the employed population commutes to the CMA or CA" (Bollman, 2016, p. 3).

References

Bollman, R. (2016). Rural Demography Update. Retrieved June 12, 2018 from www.ruralontarioinstitute.ca/file.aspx?id=26acac18-6d6e-4fc5-8be6-c16d326305fe.

Briceño-Ruiz, J., & Morales, I. (Eds). (2017). *Post-Hegemonic Regionalism in the Americas: Towards a Pacific-Atlantic Divide?* Abingdon, OX: Routledge.

Canadian Rural Revitalization Foundation. (2015). State of Rural Canada 2015. Retrieved March 12, 2018 from http://sorc.crrf.ca

Douglas, D. (2006). Rural regional development planning – Governance and other challenges in the new E.U. *Studia Regionalia, 18*, 112–132.

Gibbs, D., & Jonas, A. (2001). Rescaling and regional governance: The English regional development agencies and the environment. *Environment and Planning C -Government and Policy, 19*(2), 269–288.

Hanson, K. T., Puplampu, K. H., & Shaw, T. M. (Eds). (2018). From Millennium Development Goals to Sustainable Development Goals: Rethinking African Development. Abingdon, OX: Routledge.

Hettne, B. (2005). Beyond the "new" regionalism. *New Political Economy, 10*(4), 213.

Jones, A. Q., Dewey, C. E., Dore, K., Majowicz, S. E., McEwen, S. A., Waltner-Toews, D., & Mathews, E. (2007). A qualitative exploration of the public perception of municipal drinking water. *Water Policy, 9*(4), 425–438.

Lovering, J. (1999). Theory led by policy: The inadequacies of the "new regionalism" (illustrated from the case of Wales). *International Journal of Urban and Regional Research, 23*, 379–395.

Markey, S., Halseth, G., & Manson, D. (2008). Challenging the inevitability of rural decline: Advancing the policy of place in Northern British Columbia. *Journal of Rural Studies, 24*(4), 409–421. Doi: 10.1016/j.jrurstud.2008.03.012.

Roberts, E., & Townsend, L. (2015). The contribution of the creative economy to the resilience of rural communities: Exploring cultural and digital capital. *Rural Sociology, 56*(2), 197–219.

Savitch, H. V., & Vogel, R. K. (2000). Introduction: Paths to new regionalism. *State & Local Government Review, 32*(3), 158–168.

Savoie, D. (1992). Regional Economic Development: Canada's Search for Solutions. Toronto: University of Toronto Press.

Savoie, D. (2017). Looking for Bootstraps: Economic Development in the Maritimes. Halifax: Nimbus Publishing Limited.

Scott, J. W. (Ed). (2009). De-Coding New Regionalism: Shifting Socio-Political Contexts in Central Europe and Latin America. New York, NY: Routledge.

Simmie, J., & Martin, R. (2010). The economic resilience of regions: Towards an evolutionary approach. *Cambridge Journal of Regions, Economy and Society, 3*(1), 27–43.

Statistics Canada. (2008). Provinces and Regions. Retrieved March 14, 2018 from www.statcan.gc.ca/pub/91-003-x/2007001/4129908-eng.htm.

Statistics Canada. (2016). Census of Population. Retrieved June 12, 2018 from www12.statcan.gc.ca/census-recensement/index-eng.cfm.

Truth and Reconciliation Commission of Canada. (2015). Honouring the Truth, Reconciling for the Future: Summary of the Final Report of the Truth and Reconciliation Commission of Canada. Retrieved June 5, 2018 from www.trc.ca/websites/trcinstitution/index.php?p=890.

Wallis, A. (2002). The New Regionalism: Inventing Governance Structures for the Early Twenty-First Century. Retrieved from www.miregions.org/Strengthening%

20the%20Role/The%20New%20Regionalism%20Paper%20by%20Wallis%20at%20CUD.pdf.

Wheeler, S. (2002). The new regionalism: Key characteristics of an emerging movement. *Journal of the American Planning Association, 68*(3), 267–278.

Wolfe, D. A. (2010). The strategic management of core cities: Path dependence and economic adjustment in resilient regions. *Cambridge Journal of Regions, Economy and Society, 3*(1), 139–152.

Yamamoto, D. (2011). Regional resilience: Prospects for regional development research. *Geography Compass, 5*(10), 723–736.

Zirul, C., Halseth, G., Markey, S., & Ryser, L. (2015). Struggling with new regionalism: Government trumps governance in Northern British Columbia, Canada. *Journal of Rural and Community Development, 10*(2), 136–165.

2 Regional development in Canada
Eras and evolution

Sarah-Patricia Breen, Sean Markey, and Bill Reimer

1 Introduction

Regional development in Canada has undergone a variety of forms and levels of intervention in the post-WWII era. Each of these phases is a reflection of a complex interplay of political ideologies, development theory, policy goals, external forces, and regional conditions. Understanding the past context of regionalism in Canada provides an important basis for interpreting and improving current and future policies and practices.

The historical context of regional development in Canada was shaped predominantly by the culture, practices, and structures of two groups: Indigenous peoples and European settlers (predominantly English and French) (Hodge, Hall, & Robinson, 2016). While interaction between these two groups has been seen throughout Canadian history, it is important to note the fundamental differences in worldviews between them. Indigenous governance systems typically focus on a connection to land rooted in stories, places, and experiences and are characterized by communal rights (Hodge, Hall, & Robinson, 2016; Saul, 2009). This contrasts significantly with the European introduction of the Judeo-Christian perspective emphasizing human "dominion" over the earth, colonial assumptions of ownership and social hierarchy (including assessments of Indigenous peoples as "savages" and remote places as "wilderness"), the individualism of the industrial revolution and the equating of material accumulation with personal and social fulfillment. As noted in Chapter 1, owing to the scope of the project, the contextual differences between the two systems and the period of time considered, we focus here on the evolution and history of the European settler context. However, we recognize that the two systems are both different and intertwined. As our findings in the subsequent chapters show, there is increasing recognition of Indigenous perspectives, rights, title, and systems of governance (see Chapter 5).

Regional development as a formal policy intervention has a relatively recent history in Canada. Prior to WWII, many Canadian government initiatives were regionally relevant, but they were framed in the language of nation-building and national prosperity. It was only following WWII that regional development policy was formally articulated as a justification for programs. Our current focus on regional development policy as a way to assist economically lagging rural regions or to anchor regionalist investment with key projects emerged from this latter framework.

The purpose of this chapter is to present a framework for understanding the major historical events and concerns that have guided regional development policy in post-colonial Canada. Our intent is not to provide a detailed list of departments, programs, and initiatives, since this is well done in other volumes (e.g., Brodie, 1990; Hodge, Hall, & Robinson, 2016; Savoie, 1992, 1997). Rather, we propose a framework comprised of broad strokes to represent regional development eras. We also use these trends to organize and interpret our critique of regional development before the recent emergence of new regionalism perspectives, and to identify some key lessons to inform future policy decisions. For consistency throughout the volume, we define regional development as a purposeful and systematic intervention through public policy(ies), programs, projects, and a variety of practices in planning and management in order to influence the course of change within a large, but sub-national context, toward a set of desired development outcomes in order to enhance well-being (see Chapter 1).

2 Eras of regional development in Canada

Regional development policy in Canada emerged from a history of resource extraction and commodification built on colonization and mercantilism. The arrival of Europeans stimulated trade in fish, furs, timber, dairy products, agricultural produce, minerals, and energy in increasing quantities, paralleled by the emergence of a trade infrastructure that has structured the country's economic system to the present day. Europeans arrived in North America to a territory already managed by an elaborate system of trade – organized by multiple Indigenous groups along the many waterways of the continent. This system was gradually co-opted by the newcomers for the extraction of natural resources according to shifting European market demands.

The Europeans also brought their political and mercantile interests that served to define and redefine the organization of the territories. Primary among these were the French and English conflicts and agreements that imposed formal rights over land, controlled by European jurisprudence, law, and power. With the American war of independence, these conflicts became a three-way struggle for territorial control. As a result, the early history of Canadian regional development was infused with two primary struggles: the protection of trade and control through the St. Lawrence River system (as opposed to the Hudson and Mississippi networks) and the normalization of relations between the predominantly French-speaking population of Lower Canada and the English-speaking population of Upper Canada.

Dealing with both of these challenges involved territorially based initiatives and policies, which heavily condition the Canadian approach to regional development today. Controlling the St. Lawrence route meant ensuring the safe movement of goods to the east and the expansion of trade from the west. The former contributed to the Act of Union in 1867, and the latter to the inclusion of British Columbia in 1871 and Alberta in 1905. In these negotiations, the matter of regional fairness and equity was a major issue – first in the Confederation agreements and later in more formal system of equalization payments in 1957. The Canada Act of 1982 ensured that this issue was enshrined in the Canadian Constitution to respond to the different fiscal conditions of provinces that vary significantly in terms of size, population, resources, and economic activities.

Dealing with language issues in Upper and Lower Canada meant turning once again to territory-implicated solutions – this time with respect to language and culture. By providing provinces with the right of control over language, culture, education, health, and welfare in addition to natural resources, related social conflicts were managed by their institutionalization (Jackson, 1975), but it ensured that they would forever come under negotiation when territorial concerns occurred. As a result, regional issues became a part of the Canadian Constitution – with an initial focus on provinces, managing fiscal inequities, language, and natural resources. All of these issues involved territorial points of reference and structured the preoccupation with regional development.

3 Eras of development: a national framework

Our analysis begins with an examination of national-level regional development policies, their core themes, and the points at which we can observe relatively sharp shifts in policy direction. We identify four eras of relative stability during which federal regional development-related policies were fairly constant, and three shifts when major challenges emerged that transformed the policy orientation (see Figure 2.1). In some cases, the crises driving the shift were external to the policies, while in others they were largely generated by the limitations of the policy regimes themselves.

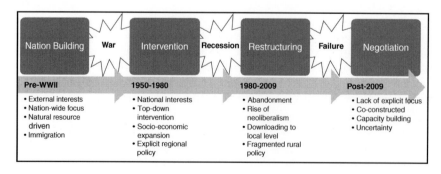

Figure 2.1 National eras and periods of crisis

We acknowledge that these phases are not exclusive, often overlap, and that there are other ways of dividing the temporal markers of different policy eras. However, our framework corresponds to critical phases of impact on regional development and restructuring at the federal level, as reflected in an extensive analysis of the Canadian regional development literature (see Sections 3.1–3.5). Using an examination of the literature, we identify phases and shifts that best represent the majority of those materials – recognizing that the results will be approximate at best. This trajectory often manifests differently at a provincial level according to institutional and historical legacies.

3.1 Era: nation-building

The first period (pre-WWII) reflects the many policies designed to build the nation from the Atlantic to the Pacific – largely driven by mercantilist policies and interests from Europe (Innis, 1930). The demand for raw materials drove the expansion of transportation routes by water, rail, and road. It also created conditions for massive immigration programs that helped to settle the prairies and feed the growth of cities. The urbanization of Canadian society began in earnest during this period and has continued unabated to the present. Most projections suggest that this trend will continue into the future – reinforcing the current preoccupation with urban-focused challenges and the reorganization of political power to urban populations (Bryant & Joseph, 2001; Reimer, 2013).

3.1.1 Shift: World War II

The demands of WWII for resources, manufactured goods, and labour created a level of industrialization that transformed this period by creating the physical and institutional infrastructure for sustained, and relatively independent, national growth. Under the influence of Cabinet Minister C.D. Howe, the entire country was put on a materials and foodstuffs production footing, and the level of industrial and corporate development was significantly increased in concert with the war effort. It was a transformation that brought the state and the corporate sector together in a way that created conditions for the next policy regime in our framework.

3.2 Era: intervention

The rapid industrialization of WWII and post-WWII patterns such as the return of veterans, a rapid increase in immigration, and the baby boom stimulated a period of state intervention that included both economic and social initiatives. It was dominated by the organization and reorganization of governments, state-supported infrastructure expansion in transportation, housing, and energy, and the emergence of welfare state policies that reorganized education, health, and labour legislation. Consumer goods became a more important element of the economy as the middle class grew in wealth and power (Douglas, 1994). The

Fordist approach to industrial organization reinforced the compromise among state, capital, and labour that had emerged during WWII to reorganize transportation, production, and the commodity industries to supply the growing urban markets. This period also witnessed a considerable expansion of regional development programs (Savoie, 1992).

3.2.1 *Shift: 1980s recession*

When major economic recessions occurred in the 1980s and again in the 1990s, the policies and programs of the earlier period came under attack. This coincided with the rise of neoliberal ideologies that were emerging in the USA and Britain, which led to the period of restructuring that spread among many industrialized nations (Young & Matthews, 2007). As industry and governments responded to the recession, there were fundamental shifts in the Fordist compromise that linked industry and government with labour and, indirectly, with rural regions during the intervention era (Barnes & Hayter, 1997). Hayter (2000) describes the economic crisis, particularly for rural regions, as being exacerbated by a variety of additional forces, including environmental debates, consumer demands for more specialized products and low cost goods, rising relative labour costs, and increasing competition from low cost global competitors.

3.3 Era: restructuring

The Canadian government began the process of dismantling the welfare state as it championed the individual-focused policies of neoliberalism. It was asserted that the state was becoming too great a burden, so spending less, privatizing more, and reducing services were the only ways to bring deficits and debts under control while letting the assumed superiority of market forces allocate public resources and set most priorities (Fairbairn, 1998; Savoie, 2003; Young & Matthews, 2007).

Using a "client" model of assessment, governments determined that the low density and long-distance qualities of rural places meant that many of their services were the first to be reduced. Education, health, postal services, labour, and rural development support programs were all affected. The federal government, with its rural-biased legacy of parliamentary representation, was faced with the dilemma of rural vulnerability in the face of fiscal restraints and urban challenges. The call for greater community and regional autonomy provided a convenient option for this dilemma and senior-level governments sought ways to download some of their responsibilities to local government and other local agencies (Harrison, 2006). However, this downloading was done without compensatory resources or capacity (Douglas, 2005). This strategy required initiatives to improve the economic and political capacity of those places, and a number of federal rural economic development agencies such as the Rural Secretariat emerged as a result.

3.3.1 Shift: global recession (2007–2008)

By the time the 2008 financial crisis occurred, there were signs that the restructuring-era strategies were not yielding the predicted results (e.g., documented failures of "New Public Management" approaches) (Aucoin, 1995; Hanlon & Rosenberg, 1998; Osborne & McLaughlin, 2002). The efforts by central governments to download responsibilities to local communities – in turn imposing market-oriented solutions – were often thwarted by the lack of capacity in many rural and small-town settings. In keeping with prevailing perspectives, mainstream policy responses often sought to encourage business development as opposed to social and organizational approaches. This approach had only modest success, especially where the distance from markets was long and basic skills were lacking. Neither the vision nor the resources were adequate to address issues of market failure, or the more fundamental issues of individual and community capacity.

The combined impacts of increasing urban demands, neoliberal-inspired reductions in government services, and the occurrence of the global recession meant that rural and northern places were largely left to fend for themselves with diminished supports. This shift in approach was exemplified by the Conservative government's 2013 dismantling of the Rural Secretariat, a federal agency mandated to represent, convene, and support rural development across the country (Hall, Vodden, & Greenwood, 2017).

3.4 Era: reactionary negotiation

While there is considerable evidence of the continuation of post-recession policies of neoliberalism, there is also evidence of change. Halseth and Ryser characterize the current chaotic period as "reactionary":

> With the breakdown of a neoliberal policy approach, there has been an incoherent re-deployment of state support (usually debt and deficit-derived support), and a reconfiguration of industry roles relative to communities and regions to deal with the contradictions – and real life implications – of decades of neoliberal-inspired restructuring. In light of these shifts, the question is how we might characterize the current policy period for resource-dependent rural and small town places and regions? The blending of ongoing commitments to neoliberalism with a chaotic return to almost neo-Keynesian public investment policy, along with a downloading of governance responsibilities to industry and communities, is creating a different policy model or framework. But the actions are too chaotic and idiosyncratic to each circumstance or jurisdiction to be explained by the kind of logic or coherence implied by the terms "model" or "framework". Instead, we would label this new public and corporate policy period or era as "reactionary".
>
> (Halseth and Ryser, 2017, p. 110)

We propose an added dimension to this reactionary phase: that it is accompanied by the necessity of *negotiation*. While this is not yet a clear departure from former federal policy approaches, there is evident pushback to neoliberalism. "Negotiation" suggests that this may manifest as a post-neoliberal phase or possibly an adaptation of neoliberalism to new circumstances. Regions, communities, and organizations are largely left on their own to negotiate their fates as best they can with federal, provincial, territorial, and regional governments (and industry) in largely bilateral, but occasionally multilateral, arrangements. Some communities and regions have done well at organizing themselves and their assets to negotiate successfully with both governments and industries, thereby enhancing the well-being of residents. However, others lack the necessary capacity to manage or sustain a more independent future. The current period of reactionary negotiation presents both challenges and opportunities for regions, depending upon their capacity, preparedness, vision, and available supports from upper-level governments. This is the era within which our project as a whole sought to find evidence of new regionalism in policy or practice. Such evidence could provide a strong basis for improving the nature and outcomes of regional strategies and outcomes.

4 Comparative themes in Canadian regional development

Our defined eras primarily represent broad federal policy characteristics. While these broad eras hold true across the country, they are significantly influenced by differing provincial contexts and governments. To analyze these trends, we proceeded in two steps. First, we compiled a table of key events in regional development policy history within each of the four case study provinces and used these to guide our discussions. Second, using national trends as reference points, we compared how these major eras and shifts manifested at the provincial and regional levels within our case provinces – coding the table for key patterns. We searched for the ways in which provincial policy and program responses complemented or differed from national trends. The results of this process were explored by the project team, with discussions focusing on common themes among the provinces.

From this analysis we identified four themes: 1) the provinces' different institutional legacies; 2) the visions they communicated for provincial development; 3) the extent to which their policies and programs enhanced or inhibited the governance capacity of actors at the sub-provincial level; and 4) shortcomings associated with the post-WWII period of regional development. It is important to note that for each of these broad themes there are both exceptions and outliers across and within the provinces.

4.1 Institutional legacies

The first theme is the legacy of institutional structures within the provinces. While the provinces share a traditional, top-down governance structure, differences are particularly noticeable in the division and management of territory and the structure and function of regional governance and governments. These institutional legacies modify the impacts of national policies and international events in significant ways by conditioning and directing the infrastructure options, information flows, decision-making approaches, and opportunities for action at the provincial and sub-provincial levels.

A comparison between Québec and the other three provinces illustrates the impact of these institutional legacies. Unlike the other provinces, governance in (primarily southern) Québec was historically based on the French seigneurial system with a regional organization dominated by the Catholic Church. When it made the transition to a municipal system of government in the 1840s, the parish system served as the historical basis for over 300 municipalities – especially in the regions outside the urban centres.

From 1847 to 2002, there were only minor alterations to the regional administrative structures in Québec (Municipal History of Québec, 2016). The influence of the Church remained until the Quiet Revolution of the 1960s, which brought about the transition from church to state. Although this transition represented a major shift in power and control, it continued to rely on the social networks, institutions, place-based identities, and infrastructure largely established by the Catholic Church over four centuries. The continuation of these ecclesiastical legacies thereby reinforced the traditional structure and traditions of regional decision-making that persist in Québec's social and political landscape today. The structure and form of today's rural Municipalitiés régionales de comté (MRC) are largely built on the legacy of social structures established over 160 years ago (Reimer, Dionne, & Jean, 2017).

The establishment and change of institutional structures in British Columbia (BC) are dominated by a different time period than that of Québec, and by different drivers. Unlike the historical and socio-cultural factors shaping Québec's municipal structure, it was the push for economic development, particularly natural resource development, that most prominently shaped BC's local governments. In many cases, only marginal attention was paid to the regional networks and institutions that structured life in the regions. While the first municipal act in BC came in 1872, not long after Québec's "Code Municipale", BC's history of western settlement prior to joining confederation in 1871 was shorter, less settled, and more focused on exploration and resource extraction. BC's Municipal Act was revised and re-written a number of times during the nation-building era, along with the 1914 establishment and growth of The Department of Municipal Affairs.

The intervention period saw further change to the institutional structure of local government in BC, including a growing focus on regional government to address governance in unincorporated rural areas. In 1957 there was a new municipal act, followed in 1965 by the establishment of the Regional District system and the Instant Towns policy, which brought "instant" municipal status and more deliberate, industry-led community planning to rural areas. Today the Regional Districts continue to provide local- and regional-level governance and government. Many former instant towns persist – like Elkford in the East Kootenays – often still economically oriented towards the same natural resources that led to their establishment. Within this structure, the BC government introduced several municipal reforms that reflected the trend of provincial downloading and federal withdrawal (e.g., 1998: Municipal Act reform; 2000: Local Government Act; 2004: Community Charter).

Further differences are found in the other two case study provinces. Ontario (ON) also has a lengthy history of European-inspired settlement, but lacked the socio-cultural uniformity of Québec. While the original institutional structure of local governments reflected the county model imported from England (Baldwin Act, 1849), its development changed to fit an increasingly diverse socio-cultural context. The region has seen periods of "reform" with the introduction of two-tier Regional Municipalities in the 1970s, aggressively implemented amalgamations in the 1990s (Douglas, 2005), and continuing processes of downloading from the provincial government.

The final case study province, Newfoundland and Labrador (NL), joined confederation in 1949, experiencing a development history similar to BC in its focus on building a natural-resource-based industrial economy and the late establishment of local government and governance institutions. Yet the new province was also shaped by differing structural influences, including the settlement patterns of remote fishing communities clustered along the coasts and historic reliance on a three-tiered society of merchants, planters (e.g., small boat/facility owners, farmers, tradesmen, artisans), and fishers. This was followed by a series of resettlement programs during the intervention era that re-drew the municipal map using economic and fiscal criteria for modernization and urbanization over social and functional ones.

The institutional legacy of each province creates both opportunities and constraints for subsequent changes and interventions. If the institutional structure and resulting settlements are built on international trade and economic development criteria, as in BC or NL, it can easily conflict with the day-to-day livelihood of local households or undermine more informal social supports and services that cut across established boundaries. It is also worth noting that more remote and northern areas were, and in some cases continue to be, treated as resource banks and subsidiary entities to southern, urban areas where much of the decision-making takes place.

The networks, modes of collaboration, negotiations, and decision-making that make regional governance possible do not develop overnight, but require the establishment of long-term institutions that facilitate engagement. Québec, for example, has been able to use these structures even as the priorities of governments have changed (Reimer, 2010). Unlike Québec, most of the other provinces in our study have undermined their own legacies over the last 30 years by frequently changing the jurisdictional boundaries and institutional design so that a dependable framework for long-term negotiations and compromises becomes difficult to find. New policies and programs must recognize these institutional legacies as potential assets for territorial development, whether economic, social, or governance related.

4.2 Vision as a platform for policy

Our second cross-cutting theme concerns the nature and coherence (or lack) of provincial vision for regional development during the different periods identified. When they are formed in an inclusive and forward-looking manner, visions are important tools for communicating and establishing a shared perspective about future directions (Markey, Halseth, & Manson, 2012). They can enable institutional stability at all levels over the long periods required for development. This can help to mediate internal tensions and facilitate continuity and capacity building, potentially reinforcing the vision itself.

In the absence of a coherent vision, policies and programmatic shifts are much less robust and may fall victim to hasty reactions to external and internal forces. Expedient short-term initiatives, rather than strategic long-term collaborative planning, are more likely to occur as communities, groups, and individuals attempt to gain benefits in the face of an uncertain future. The extent to which a vision itself is robust and attractive to different levels of government and other governance actors may also dictate its longevity and flexibility across different political administrations. In the following section, we provide three examples that illustrate the variable development implications associated with articulating and sustaining a vision for regional development.

First, in the post-WWII province-building era in BC we see how a strong vision for post-war rural regional development was actively supported by the coordination of different development functions (e.g., health, education, industrial policy) and active, interventionist investment in rural infrastructure and services by government and industry. The era borrowed heavily from the lessons of industrial transformation in Ontario, which advocated for a series of key development principles: the maintenance of public ownership of resource lands; the security of industrial investment via long-term lease rights; attention to critical infrastructure investments by the public purse to support private resource development; and finally, an emphasis on steady flows of resource revenues to the provincial coffers as well as the creation of local employment to stimulate regional economies (Nelles, 2005).

BC's influential post-WWII Premier, W.A.C. Bennett (1952–1972) was a member of the Post-War Rehabilitation Council that was responsible for developing a peacetime development strategy for the country (Markey, Halseth, & Manson, 2012). The Council enabled Bennett to travel throughout rural areas in BC, granting him particular insights into the potential of rural resource regions. This experience, combined with his own inherent pragmatism, helped to create a strong vision for regional development in BC, to be implemented over a period of two decades.

The implementation of this vision included three main components: ministries tended to work in an integrated, rather than siloed or sectoral fashion to foster development, the government took a pragmatic and flexible approach to development, and the vision for the province was supported by a two-decade run in power by the Bennett government. Whether by design or happenstance, we now recognize the importance of these characteristics for effective development policy.

A second example concerns common characteristics evident in the most recent restructuring period within BC, ON, and NL, and indeed in most other Canadian jurisdictions. The policy response during this period may be best characterized as state withdrawal from rural development in both social and economic terms. First, this response is characteristic of a shift in government policy across Canada, and in other industrialized countries: from an *equity-based* orientation to less defined attempts at *enabling* regional development (Polèse, 1999). This means that successive governments gradually withdrew from a commitment to provide equitable access to standardized public services across the province, while making modest (and incomplete) efforts to assume a secondary role of facilitating transition through various community and regional development programs (Markey, Halseth, & Manson, 2012).

It is possible to interpret this period as one where a *laissez-faire*, market-oriented approach to development became the dominant vision. Regions within this approach succeeded (or not) depending on their competitive capacity to attract and retain both capital and people. Under such a model, government action would be necessary only for those conditions where market failure was likely to occur. However, the lack of strategic action where such failure occurs (e.g., regarding environmental and social damage) belies the claim that this was a coherent or integrated vision.

The third example of provincial vision can be seen in Québec's pursuit of a robust, territorial approach to rural policy development spanning across the restructuring and negotiation eras (2001 to 2014). During the early 1990s, Québec established 86 regional organizations based on traditional boundaries and 18 territories that were equivalent to an MRC (TEs: *territoires équivalents à une MRC*). These boards provided a forum where municipal representatives met to debate and make decisions about development issues, including social programs, territorial planning, economic development, and employment assistance (OECD, 2010; Reimer, 2010).

In 2001, this approach was formally articulated as a provincial rural policy, or *Politique Nationale de la Ruralité* (PNR) (OECD, 2010). The approach reflected the comprehensive and coordinated policy witnessed in the post-WWII period of BC since it linked social and economic development. It extended this model to support and privilege territorial development with deep commitments to building both social capital and capacity at the extra-local level to enable rural regional development. From a macro perspective, the PNR is now in its third planning cycle, illustrating significant durability across different political mandates. At the meso level, the consistency of the vision has enabled the development of robust regional planning to build relationships and capacity over a 14-year period. It remains to be seen whether this capacity will continue under the severe cutbacks to the PNR that were imposed in 2014 (Reimer & Jean, 2015).

4.3 Regional governance organization

The third theme for our analysis is the way in which provincial governments vary in their organization of regional governments and associated organizations. This includes the authority given to municipalities, regional agencies, departments, and organizations; the responsibilities bestowed on them; and the resources they have available to act on behalf of their constituencies (Jacob et al., 2008).

The federal government is involved in organizing regional development, but primarily in indirect ways, via the implications of the Canadian Constitution with its related acts and traditions. Watersheds and watercourse legislation that cross provincial boundaries, international and inter-provincial trade, the array of labour, health, environmental, and employment legislation designed to ensure inter-provincial mobility for labour, and equalization payments to offset fiscal imbalances are all examples of areas of federal action and/or responsibility that touch on regional development. The significant economic inequalities from one part of the country to another and constitutional obligations for relative equality across the country have also been used to justify specific development programs offered through federal departments.

In line with the interventionist and top-down approach in favour at the time, these programs typically championed large-scale investments as a solution to economic disparity. The 1957 Royal Commission on Canada's Economic Prospects (the Gordon Commission) explicitly identified regional disparity as a looming problem for Canada and the federal government responded with the first of many large-scale initiatives – the Agricultural Rehabilitation and Development Program (ARDA) (Savoie, 2003). Although initially focused on agriculture, these initiatives gradually expanded to other sectors and in some cases took on a place-focused element that reinforced regional concerns in significant ways. With acronyms like ADA, FRED, DREE, RDA, LIP, LEAP, and DRIE, these departments or programs became sources of revenue and intelligence for provinces and municipalities that had insufficient capacity. They created opportunities for places to receive funding for specific projects as well as unprecedented access to planners, agents, and development officers with expertise and focus on municipalities and small regional governance organizations (Fairbairn, 1998). The most recent set of federal regional development agencies, including Western Economic Diversification (WD), FedNor, and the Atlantic Canada Opportunities Agency (ACOA) were formed in 1987. After more than thirty years, the surviving agencies continue to serve as important sources of support for regional development activities and organizations in their respective regions today.

Each province has interpreted its internal sub-regional mandate differently. In general, the primary focus has been on settlements such as municipalities or villages, with additional responsibilities allocated to counties or districts of lower population density. In Canada, municipalities and regional governments have been created and operated under the jurisdiction of the provinces (Tindal & Tindal, 2009). The mandates for the associated councils and boards have traditionally focused on local service provision such as water, solid and liquid waste management, fire prevention, policing, housing, road maintenance, land use, and recreation. Transfer payments along with land and business taxation have provided the major sources of revenue for regional services. When com pared internationally, local government in Canada is weak, having a narrow revenue base with an expanding array of services, and little actual decision-making power (Douglas, 2006, 2016).

By the end of the nation-building era, all provinces except NL had municipal acts in place with responsibilities and powers primarily focused on local municipal services. Health, education, welfare, and economic development were largely left in the hands of the provincial government with little statutory input from municipalities, especially those outside larger urban regions. WWII and the intervention era merely solidified this approach in most provinces so that municipal and regional bodies were treated as service delivery agents for the more general social and economic initiatives of provincial and federal programs.

As the inadequacies of large-scale interventions became apparent and the 1980s recession hit, federal and provincial government attention shifted from growth poles[1] to improving employment opportunities through community initiatives. Local community development discourse often emerged via practitioners supported by the funds and regulatory requirements of regional development programs. It was eventually integrated into the federal government rhetoric and approached as a promising direction for overcoming the backlash from failed large-scale investments. Local development had the added attraction of shifting the responsibility for development to regions and municipalities.

During this period, the provinces were modifying their regional government structures and opportunities in a variety of ways. BC organized its regional health, education, and planning infrastructure to complement the industrial growth of the province during the intervention era, but was faced with massive forest sector layoffs during the 1980s recession. It wasn't until the New Democratic Party (NDP) government took over BC in the 1990s that regional initiatives favouring local community and regional development were implemented. These initiatives blended well with the federal regional development programs at that time, but were gradually eroded by the neoliberal policies of the Liberal provincial government after 2001. The subsequent restructuring reinforced the sectoral dominance of regional development policy and attempts to reconcile overlapping regions resulted in large administrative boundaries that weakened local autonomy. This pattern was reinforced by the financial crisis of 2008.

A unique feature of recent BC regional development is the plethora of Indigenous peoples' land and governance negotiations taking place. When the provincial and federal courts began to support ancestral rights, it led to many claims and counter-claims in BC and the Yukon where, unlike in most other provinces, treaties and agreements have not been signed. This policy vacuum has provided the opportunity for First Nations in BC and Yukon to negotiate new treaties, often taking on considerable self-governance capacity in doing so. These initiatives have challenged the relative autonomy of provincial and regional actors, but have also created a basis for new regional governance for the future characterized by co-existence between settler communities and semi-autonomous Indigenous regional governments.

As outlined above, Ontario followed similar visions to that of the federal government, establishing the Ontario Development Corporation in 1966 and in 1982 reducing provincial control over municipal decisions. The federal regional development agencies played an important part in the programs and policies of ON – particularly with the establishment of FedNor, a region-specific development agency dedicated to northern Ontario. Community Futures initiatives flourished and the rhetoric of local community development was found in most policy documents related to regional issues. However, due to the 1980s recession and ideological shifts, the provincial government looked to the amalgamation of municipalities and counties as a measure to reduce costs relating to municipal operations, including the closure or amalgamation of existing regional municipalities that were established in the 1970s.

The regional organization of Québec is relatively unique. Although it has been faced with the same eras and shocks, the impacts have been modified or delayed in significant ways. As outlined previously, during the intervention period most of the regional-related initiatives were convoluted with the secularization of the Quiet Revolution. Provincial control of social and economic activities blended well with the interventionist tendencies of the post-WWII era, and the 1980s recession was largely interpreted as evidence for the promise of independence from Canada. The regional and municipal infrastructure inherited from the Church made it relatively easy to form a regional-focused governance structure when the federal policy focus shifted to a more local and distributed approach during the restructuring era. The MRCs were well supported until 2014 when the government introduced a severe program of austerity and cut a major portion of their funds and personnel resources (Reimer, Dionne, & Jean, 2017).

Newfoundland and Labrador's 1949 entry into confederation meant that it was isolated from federal policies up to the post-WWII period. Therefore, it entered under the interventionist era with an emphasis on top-down governance (government) that was particularly aggressive for a province perceived as "behind" in its development. The grassroots establishment of Rural/Regional Development Associations (RDAs)[2] in the 1960s provided some of the first signs of resistance to the top-down approach, and became a basis for regional governance over the following decades. In the 1990s the RDAs came under criticism and were faced with significant funding cuts. The provincial government established the Regional Economic Development Boards (REDBs) in 1995, but the massive reorientation of the NL economy toward oil and gas meant the governance of the regions began in a state of conflicting jurisdictions and interests.

Multiple regional organizations added through the 1990s and early 2000s added to what was later described as a "maze of regions and organizational structures and processes across the province" (Vodden, Hall, & Freshwater, 2013). The establishment of the provincial Rural Secretariat in 2004 became an attempt to rationalize provincial regional governance and established nine regions with a staff and council made up of volunteers appointed by the provincial government. In 2011 the funding for the REDBs was discontinued, followed by the dismantling of the provincial Rural Secretariat and its nine volunteer regional councils (Hall, Vodden, & Greenwood, 2017).

5   Conclusions

We have identified and used the core themes of institutional legacies, vision, and regional government organization as a way to illustrate the different phases of regional development in Canada, and the complex way that federal policy influences provincial regional development. Within each theme, it is apparent that Québec has remained an outlier in terms of rural regional development due to the legacy of the established Church infrastructure, a clearly formulated provincial vision, and the close association of the nationalist agenda with rural vitality – at least until recent challenges under austerity measures and urban demands. Conversely, ON has, with some exceptions, shown a fragmented and frequently changing vision of rural regional development, equivocation about institutional boundaries, and the dominance of urban priorities. Different again is BC. It had the advantage of being a latecomer in terms of regional development and visioning, which provided an opportunity to evaluate initiatives from early adopters. However, formerly strong regional initiatives have been hampered by frequently changing regional boundaries and institutions, combined with the short-term nature of many provincial projects. NL is another latecomer to regional development and visions, as well as having the economic cushioning provided by offshore oil during the recession periods and after the 1992 cod moratorium. However, it is also challenged by a lack of coherent regional development vision, a legacy of centralized, resource-industry-driven decision-making at the cost of traditional structures, and frequently changing institutional boundaries.

Currently, political pressures and policies are at odds between seeking to construct flexible, adaptive, context-appropriate, informed development policy for a more regionally resilient future and reverting to the past, whether it be nostalgic references to the interventionist period, or a continuation of a neoliberal restructuring agenda. Policy failure over the past thirty years is often attributed to an inability or unwillingness to implement the neoliberal approach.

The conditions and legacies of the past provide several implications for current and future policy. This is particularly important since the short-term, politicized responses prominent during the restructuring era can be understood to be failing because of the inability to recognize how path dependency frames the capacity for change in the present. In the past, critical shifts such as WWII or the 1980s recession necessitated a break from the former dominant policy path. Just as these crises in the past created conditions for major policy shifts, we are now at a point where new options can emerge.

The 2007–2008 global recession, combined with our knowledge of the failures during previous time periods, may provide the most recent opportunity to shift the dominant path. As we have seen in the past, however, it may be that the current era is a continuation of the pre-financial crisis restructuring era, conditioned by pre-existing path dependence – thus the reference to reactionary negotiation. If so, we may be experiencing the kind of rigidity and overall incoherence in the policy system that resilience researchers warn can lead to system collapse (Vodden, 2009).

This research reinforces the idea that lessons learned in one context cannot be simplistically transferred and used unaltered in another. At the same time, it points to features of provincial-level legacies that should be taken into account when considering the transfer, adaptation, and mutual learning of lessons for regionalist policy. From a research perspective, future inquiry should focus on an investigation of what aspects of the provincial and regional conditions are most important for modifying and engineering shifts from path dependence. For practitioners and activists, this work points to key assets for regional development and action: institutional legacy, vision, and local or regional capacities to respond to change.

Notes

1 An economic development approach where it was assumed that by supporting the concentration of business and industry in a specific location, growth would spread to its surrounding region (Savoie, 2003).
2 The RDAs have been referred to in some official documents and in practice as Rural Development Associations and as Regional Development Associations in others (Vodden, Hall, & Freshwater, 2013).

References

Aucoin, P. (1995). *The New Public Management: Canada in Comparative Perspective*. Montreal: Institute for Research on Public Policy.

Barnes, T., & Hayter, R. (1997). *Troubles in the Rainforest: British Columbia's Forest Economy in Transition*. Victoria: Western Geographical Press.

Brodie, J. (1990). *The Political Economy of Canadian Regionalism*. Toronto: Harcourt Brace Jovanovich.

Bryant, C., & Joseph, A. (2001). Canada's rural population: Trends in space and implications in place. *The Canadian Geographer*, 45(1), 132–137.

Coffey, W.J., & Polese, M. (1984). The concept of local development: A stages model of endogenous regional growth. *Papers of the Regional Science Association*, 35, 1–12.

Douglas, D.J.A. (1994). *Community Economic Development in Canada: Volume 1.* Toronto: McGraw-Hill Ryerson.

Douglas, D.J.A. (2005). The restructuring of local government in rural regions: A rural development perspective. *Journal of Rural Studies*, 21(2), 231–246.

Douglas, D.J.A. (2006). Rural regional development planning: Governance and other challenges in the new EU. *Studia Regionalia*, 18, 112–132.

Douglas, D.J.A. (2016). Power and politics in the changing structures of rural local government. In M. Shucksmith & D.L. Brown (Eds.), *Routledge International Handbook of Rural Studies*. London: Routledge, 601–614.

Fairbairn, B. (1998). *A Preliminary History of Rural Development Policy and Programmes in Canada, 1945–1995.* Saskatoon: University of Saskatchewan, NRE Program.

Hall, H., Vodden, K., & Greenwood, R. (2017). From dysfunctional to destitute: The governance of regional economic development in Newfoundland and Labrador. *International Planning Studies*, 22(2), 49–67.

Halseth, G., & Ryser, L. (2017). *Toward a Political Economy of Resource Dependent Regions.* New York, NY: Routledge Press.

Hanlon, N., & Rosenberg, M. (1998). Not-so-new public management and the denial of geography: Ontario health-care reform in the 1990s. *Environment and Planning C: Government and Policy*, 16, 559–572.

Harrison, J. (2006). Re-reading the new regionalism: A sympathetic critique. *Space and Polity*, 10, 21–46.

Hayter, R. (2000). *Flexible Crossroads: The Restructuring of British Columbia's Forest Economy.* Vancouver: UBC Press.

Hodge, G., Hall, H., & Robinson, I. (2016). *Planning Canadian Regions* (2nd ed.). Vancouver: UBC Press.

Innis, H.A. (1930). *The Fur Trade in Canada.* Toronto: University of Toronto Press.

Jackson, J.D. (1975). *Community and Conflict: A Study of French-English Relations in Ontario.* Montréal: Holt, Rinehart & Winston.

Jacob, B., Lipton, B., Hagens, V., & Reimer, B. (2008). Re-thinking local autonomy: Perceptions from four rural municipalities. *Canadian Public Administration*, 51(3), 407–427.

Markey, S., Halseth, G., & Manson, D. (2012). *Investing in Place.* Vancouver: UBC Press.

Municipal History of Québec. (2016). *Wikipedia, the Free Encyclopedia.* Retrieved April 9, 2018 from https://en.wikipedia.org/w/index.php?title=Municipal_history_of_Québec&oldid=714431154.

Nelles, H.V. (2005). *The Politics of Development: Forests, Mines and Hydro-Electric Power in Ontario, 1849–1941* (2nd ed.). Montreal: McGill-Queen's University Press.

OECD. (2010). *OECD Rural Policy Reviews: Québec, Canada 2010.* OECD Rural Policy Reviews. Paris: OECD Publishing. Doi:10.1787/9789264082151-en.

Osborne, S., & McLaughlin, K. (2002). A new public management in context. In K. McLaughlin, S. Osborne, & E. Ferlie (Eds.), *New Public Management: Current Trends and Future Prospects*. London: Routledge, 7–14.

Polèse, M. (1999). From regional development to local development: On the life, death, and rebirth(?) of regional science as a policy relevant science. *Canadian Journal of Regional Science*, 22(3), 299–314.

Reimer, B. (2010). Space to place: Bridging the gap. In G. Halseth, S. Markey, & D. Bruce (Eds.), *The Next Rural Economies: Constructing Rural Place in Global Economies.* Cambridge, MA: CABI, 263–274.

Reimer, B. (2013). Rural–urban interdependence: Understanding our common interests. In J. Parkins, G. Maureen, & M. Reed (Eds.), *Social Transformation in Rural Canada: Community, Cultures, and Collective Action.* Vancouver: UBC Press, 91–109.

Reimer, B., Dionne, J., & Jean, B. (2017). Québec's approach to regional government: An overview and critical reflections. In *RPLC Webinar Presentation,* June 14, 2017. Retrieved May 22, 2018 from www.youtube.com/watch?v=5ZjdRc585V8

Reimer, B., & Jean, B. (2015). Québec's approach to regional development: A successful rural policy under budgetary pressure. In *Presentation to the Water-Food-Energy-Climate Nexus: An Emerging Challenge for Rural Policy, OECD/ICRPS/RPLC Preconference.* Memphis, TN.

Saul, J.R. (2009). *A Fair Country: Telling Truths about Canada* (Reprint ed.). Toronto: Penguin Canada.

Savoie, D. (1992). *Regional Economic Development: Canada's Search for Solutions.* Toronto: University of Toronto Press.

Savoie, D. (1997). *Rethinking Canada's Regional Development Policy: An Atlantic Perspective.* Ottawa: The Canadian Institute for Research on Regional Development.

Savoie, D. (2003). *Reviewing Canada's Regional Development Efforts.* Ottawa: Royal Commission on Renewing and Strengthening Our Place in Canada.

Tindal, C.R., & Tindal, S.N. (2009). *Local Government in Canada* (7th ed.). Toronto: Nelson Education.

Vodden, K. (2009). *New Spaces, Ancient Places: Collaborative Governance and Sustainable Development in Canada's Coastal Regions.* Burnaby: Simon Fraser University.

Vodden, K., Hall, H., & Freshwater, D. (2013). *Understanding Regional Governance in Newfoundland and Labrador: A Survey of Regional Development Organizations.* Memorial University of Newfoundland. Retrieved January 31, 2018 from http://research.library.mun.ca/1966/1/Understanding_Regional_Governance.pdf.

Young, N., & Matthews, R. (2007). Resource economies and neoliberal experimentation: The reform of industry and community in rural British Columbia. *Area,* 39(2), 176–178.

3 What is new regionalism?

Jen Daniels, David J.A. Douglas, Kelly Vodden, and Sean Markey

1 Introduction: roots and characteristics

New regionalism has been described and defined through a variety of theories, concepts, and general descriptors that attempt to explain the evolution of a regional development regime from the 1950s to the present. The earlier version dominated the era of state intervention described in Chapter 2 as "old regionalism", which was replaced by one that emerged in the 1980s and 1990s as the former faltered. Hettne (1999) and Scott (2016), for example, have described new regionalism as both a process of region-building and a package of policies that has several aims, from enhanced territorial control and democratic governance, to fostering regional cooperation, integration, and identity, and increasing "economic and environmental viability" (Scott, 2016, p. 21). This *new* regionalism is presented as a significant shift in the intellectual trajectory of regional development discourse and practice.

The era of restructuring in the final quarter of the 20th century saw the ascendancy of neoliberalism and the hegemony of the market perspective as primary informants of public policies. This was in turn associated with a selective "hollowing out" of the state (Jessop, 1994), and refocusing of the state's development activities on facilitating competitive advantage, accumulation, and regulation (e.g., Keating, 1998; Brenner, 1999; MacLeod, 2001). This facilitated the selected decentralization and downloading of government and publicly supported services to the local level, while simultaneously fueling an already vibrant "localism" that saw increased self-assertion and self-reliance at the community level. This localism was fueled by (a) a broad-based disenchantment with the ineffectiveness of so-called top-down national and state/provincial regional development policies and programs, (b) a growing realization of the inadequacy of the narrow economic perspectives (e.g., comparative advantage) which dominated these policies, and (c) a shift away from the dominance of a needs-based approach to development toward a more balanced and nuanced assets-based approach. Markey (2011) refers to these shifts as "push" and "pull" factors characteristic of the terrain in which new regionalism emerged.

New regionalism, Markey (2011) argues, "occupies an intermediating position, within a dynamic tension between the abandonment of traditional patterns of top-down stewardship and the appeal of local control and place-sensitive intervention" (p. 4). This new place-particular perspective calls for more heterogeneous and flexible public policies and practices, in contrast to a generic space-based perspective, together with greater emphasis on local democracy and collaboration, integration of horizontal and vertical processes, and relational perspectives that temper or supplant older top-down controls. This emergent place-based approach, usually associated with "thick institutional" conditions (Amin & Thrift, 1994) and supportive networks of various social capitals, allows for a plurality of interests, agents, and perspectives cultivating what has come to be known as a governance approach to development (e.g., Rhodes, 1996; Stoker, 1998), in contrast to the former government-dominated approach.

New regionalism emerged in tandem with a re-assertion of the region as an appropriate and effective spatial framework for development (Douglas, 1997; Storper, 1997; Amin, 1999; Harrison, 2006; Zimmerbauer & Paasi, 2013). New regionalism provides a focus on specific territories, allowing greater sensitivity to regional particularities among theorists and regional planners (Wheeler, 2002). Yet the spatial manifestations of this emergent practice permit multi-scalar and shifting, dynamic formations and processes in identifying all manner of regional designs, in contrast to the previous "official" regions of the state and its local government apparatus.

Many authors focus on new regionalist political-economic arrangements on an international scale, with multiple countries forming alliances (e.g., the North American Free Trade Agreement, Asia-Pacific Economic Cooperation, Mercosur). In contrast, rural development scholars often speak of new regionalism as an intra-national phenomenon: occurring within provinces in the case of Canadian regional development (Markey, 2011), or within states in Australia (Peterson, McAlpine, Ward, & Rayner, 2007). In other cases, development processes are examined on local and extra-local scales, with regions constituting a network of relations as opposed to a discrete, physical geographic space (Young, 2010). New regionalism in Europe, for example, employs a regional governance model that manifests itself in sub-national administrative units, metropolitan regions and/or cultural areas with increasing degrees of political autonomy, while at the same time recognizing the significance of macro-regional dynamics within the European political economic landscape.

New regionalism embraces fluidity in how regional scale is defined; while

> the old regionalism was concerned with defining boundaries and jurisdictions ... The new regionalism accepts that boundaries are open, fuzzy or elastic. What defines the extent of the region varies with the issue we're trying to address or the characteristic we are considering.
>
> (Young, 2010, p. 3)

While we accept this openness and fluidity in regional definitions in this volume as a characteristic of new regionalist thought, our focus is on sub-provincial regions in Canada (variously defined, as we discuss further in Chapter 4), but with a recognition of the extra-local networks of which these regions are a part.

Different groups of new regionalist scholars place varying degrees of emphasis on economic and political dimensions of regional development. Some focus on regions as the key territorial unit for economic development, mobilizing concepts of embeddedness, institutional thickness, untraded interdependencies, learning, and regional innovation systems (Granovetter, 1985; Amin & Thrift, 1994; Storper, 1997; Cooke & Morgan, 1998). Others argue that regions are the key territorial unit for political action, with a focus on institutional restructuring, political mobilization, and a shift away from a state government mandate of ensuring inter-spatial equity toward an approach that enables and facilitates development (Keating, 1998; Polèse, 1999). In other words, a governance model is adopted that includes "a set of institutions and actors that are drawn from but also beyond government ... [and] ... recognizes the capacity to get things done which does not rest on the power of government to command or use its authority" but rather "sees government as able to use new tools and techniques to steer and guide ..." (Stoker, 1998, p. 18) within collaborative and multi-level collaborative governance arrangements (Gibson, 2014).

The juxtaposition between the dominant characteristics of regional development policy and practice in the highly centralist intervention era and that of the subsequent eras of restructuring, characterized by greater devolution and negotiation (as described in Chapter 2), offers insights into the elements that are seen to define new regionalism. These include bottom-up and top-down dynamics as well as reactive and proactive responses to the restructuring that began in the 1980s and continued through the 1990s and beyond, as described in the previous chapter (Hettne, Inotai, & Sunkel, 2000; Wheeler, 2002; Hettne, 2005; Buzdugan, 2006; Scott, 2007; Markey, 2011; Perrin, 2012). Table 3.1 below provides this summary comparison.

We explore the empirical bases of new regionalism in Canada through five core themes identified in the literature (multi-level collaborative governance,

Table 3.1 New regionalism versus old regionalism

New regionalism	Old regionalism
Network-based system	Hierarchy-based system
Governance	Government
Process	Structure
Open	Closed
Collaboration	Coordination
Trust	Accountability
Empowerment	Power

(Adapted from: Wallis, 2002)

place-based development, integrated development, rural–urban interdependencies, and learning and innovation). Included in these are the variously articulated themes of sustainable, integrated approaches to development and rural–urban interactions – where the rural is a central consideration. Our approach contrasts with metropolitan new regionalism, which considers city-regions as the key territorial unit for planning, governance, and global competitiveness (e.g., Savitch & Vogel, 2000; Sancton, 2001; Nelson, 2002; Wheeler, 2002; Wolfe, 2003). We argue that the pursuit of sustainable regions, particularly within the Canadian context, must include consideration of the unique development context facing rural communities (Peterson, Walker, Maher, Hoverman, & Eberhard, 2010). While much new regionalist literature has focused on urban areas (discussed further below) the rationale for a regional approach to rural community development has been thoroughly examined by Douglas (1999, 2006), with justifications for greater attention to this context for development having been more recently re-stated (e.g., Markey & Heisler, 2011; Markey, Halseth, & Manson, 2012).

2 Five key themes of new regionalism

In this section, we will discuss how each of the five themes of new regionalism introduced in Chapter 1 are discussed in the new regionalism literature. In varying degrees, these themes are interconnected throughout the different types of new regionalism, and their use also varies across different scales of regional development.

2.1 Multi-level collaborative governance

Governance, and in particular multi-level and collaborative governance, is a salient feature in all varieties of new regionalism literature. The centerpiece in the concept of governance is the acquisition of *agency*, in contexts of uncertain legitimacies and scarce resources (Stoker, 1998). Governance is a process of collaboration and coordination, and steering of interests involved in decision-making, including community, voluntary, and commercial interests within an area, across economic, social, and environmental sectors (Townsend, 2005; Gregory, Johnston, Pratt, Watts, & Whatmore, 2009; Vodden, 2015). A critical feature of governance is participation, including participation in deciding what ends and values should be chosen and how these should be pursued (Townsend, 2005; Castro, 2007). Typically, governance is characterized by self-organization and coordination among organizations, often including the participation of various scales of government through vertical (hierarchical) coordination, and through horizontal partnerships, such as between two regional groups (Townsend, 2005; Bogason & Zølner, 2007; Gregory et al., 2009). Collaborative governance often includes government actors, multilateral institutions, NGOs, businesses, academics and others working in partnerships (e.g. private-public partnerships), and networks that produce and coordinate policy decisions (Bulkeley, 2005; Bogason & Zølner, 2007). The goal of a regional governance framework is *not* the absence of government; rather it is a "better structuring of relations among governments ... to provide an institutional base to house strategic planning and a framework to allow local governments to discern a [regional] interest where one exists" (Vogel & Nezelkewicz, 2002, p. 129).

The principal drivers and characteristics of governance vary greatly across the new regionalism literature, due to the different scales of regions and forms of regionalism. The economic new regionalism discussion includes multi-level collaborative governance forms, where regional economic development is considered a key driver (Storper, 1997; MacLeod, 2001; Zimmerbauer & Paasi, 2013). This often takes the form of explicit multi-level attempts to improve regional competitiveness in the global economy, throughout Europe, the Asia Pacific, and North and South America via macro-regional policy directives and the establishment of bottom-up regional partnerships. We also find related initiatives in southern African countries, such as small, medium, and micro-finance enterprise development and other localized employment creation and community empowerment programs (e.g., Rogerson, 2001; Harrison, 2006; Scott, 2016). Other key drivers include: the desire to increase regional capacity and coordination in (political) decision-making to increase autonomy and improve community quality of life (Bellamy & Brown, 2009; Keating & Wilson, 2014), and the desire to tackle complex environmental and social issues that are difficult for government alone to address (Bulkeley, 2005; Clarke, 2016). A survey of the primary characteristics of and actions for regional governance are included in Table 3.2.

The critiques posed to regional governance are similar to those that challenge new regionalism itself, namely a lack of clarity around the definition of the region and the challenges posed by shifts in scale. Frisken and Norris (2001) argue that new regionalism proponents only vaguely define what they mean when they use the term "regional governance", and have historically leaned too strongly on the idea of cooperation, which they argue in and of itself is insufficient for achieving sustainable regional governance, whether in the form of economic competitiveness or greater political autonomy. Breen and Minnes (2014) note that rescaling governance is difficult, "particularly as giving power to the local level without accompanying capacity can have opposing effects to what is intended" (p. 8). Such initiatives can alter power imbalances and sharpen dichotomies between "winners" and "losers" (Bakker & Cook, 2011). As well, in light of the issue of a "relativization of scale", or hollowing out of the state, (Jessop, 1994) with "no privileged level yet assuming a preeminent role in the meta-governance of socioeconomic affairs" (MacLeod, 2001, p. 824), Morgan (2004) argues that conceptualizations of multi-level collaborative governance often pay too little attention to the inter-dependencies at work. To mitigate this issue, regionalist scholars and practitioners must pay close attention to the role of the state and international governing bodies (in addition to those on the ground or in the region), the interplay between levels of governance and the power imbalances, inequalities, social and environmental costs – and overall unequal geographies – that result from governance practices (MacLeod, 2001; Morgan, 2004).

Table 3.2 Regional governance characteristics in the new regionalism literature

Characteristic	Cited in (not exhaustive)
Multi-level partnerships and associations, including vertical and horizontal linkages	Savitch & Vogel, 2000; Gainsborough, 2001; Gibbs & Jonas, 2001; Healey, 2004; Bulkeley, 2005; Townsend, 2005; Harrison, 2006; Pahl-Wostl, Gupta, & Petry, 2008; Bellamy & Brown, 2009; Pitschel & Bauer, 2009
Adaptive and flexible	Savitch & Vogel, 2000; Bellamy & Brown, 2009; Scott, 2016
Public involvement, engagement, and participation	Gibbs & Jonas, 2001; Sancton, 2001; Townsend, 2005; Castro, 2007; Nelles, 2009; Riggirozzi, 2010
Inclusive/institutional thickness	Giordano, 2001; Bellamy & Brown, 2009; Bakker & Cook, 2011
Networks and information sharing	Bulkeley, 2005; Bogason & Zølner, 2007; George & Reed, 2015; Scott, 2016
Calls for increased institutional and structural capacity and support	Gainsborough, 2001; Bulkeley, 2005; Harrison, 2006; Maxwell, 2008; Pahl-Wostl et al., 2008; Clarke, 2016
Calls for civic capital and inter-municipal cooperation and agreements	Savitch & Vogel, 2000; Pahl-Wostl et al., 2008; Nelles, 2009
Need for co-construction of regional policies and governance arrangements	Zirul, Halseth, Markey, & Ryser, 2015

(Adapted from: Breen & Minnes, 2014)

As evident throughout this section, governance is highly interconnected with several other themes in our new regionalism framework (see Figure 1.1). Regional identity and the role of a place-based development are reflected in many of the characteristics present in governance, for example, especially public participation and consent in defining values and the goals of governance structures (Reimer, 2005; Makoni, Meiklejohn, & Coetzee, 2008; George & Reed, 2015). Shared learning and networks are also important to ensuring successful regional governance, while the pursuit of economic growth and competition should be accompanied by considerations of social and environmental factors and their role in regional resilience and sustainable governance (MacLeod, 2001; Christopherson, Michie, & Tyler, 2010). For more on our conceptualization of governance within our research and related findings, see Chapter 5.

2.2 Place-based development

Place and place-based development are integral components of the new regionalism literature. Place-based development emerged as an alternative to traditional, "top-down" development interventions and contextually obtuse strategies, including, single-sector and neoliberal approaches, wherein individuals are assumed capable of acting completely independently from the community/place in which they exist (Markey, 2010; Barca, McCann, & Rodríguez-Pose, 2012). Here, place can be defined as a spatial entity co-constructed for particular negotiated purposes, and not assumed to be fixed or otherwise immutable (Douglas, 2006; Escobar, 2008). Acknowledging places as sites where people and bio-physical landscapes converge in personally relevant, historically embedded and dynamic ways is critical to understanding how place influences regional economic development (Cheng, Kruger, & Daniels, 2003; Gregory et al., 2009; Daniels, Baldacchino, & Vodden, 2015). Within the new regionalist literature, places are considered to be endowed with inherent assets – above and beyond economic capital (Markey, 2010). Critical in the utilization of a place's assets are the leadership and participation of local community and regional actors, with an emphasis on the agency of these actors, as opposed to the structures in which they operate (Markey, Halseth, & Manson, 2008; Reimer & Markey, 2008; Halseth, Reed, & Reimer, 2010; OECD, 2010). There is also a need to identify and select place-sensitive policy tools in order to best utilize resources and respond to threats (Reimer, 2006). Regional identity, that is, the extent to which people are bonded to a particular place, and its influence on development, is also a recurrent theme in the new regional literature (see Table 3.3).

The main drivers and priorities for place-based development may extend from social inclusion, environmental challenges, or economic competitiveness, to public health, physical infrastructure issues, and education. Storper (1997) has noted, for example, that the new political economic realities of the post-Fordist reflexive capitalism mean that firms, governments, and notably regional interests have to construct context specific "frameworks for action" to deal with the radical economic uncertainties they face. The prevailing institutional environment, both necessary for and engendered by these collaborative, opportunistic spatial arrangements, is one including local, place-specific governance relationships and practices. Examples of such place-based arrangements include: regional-scale approaches to watershed governance, water management, and forest management in Canada (Bakker, 2007; George & Reed, 2015); regionally specific development policies using specific regional contexts, and local knowledge and experiences from key regional actors in the EU (Barca, 2009); "smart-specialization" utilizing place-based innovations and knowledge in economic development strategies in Europe and North America (Wolfe, 2011; Hildreth & Bailey, 2014); and the development of a program for the implementation of social and welfare projects for ALBA (Bolivarian Alliance for the Peoples of Our America) countries (Riggirozzi, 2010).

The role of regional identity in development is highly place-dependent. Identity may foster or hinder region-building, depending on whether the change is externally or internally prompted, the strength of regional affiliations, and the historical, cultural, and political context (Zimmerbauer & Paasi, 2013). Since regional identity is complex, the diversity of regional expression is better considered through a multi-dimensional framework (Centellas, 2010).

Table 3.3 Place-based development characteristics in the new regionalism literature

Characteristic	Cited in (not exhaustive)
Regional identity key in development (positive or negative, in the case of lack of identity)	Cheng et al., 2003; Centellas, 2010; Peterson et al., 2010; Riggirozzi, 2010; Berkes & Ross, 2013; Faludi, 2013; Paasi, 2013; Gill & Larson, 2014; Devlin et al., 2015
Place holistically defined (social, cultural, environmental, economic etc.), relational and territorial	Wheeler, 2002; Paasi, 2004; Harrison, 2006; Frisvoll & Rye, 2009; Jonas, 2013; Zimmerbauer & Paasi, 2013; Huggins & Thompson, 2014; Markey, Breen, Vodden, & Daniels, 2015
Assets and capacities influencing development (e.g., social, cultural, physical, environmental)	Hirst, 1997; Scott, 1998; Grant, 2004; De Loë & Kreutzwiser, 2005; Reimer, 2006; Bakker, 2007; Frisvoll & Rye, 2009; Huggins & Clifton, 2011
Place-based development strategies linked to enhanced competitive advantage	Markey, 2010; Tomaney, 2010; Huggins & Clifton, 2011; Markey et al., 2012
Local management and governance control	Gibbs & Jonas, 2001; George & Reed, 2015
Importance of local knowledge	Peterson et al., 2007, 2010
Need to recognize scale interdependencies, local-global connection	Hudson, 2007; Reimer & Markey, 2008; Harrison, 2013
Need for local participation in policy/governance co-construction	Markey, 2010

(Adapted from: Breen & Minnes, 2014)

One criticism of place-based development is that while regional groups and small governments can often identify an array of assets that afford development opportunities (including identity), the strategic application of these is often limited (De Loë & Kreutzwiser, 2005; Vodden, 2015). This can occur, for example, because higher levels of government and regulations may control the development of local assets. Researchers and scholars must also remain cognizant of the political interests related to defining and utilizing an asset. For example, assets such as social capital are not apolitical entities, but rather have specific socio-political geographies that include and exclude people, groups, and initiatives in particular ways (Hadjimichalis, 2006). The new regionalist research has sought to integrate social, cultural, and environmental aims in development, in addition to enhancing economic competitiveness, acknowledging territoriality, and territorial and regional identity politics – that is, the diversity of people, groups and non-human agents involved – to resist a more narrow neoliberal agenda (Hadjimichalis, 2006; Riggirozzi, 2010). Our findings with respect to these dynamics of place and place-based development in Canada are presented in Chapter 6.

2.3 Integrated development approaches

Integration is a key component of new regionalism, which highlights, among other things, the need for interlocking policy frameworks at different levels of government (Wheeler, 2002). According to Gregory et al. (2009, p. 1), integration is the "creation and maintenance of intense and diverse patterns of interaction and control between formerly more or less separate social spaces", and thus, brings together different systems of meaning and action. Within the regional development context, the integrated theme can also be thought of as a linkage of diverse systems, such as social, cultural, ecological, and health systems, to counter fragmentation (Lubell, Schneider, Scholz, & Mete, 2002; Bellamy & Brown, 2009; Hudson, 2009; Berkes & Ross, 2013).

From a sustainable development perspective, integration brings together environmental, economic, and social priorities in decision-making. New regionalism posits that regions are the key territorial unit for sustainable integrated development (Wheeler, 2002; Rainnie & Grobbelaar, 2005; Bradford, 2010; Devlin et al., 2015). Peterson et al. (2010) argue that this more encompassing and holistic version of new regionalism entails

> a focus on specific geographic regions and place making; an active approach based on improved governance arrangements; the adoption of more holistic and integrated frameworks that incorporate environmental concerns; inclusion of normative approaches; acknowledgement of the importance of regional design and physical planning.
>
> (p.132)

In these terms, new regionalism is a normative project based on principles of sustainable and integrated development.

The main priority of integrated development is the movement toward more holistic, place-particular planning and regional development approaches that recognize interdependencies across different sectors, scales, levels of governance, and regions (Wheeler, 2002). One of the key characteristics of integrated development is the coordination of governance and policy approaches around a resource (see Table 3.4). Breen and Minnes (2014) illustrate this process using regional approaches to water and watershed management across Canada. Other examples of integrated development in practice include place-based governance approaches of model forests and biosphere reserves in eastern Canada, which have sought to address social sustainability in developing policies. These approaches include procedural justice and community involvement in the pursuit of social sustainability as components, including concerns for social needs, equity, and public health while attending to environmental challenges (George & Reed, 2015). Other examples include the urgent need to connect local government "reform" to the overall rural development agenda itself (Douglas, 2016). The "New Urban Planning" paradigm emerging out of the 2006 World

Planning Congress in Vancouver provides a further illustration of an integrated approach. This paradigm recommends integrative planning approaches with broad community input to develop regional development strategies (Illsley, Jackson, Curry, & Rapaport, 2010). Another example can be found in the establishment of "peace parks" in the Maputo Development Corridor (MDC) linking nature reserves along the borders of South Africa and Mozambique. These parks provide an opportunity for eco-tourism and continued environmental protection (Rogerson, 2001). Other key characteristics of the integrated theme are listed in Table 3.4.

While there is evidence of the integrated concept in the new regionalism literature, in practice policy and program integration have been relatively rare, particularly in the Canadian regional development context (Douglas, 2014b). Likewise, there is a minimal response within development practice to balancing the issue of economic growth with social equity (Vodden, 2015). Genuine policy and plan integration are difficult to achieve. For example, in regional water management success in integration is often lacking due to the complexity of the issue and difficulty in appealing to all stakeholder groups (Castro, 2007; Cohen, 2012). The application of these ideas and challenges encountered in doing so are explored further drawing from our research findings in Chapter 7.

Table 3.4 Integrated characteristics in the new regionalism literature

Characteristic	Cited in (not exhaustive)
Includes different arenas: economic, political, cultural, natural/ecological, environmental, health	Gibbs & Jonas, 2001; Pezzoli, Marciano, & Zaslavsky, 2001; Wheeler, 2002; Peterson et al., 2007; Ferreyra, de Loë, & Kreutzwiser, 2008; Bellamy & Brown, 2009; Gregory et al., 2009; Illsley et al., 2010; Berkes & Ross, 2013; George & Reed, 2015; Douglas, 2016
Balancing questions of regional economic development and social equity	Hadjimichalis, 2006; Riggirozzi, 2010
Multi-level, interdependent scales	Wheeler, 2002; Bellamy & Brown, 2009; Grigg, 2012
Normative model	Pezzoli et al., 2001
Uneven processes	Hudson, 2007; Gregory et al., 2009
Use of sustainable, place-based planning and development principles	Gibbs & Jonas, 2001, Pezzoli et al., 2001; Morgan, 2004; Peterson et al., 2007
Movement toward policy coordination and need for coordination approaches to the same issue/resource	Mitchell, 2005; Bakker, 2007; Maxwell, 2008; Bellamy & Brown, 2009; Illsley et al., 2010; Bakker & Cook, 2011; George & Reed, 2015

(Adapted from: Breen & Minnes, 2014)

2.4 Rural–urban interdependence

New regionalism has primarily been examined in urban-centred settings with a focus on key concepts such as: smart growth, new urbanism, regional planning, regional transportation, regional service provision, economic competitiveness, and efficiencies (Sancton, 2001; Windsheimer, 2007; Rodríguez-Pose, 2008; Wolfe, 2010). At the same time, there is much discussion in the literature that focuses on the (perceived) power imbalance and conflict between rural and urban areas, and a hierarchical spatial order that privileges urbanized areas over rural counterparts in terms of public policy and institutional representation (Reimer, 2005; Overbeek, 2009; Tsukamoto, 2011). Yet we argue that the academic focus on ongoing rural–urban conflict – often arising from challenges over resources – does not adequately reflect the interdependence between the two (Reimer, Vodden, & Brett, 2011). Table 3.5 illustrates a broader focus for such interdependence discussions.

Within new regionalism, rural–urban interdependence scholars examine the interdependence of rural and urban areas both within and between regions (Tacoli, 1998; Gallent, 2006). Sources of interdependence include: trade of resources and people, institutional integration and influences, environmental concerns such as air pollution, greenhouse gases, and water quality, as well as identity formation and management (Reimer, 2005; External Advisory Committee on Cities and Communities, 2006; Robinson et al., 2008). The rural provision of

Table 3.5 Rural–urban interdependence characteristics in the new regionalism literature

Characteristic	*Cited in (not exhaustive)*
Rural communities valuable in terms of recreation and environmental assets	Reimer, 2005; Hamin & Marcucci, 2008; Ortiz-Guerrero, 2013; Breen, 2016
Rurally located resources as a base for urban economic growth	Baxter, Berlin, & Ramlo, 2005; Hamin & Marcucci, 2008; Reimer et al., 2011, Tsukamoto, 2011
Four spheres of interdependence: trade and exchanges, institutions (policies, design), environment, identity	Reimer, 2005; Hamin & Marcucci, 2008; Reimer et al., 2011; Ortiz-Guerrero, 2013
Three types of rural–urban relations: flows between, different territorial bounds, different functional relations	Overbeek, 2009
Need for shift to emphasize interrelationships (governance) and functional interdependencies as opposed to the more conventional conflict that occurs	External Advisory Committee on Cities and Communities, 2006; Freshwater, Simms, & Vodden, 2011; Devlin et al., 2015; Breen, 2016
Interdependencies are important for consideration in planning (e.g., the RU fringe areas)	Wheeler, 2002; Gallent, 2006;; Freshwater et al., 2011; Vodden, 2015

resources, labour, recreational opportunities, and environmental stewardship serves as a base for urban growth while urban areas provide markets, technology, financial capital, manufactured goods, services, and policies, and actions around these have implications for both rural and urban areas (Reimer et al., 2011)

A key driver for exploring rural and urban interdependence is the major influence that land and natural resource development policies have on people's lives and the environment, from a macro-scale to the local level. This is perhaps no more evident than when considering water systems. To illustrate, approximately 70% of the Canadian population is in an urban watershed, with headwaters that extend far into rural areas. Rural–urban dialogue is therefore essential in adequately governing such watershed regions (Rothwell, 2006).

In general terms, Wheeler (2002) suggests that there is a lack of under-standing of the interdependence between rural and urban areas in regional development, and more specifically new regionalism literature. In light of available evidence to support critiques of urban-centric new regionalism, further scholarly and practitioner attention needs to be paid to rural regions, and their impact on urban places (Ortiz-Guerrero, 2013; Vodden, 2015). At the same time, it must be recognized that the differing contexts of rural areas can make the transference of new regionalist ideas emerging from urban settings difficult (Sancton, 2001; Wheeler, 2002; Ward & Jonas, 2004; Rast, 2006; Scott, 2007; Heisler, 2012; Ortiz-Guerrero, 2013; Zimmerbauer & Paasi, 2013). We explore these ideas further in Chapter 8.

2.5 Innovation and knowledge flows

Learning, knowledge flows, and innovation are considered to be central fea-tures of new regionalism (Bunnell & Coe, 2001; Amdam, 2002; Morgan, 2004; Allen & Cochrane, 2007; Brett & MacKie, 2012; Carter & Vodden, 2017). Innovation refers to the introduction of new phenomena such as con-cepts, objects, or practices into products or processes (Gregory et al., 2009; Vodden et al., 2013). Other definitions describe innovation as the creation and diffusion of new ways of doing things (Vodden et al., 2013), including original policy ideas (Berry & Berry, 2007), or changes to products, processes, or organization (Bunnell & Coe, 2001). Learning and knowledge flows are closely related to innovation and are often considered critical to development outcomes (Allen & Cochrane, 2007; Vodden et al., 2013). Harnessing learn-ing and knowledge flows, from a regional development perspective, can result in novel ways of organizing, sharing information within and across organizations, developing new strategies for addressing local challenges and opportunities, or mobilizing new forms of investment (Grant, 2004; Vodden et al., 2013).

Aspects of innovation in regional development include learning networks, which can help alleviate potential path dependencies, and territorial innov-ation systems such as industrial districts, innovation milieux, regional innovation systems, and clusters (Vodden et al., 2013). These can range from formal to informal networks, originating or being developed in highly urban hubs to "quiet" and pragmatic innovation in rural communities, households, enterprises, and organizations (Vodden, 2015). Innovative learning systems are important for regional organizations to reflexively and strategically adopt new governance models, as in the case of "double and triple-loop" learning in resource conservation and management organizations in New South Wales, Australia (Mitchell, 2013). Regional innovation systems are a set of relationships in an area which generate a collective learning process leading to the rapid diffusion of knowledge (Vodden et al., 2013).

The main drivers, and key characteristics, of innovation and enhanced learning flows illustrated in the new regionalism literature tend to be economic in nature. Researchers have noted that innovation and knowledge contribute to competitive advantage (Amin & Thrift, 1994; Storper, 1997; Grant, 2004; Cooke & Leydesdorff, 2006; Wolfe, 2011; Vodden et al., 2013). Competition demands continuous innovation (Council on Competitiveness, 2010), and similarly, as globalization accelerates, there is a diffusion of technology and increase in innovations, whereby innovation translates into a driver of economic growth via investments and labour-force development (International Labour Office, 2010). Additionally, the new regionalist literature supports the notion that knowledge itself is an integral component of the economy and consequently regional development. The knowledge economy is characterized by a shift toward information handling, knowledge accumulation, and knowledge goods, with linkages to regional innovation systems (Rainnie & Grobbelaar, 2005). Territorially specific innovations are deemed critical to regional economic competitiveness. In practice, this can be translated into the development of strategic economic development policies, i.e., focused on clear regional priorities for the use of limited public funds, which in the EU is referred to as "smart specialization" (Wolfe, 2011; Foray et al., 2012). Regional innovation strategies can also play a role in assisting less favoured regions (Morgan, 2004).

A survey of the primary characteristics of and actions for innovation and learning flows in the new regionalism literature are included in Table 3.6.

While innovation can provide opportunities and potential solutions for regional development, the context and extent to which various strategies can be applied and/or succeed varies (e.g., Morgan, 2004; Rainnie & Grobbelaar, 2005). Small or rural systems face difficulties when the required technological innovations are beyond their capabilities (Maxwell, 2008). Further, simply investing in knowledge infrastructure does not automatically lead to better outcomes – a complex interaction of people and actions may be required to make it work (Vodden et al., 2013).

The majority of innovation research in the new regionalism literature has been urban-centric. Vodden et al. (2013) note, however, that innovation research in rural regions must pay attention to the rural context, acknowledging the importance of scale interdependency for example, and that policy

Table 3.6 Innovation and knowledge flows characteristics in the new regionalism literature

Characteristic	Cited in (not exhaustive)
Knowledge building (including learning networks)/understanding existing knowledge levels	Morgan, 1997; Amin, 1999; Giordano, 2001; Rainnie & Grobbelaar, 2005; Bakker, 2007; Maxwell, 2008; Herrschel, 2009; Bradford, 2010; Mitchell, 2013; Ortiz-Guerrero, 2013
Different sources of knowledge (e.g., local knowledge)	Muys, 2000; Bakker, 2007; Maxwell, 2008; Illsley et al., 2010; Bakker & Cook, 2011
Innovation as a social process (versus technical)	Ehrenfeucht, 2002; Grant, 2004; Morgan, 2004; Bradford, 2010; Riggirozzi, 2010; Shearmur, 2010; Mitchell, 2013
Innovation systems stress links between firms, education/research institutions, and government	Grant, 2004; Ridley, Yee-Cheong, & Juma, 2006; Ortiz-Guerrero, 2013
Synergism/urban agglomerations coming together (clustering people/economic activities), promoting innovation	Cooke & Morgan, 1998; Amin, 1999; Ehrenfeucht, 2002; Ortiz-Guerrero, 2013
multi-scale, reflexive approach (innovation systems, learning, and interdependence across scales)	Bunnell & Coe, 2001; Morgan, 2004; Vodden et al., 2013

(Adapted from: Breen & Minnes, 2014)

levels important for economic development outcomes exist at levels beyond regional control.

The innovation and knowledge flows theme (discussed further in Chapter 9) is highly interconnected with the other new regionalism themes. Innovation is a spatial phenomenon with geographic, spatial, and place elements (Shearmur, 2010). Further, a growing body of evidence demonstrates that innovation depends on "networked relationships and organizational synergies that flow through face to face interaction and ongoing dialogue among geographically proximate actors" (Wolfe, 2010, p. 1; cf. Barca, 2009). This place element also links to rural–urban interdependencies since the conditions for innovation are better met in some regions than others. Proximity to urban areas is a significant factor (Shearmur, 2010). Finally, the need for inclusion of innovation, as well as deliberate attention to knowledge as a resource to be fostered and well managed, is critical to an integrated approach to governance (Bakker & Cook, 2011; Mitchell, 2013).

3 Considering critiques

Several critiques of the new regionalist body of work merit careful consideration and response. The following section will present and respond to four primary critiques: vague definitions within new regionalism; the insular focus on the regional scale; the lack of transferability, cohesion, and clear methodological focus; and, its purported facilitation of a neoliberal agenda (Brett & MacKie, 2012). We also provide responses to these critiques that in our view are sufficiently powerful to warrant the adoption of new regionalism as a central theoretical framework for the recent Canadian research presented in this volume.

One of the chief criticisms of new regionalism is its purported lack of a strong conceptual connection within the related literature, as well as a vague idea of "the region" itself. Indeed, since its emergence over two decades ago, a widely accepted definition of new regionalism remains elusive and the question of to what extent substantive differences exist between the "new" and "old" continues to be posed (Rainnie & Grobbelaar, 2005; Buzdugan, 2006; Brett & MacKie, 2012). Lagendijk (1997) suggests "the success of new regionalism is attributed to the variation in concepts which, while evolving individually, have all converged by invoking a network metaphor" (p. 2). New regionalism, we further argue, is held together through two key factors. The first is that it speaks to the need for a re-imagined framework that addresses the shortcomings of the "old regionalism" that dominated the interventionist era. Secondly, unifying this framework is a normative drive for social democratic forms of governance and economic equity through devolution and place-based development. For some, particularly in sustainable new regionalism, sustainable development is the objective. We grant, however, that given the diversity among new regionalist scholars and policy these points of unity are tenuous.

A related critique is the lack of a clear definition of the region as "the supposedly foundational concept of the new 'paradigm'" (Lovering, 1999, p. 383). As discussed above, the extent to which the term new regionalism is deployed ranges from discussion of macro-scale globalization and multinational economic integration to (rural) development-focused, conservation-minded, micro-economic geographies (Ethier, 1998; Mansfield & Milner, 1999; Peterson et al., 2007; Väyrynen, 2003; Young, 2010).

A second line of critique is that regionalist scholars and practitioners, even those who align themselves with new regionalism, tend to conceptualize the notion of the region in insular terms and/or overemphasize its importance and thus underestimate the impact of other scalar units in regional development (Harrison, 2006; Allen & Cochrane, 2007; Brett & MacKie, 2012). According to Harrison (2006), "*the* major issue facing the new regionalism today is the need to consider the region in relation to its interconnectedness with other scales and other sites of economic organization" (p. 38, emphasis added). To illustrate, Brett and MacKie (2012) point to an OECD (2010) rural development report that fails to discuss the role of the federal government in rural development policy in Québec, limiting analysis to municipal, inter-provincial, and provincial actors, and a mid-1990s instance where the Federation of Canadian Municipalities (FCM) focused so much on the micro-scale region that it largely negated the regulatory role of international trade, the interconnectivity of sub-national to the multi-national scales, and their subsequent impact on regional development (Corrigan, 2007; Brett & MacKie, 2012). Considering that the emergence of new regionalism aligns with a period of rapid globalization and economic reconfiguration, it is critical for scholars and practitioners to acknowledge the interconnected and dynamic influences occurring across multiple scales of analysis impacting regional development (Brenner, 1997; Mahon & Johnson, 2005). In fact, many do. While some new regionalist scholars are censured for insularity, it is also argued that adopting a more open-ended, dynamic, and contingent understanding of region and focusing on relational phenomena such as economic clustering and governance-like decision-making as the main variables of interest may divorce the region from its territorial conceptualization (Jones & MacLeod, 2004; Deas & Lord, 2006; Allen & Cochrane, 2007; Brett & MacKie, 2012).

The third criticism of new regionalism refers to its methodological ambiguity concerning how best to measure its preence or characteristics as well as the extent to which empirical work may be transferred to policy. This concern may also be attributed to post-structural economic geography as a whole, due to the complex and simultaneously conflicting forces posed by globalization (Harrison, 2006; Jonas, 2006). As illustrated by Brett and MacKie (2012):

> while a Keyensian-period staples approach could actually impact large blocks of industry and infrastructure through the fulcrum of the state, and [the state] was thereby more aware of what data and administrative needs were required, the contemporary economic and political landscape implies much more uncertainty and evinces much more complex networks, so as to obscure exactly what the goal/state of a "region" should be and what data must therefore be gathered.
>
> (p. 9)

The ability to draw generalizable conclusions from new regionalist research to inform policy is further confounded by an absence of an explicitly defined method for capturing data, reflected in open-ended methodological designs adhering to principles of contingency, specificity, and uniqueness of each region under study (McGuirk, 2007; Young, 2010; Brett & MacKie, 2012). There are also instances where policy objectives inform particular methodological choices (e.g., Prytherch, 2006; Peterson et al., 2007; Young, 2010), bringing about Lovering's (1999) concern that new regionalism is the "policy tail wagging the theoretical dog" (p. 390).

Finally, a common critique made of new regionalism is that it directly or indirectly serves as a vehicle for neoliberalism (Bowles, 1997; Jayasuriya, 2003; Rainnie, 2004; Rainnie & Grobbelaar, 2005; Hadjimichalis, 2006). Brenner states that new regionalism is "often interpreted in terms of a normative 'neoliberal' vision of governance: one in which self-organization and consensus, displaces state intervention as a response to social and economic challenges" (p. 20). This normative foundation is thought to favour de-centralization, flexibility, and entrepreneurial governance, in practice and theory (cf. Scott,

2016). Hadjimichalis (2006) argues that the conceptualization of social capital used by new regionalists tends to treat social interactions as conflict-free, depoliticized encounters that can mobilize for the benefit of all, neglecting the issues of inequality in regional development and that the prosperity apparent in many "thriving regions" is bifurcated between groups and dependent on the exploitation of people based on gender, race, and class (MacLeod, 2001; Rainnie, 2004; Hadjimichalis, 2006). Further, the lexicon used by regionalist scholars in the late 1990s began to treat regions as though they were firms (e.g., learning firm, learning region, competitive firm, competitive region), creating a "dangerous shift from the rationality of the firm as an instrumental actor, to the rationality of the region as an instrumental actor" (Hadjimichalis, 2006, p. 698). These comparisons bely the inherent undertones of capitalism and uneven development. However, while Lovering (1999) claims that new regionalism is a reformist response to neoliberalism, Brenner (2004) suggested that new regionalism is primarily motivated by a policy and democratic-socialist oriented approach to "mediate between capitalism, group interests, and society at large in an attempt to mitigate the negative effects of economic activity and societal development" (cf. Scott, 2016, p. 20). Given the realities of neoliberalism, it is arguable that the new regionalist framework is deployed in an attempt to mitigate the worst of its effects, that is, it is *responsive to* rather than dominated *by* contemporary systems of capital accumulation (Brett & MacKie, 2012). It must be acknowledged that the record of planning in the public domain, at all spatial scales, has long been associated with processes to alleviate the worst attributes of market capitalism (e.g., Friedmann, 1987).

4 Conclusion

We present new regionalism as an assemblage of five core themes: multi-level collaborative governance, innovation and knowledge flows, place-based development, integrated development, and rural–urban interactions. Each of these has relevance to Canadian rural contexts – particularly in terms of pursuing regional planning and development that aspires to be economically sustainable and environmentally and socially just. The remainder of this volume will critically explore the degree to which these conceptual themes in the new regionalism framework posited here are evident in Canadian regional development policy and practice – and will further consider the criticisms that have been posed to new regionalism, as presented in this chapter, through this exploration.

References

Allen, J., & Cochrane, A. (2007). Beyond the territorial fix: Regional assemblages, politics and power. *Regional Studies*, *41*(9), 1161–1175.

Amdam, R. (2002). Sectoral versus territorial regional planning and development in Norway. *European Planning Studies*, *10*(November 2012), 37–41.

Amin, A. (1999). An institutional perspective on regional economic development. *International Journal of Urban and Regional Research*, *23*(2), 365–378.

Amin, A., & Thrift, N. (1994). *Globalization, institutions and regional development in Europe*. Oxford: Oxford University Press.

Bakker, K. (Ed.). (2007). *Eau Canada*. Vancouver: UBC Press.

Bakker, K., & Cook, C. (2011). Water governance in Canada: Innovation and fragmentation. *International Journal of Water Resources Development*, *27*(2), 275–289.

Barca, F. (2009). An agenda for reformed cohesion approach to meeting policy: A place-based European Union challenges and expectations. *Independent Report Prepared at the Request of Danuta Hubner, Commissioner for Regional Policy*. Brussels, European Commission.

Barca, F., McCann, P., & Rodríguez-Pose, A. (2012). The case for regional development intervention: Place-based versus place-neutral approaches. *Journal of Regional Science*, *52*(1), 134–152.

Baxter, D., Berlin, R., & Ramlo, A. (2005). The urban futures institute report 62. In D. Baxter, R. Berlin & A. Ramlo (Eds.) *Regions & resources: The foundations of British Columbia's economic base*. Vancouver: Urban Futures Institute.

Bellamy, J., & Brown, A. J. (2009). Regional governance in rural Australia: An emergent phenomenon of the quest for liveability and sustainability? *Proceedings of the 53rd Annual Meeting of the International Society for the Systems Sciences* (pp. 1–23). Brisbane.

Berkes, F., & Ross, H. (2013). Community resilience: Toward an integrated approach. *Society & Natural Resources*, *26*(1), 5–20.

Berry, F., & Berry, W. (2007). Innovation and diffusion models in policy research. In P. A. Sabatier (Ed.), *Theories of the policy process* (pp. 223–260). Cambridge: Westview Press.

Bogason, P., & Zølner, M. (2007). *Methods in democratic network governance*. New York, NY: Palgrave Macmillan.

Bowles, P. (1997). ASEAN, AFIA and the "new regionalism". *Pacific Affairs, University of British Columbia*, *70*(2), 219–233.

Bradford, N. (2010). *Regional economic development agencies in Canada: Lessons for Southern Ontario informed by Ontario's reality executive summary*. Toronto: Mowat Centre for Policy Innovation.

Breen, S. (2016). From staples theory to new regionalism: Managing drinking water for regional resilience in rural British Columbia. PhD Dissertation. Simon Fraser University.

Breen, S., & Minnes, S. (2014). *A regional approach to drinking water management: NL-BC comparative water systems study* [Unpublished report]. Corner Brook, NL: Grenfell Campus, Memorial University of Newfoundland.

Brenner, N. (1997). Global, fragmented, hierarchical: Henri Lefebvre's geographies of globalization. *Public Culture*, *10*, 135–167.

Brenner, N. (1999). Globalization as reterritorialization: The re-scaling of urban governance in the European Union. *Urban Studies*, *36*(4), 431–451.

Brenner, N. (2004). Urban governance and the production of new state spaces in Western Europe, 1960–2000. *Review of International Political Economy*, *11*(30), 447–488.

Brett, M., & MacKie, C. (2012). *New regionalism: Critically appraising an emerging paradigm*. Draft Working Document for the project – Canadian Regional Development: A Critical Review of Theory, Practice and Potentials, Corner Brook, NL.

Bulkeley, H. (2005). Reconfiguring environmental governance: Towards a politics of scales and networks. *Political Geography*, *24*(8), 875–902.

Bunnell, T. G., & Coe, N. M. (2001). Spaces and scales of innovation. *Progress in Human Geography, 25*(4), 569–589.

Buzdugan, S. (2006). New regionalism. In M. Bevir (Ed.), *Encyclopedia of governance* (pp. 617–618). Thousand Oaks, CA: Sage.

Carter, K. L., & Vodden, K. (2017). Applicability of territorial innovation models to declining resource-based regions: Lessons from the Northern Peninsula of Newfoundland. *The Journal of Rural and Community Development, 12*(2/3), 74–92.

Castro, J. E. (2007). Water governance in the twentieth-first century. *Ambient, 10*(2), 97–118.

Centellas, M. (2010). Savina Cuellar and Bolivia's new regionalism. *Latin American Perspectives, 37*(4), 161–176.

Cheng, A., Kruger, L., & Daniels, S. (2003). "Place" as an integrating concept in natural resource politics: Propositions for a social science research agenda. *Society & Natural Resources, 16*, 87–104.

Christopherson, S., Michie, J., & Tyler, P. (2010). Regional resilience: Theoretical and empirical perspectives. *Cambridge Journal of Regions, Economy and Society, 3*(1), 3–10.

Clarke, S. E. (2016). Local place-based collaborative governance: Comparing state-centric and society-centered models. *Urban Affairs Review, 53*(3), 578–602.

Cohen, A. (2012). Rescaling environmental governance: Watersheds as boundary objects at the intersection of science, neoliberalism, and participation. *Environment and Planning A, 44*(9), 2207–2224.

Cooke, P., & Leydesdorff, L. (2006). Regional development in the knowledge-based economy: The construction of advantage. *Journal of Technology Transfer, 31*(October 2003), 5–15.

Cooke, P., & Morgan, K. (1998). *The Associational Economy: Firms, Regions, And Innovation.* Oxford: Oxford University Press.

Corrigan, K. (2007). Impact of trade agreements on subnational governments. In R. Grinspun & Y. Shamsie (Eds.), *Whose Canada? Continental Integration, Fortress North America, And The Corporate Agenda* (pp. 317–342). Montreal: McGill-Queen's University Press.

Council on Competitiveness. (2010). *Collaborate: Leading regional innovation clusters.* Washington, DC: Council on Competitiveness.

Daniels, J., Baldacchino, G., & Vodden, K. (2015). Matters of place: The making of place and identity. In K. Vodden, G. Baldacchino, & R. Gibson (Eds.), *Place Peripheral: Place-Based Development In Rural, Island And Remote Regions* (pp. 18–31). St. John's, NL: ISER Press.

De Loë, R. C., & Kreutzwiser, R. D. (2005). Closing the groundwater protection implementation gap. *Geoforum, 36*(2), 241–256.

Deas, I., & Lord, A. (2006). From a new regionalism to an unusual regionalism? The emergence of non-standard regional spaces and lessons for the territorial reorganisation of the state. *Urban Studies, 43*, 1847–1877.

Devlin, J., Vinodrai, T., Parker, P., Clarke, A., Scott, S., Bruce, B., Lipcsei, R., Deska, R., Collins, D., Bangura, T., & Sanders, K. (2015). Evaluating regional economic development initiatives: Policy backgrounder. *Report for the Ontario Ministry of Agriculture, Food and Rural Affairs, 2.*

Douglas, D. J. A. (1997). The return of regional planning: New directions? *Paper Presented to the Canadian Institute of Planners National Conference.* St. John's.

Douglas, D. J. A. (1999). The new rural region: Consciousness, collaboration and new challenges and opportunities for innovative practices. In W. Ramp, J. Kulig,

I. Townshend, & V. McGowan (Eds.), *Health in Rural Settings: Contexts For Action* (pp. 39–60). Lethbridge: University of Lethbridge.

Douglas, D. J. A. (2006). Rural regional development planning: Governance and other challenges in the new EU. *Studia Regionalia, 18*, 112–132.

Douglas, D. J. A. (2014a) "New regionalism" as the local development paradigm?: Cautionary evidence from some recent research in Canada. *Presentation to the OECD-LEED Conference*. Stockholm. Retrieved from http://cdnregdev.ruralresilience.ca/?page_id=29

Douglas, D. J. A. (2014b). "Integrated" in regional development discourse, policy, and practice. Corner Brook, NL; *Working Paper CRD – 5*, Memorial University.

Douglas, D. J. A. (2016). Power and politics in the changing structures of rural local government. In M. Shucksmith & D. L. Brown (Eds.), *Routledge International Handbook Of Rural Studies* (pp. 601–614). London: Routledge.

Ehrenfeucht, R. (2002). The new regionalism: A conversation with Edward Soja. *Critical Planning Journal, 9*(Summer), 5–12.

Escobar, A. (2008). *Territories of Difference: Place, Movements, Life, Redes*. Durham, NC: Duke University Press.

Ethier, W. (1998). The new regionalism. *The Economic Journal, 108*, 1149–1161.

External Advisory Committee on Cities and Communities. (2006). *From Restless Communities To Resilient Places: Building A Stronger Future For All Canadians*. Ottawa: Infrastructure Canada.

Faludi, A. (2013). Territorial cohesion, territorialism, territoriality, and soft planning: A critical review. *Environment and Planning A, 45*(6), 1302–1317.

Ferreyra, C., de Loë, R. C., & Kreutzwiser, R. D. (2008). Imagined communities, contested watersheds: Challenges to integrated water resources management in agricultural areas. *Journal of Rural Studies, 24*(3), 304–321.

Foray, D., Goddard, J., Beldarrain, X. G., Landabaso, M., McCann, P., Morgan, K., … Ortega-Argilés, R. (2012). *Guide to Research And Innovation Strategies For Smart Specialisation (RIS 3)*.

Freshwater, D., Simms, A., & Vodden, K. (2011). *Defining regions for building economic development capacity in Newfoundland and Labrador*. Harris Centre Report. St. John's, NL: Memorial University.

Friedmann, J. (1987). *Planning in the Public Domain: From Knowledge To Action*. Princeton, NJ: Princeton University Press.

Frisken, F., & Norris, D. F. (2001). Regionalism reconsidered. *Journal of Urban Affairs, 23*(5), 467–478.

Frisvoll, S., & Rye, J. F. (2009). Elite discourses of regional identity in a new regionalism development scheme: The case of the "mountain region" in Norway. *Norsk Geografisk Tidsskrift – Norwegian Journal of Geography, 63*(3), 175–190.

Gainsborough, J. F. (2001). Bridging the city-suburb divide: States and the politics of regional cooperation. *Journal of Urban Affairs, 23*, 497–512.

Gallent, N. (2006). The rural–urban fringe: A new priority for planning policy? *Planning Practice and Research, 21*(3), 383–393.

George, C., & Reed, M. G. (2015). Operationalising just sustainability: Towards a model for place-based governance. *Local Environment*, 1–19. doi:10.1080/13549839.2015.1101059.

Gibbs, D., & Jonas, A. E. G. (2001). Rescaling and regional governance: The English regional development agencies and the environment. *Environment and Planning C: Government and Policy, 19*(2), 269–288.

Gibson, R. (2014). *Collaborative governance in rural regions: An examination of Ireland and Newfoundland and Labrador.* PhD Dissertation. St. John's, NL: Memorial University.

Gill, R., & Larson, G. S. (2014). Making the ideal (local) entrepreneur: Place and the regional development of high-tech entrepreneurial identity. *Human Relations, 67*(5), 519–542.

Giordano, B. (2001). "Institutional thickness", political sub-culture and the resurgence of (the "new") regionalism in Italy – A case study of the Northern League in the province of Varese. *Transactions of the Institute of British Geographers, 26*(1), 25–41.

Granovetter, M. (1985). Economic action and social structure: The problem of embeddedness. *American Journal of Sociology, 91*(3), 481–510.

Grant, J. (2004). Gippsland's regional development agencies: The triumph of tribalism over regionalism. *Australasian Journal of Regional Studies, 10*(1), 49–75.

Gregory, D., Johnston, R., Pratt, G., Watts, M., & Whatmore, S. (Eds.). (2009). *The Dictionary of Human Geography. Human Geography* (5th ed.). Hoboken, NJ: Wiley-Blackwell.

Grigg, N. (2012). Integrated water management in 2050: Institutional and governance challenges. In W. M. Grayman, D. P. Loucks, & L. Saito (Eds.), *Toward A Sustainable Water Future: Vision for 2050* (pp. 66–75). Reston, Virginia: American Society of Civil Engineers.

Hadjimichalis, C. (2006). Non-economic factors in economic geography and in "new regionalism": A sympathetic critique. *International Journal of Urban and Regional Research, 30*(3), 690–704.

Halseth, G., Reed, M. G., & Reimer, B. (2010). Inclusion in rural development planning: Challenges and opportunities. In D. Douglas (Ed.), *Rural Planning and Development in Canada.* Toronto: Nelson Education, pp. 256–280.

Hamin, H. M., & Marcucci, D. J. (2008). Ad hoc rural regionalism. *Journal of Rural Studies, 24*, 467–477.

Harrison, J. (2006). Re-reading the new regionalism: A sympathetic critique. *Space and Polity, 10*(1), 21–46.

Harrison, J. (2013). Configuring the new "regional world": On being caught between territory and networks. *Regional Studies, 47*(1), 55–74.

Healey, P. (2004). The treatment of space and place in the new strategic spatial planning in Europe. *International Journal of Urban and Regional Research, 28*, 45–67.

Heisler, K. G. (2012). *Scales Of Benefit And Territories Of Control: A Case Study Of Mineral Exploration And Development in Northwest British Columbia.* Burnaby, British Columbia: Simon Fraser University.

Herrschel, T. (2009). City regions, polycentricity and the construction of peripheralities through governance. *Urban Research & Practice, 2*(3), 240–250.

Hettne, B. (1999). Globalization and the new regionalism: The second great transformation. In O. Sunkel, & A. Inotai (Eds.), *Globalism and the New Regionalism* (pp. 1–24). London: MacMillan Press.

Hettne, B. (2005). Beyond the "new" regionalism. *New Political Economy, 10*(4), 213.

Hettne, B., Inotai, A., & Sunkel, O. (Eds.). (2000). *National Perspectives On The New Regionalism In The North.* Helsinki: United Nations University, Vol. 2.

Hildreth, P., & Bailey, D. (2014). Place-based economic development strategy in England: Filling the missing space. *Local Economy, 29*(4–5), 363–377.

Hirst, P. (1997). *From Statism To Pluralism: Democracy, Civil Society And Global Politics.* London: UCL Press.

Hudson, R. (2007). Region and place: Rethinking regional development in the context of global environmental change. *Progress in Human Geography, 31*(6), 827–836.

Hudson, R. (2009). Resilient regions in an uncertain world: Wishful thinking or a practical reality? *Cambridge Journal of Regions, Economy and Society*, *3*(1), 11–25.

Huggins, R., & Clifton, N. (2011). Competitiveness, creativity, and place-based development. *Environment and Planning A*, *43*(6), 1341–1362.

Huggins, R., & Thompson, P. (2014). Culture and place-based development: A socio-economic analysis. *Regional Studies*, *49*(1), 130–159.

Illsley, B., Jackson, T., Curry, J., & Rapaport, E. (2010). Community innovation in the soft spaces of planning. *International Planning Studies*, *15*(4), 303–319.

International Labour Office. (2010). *A skilled workforce for strong, sustainable and balanced growth*. Geveva. Retrieved from www.oecd.org/g20/topics/employment-and-social-policy/G20-Skills-Strategy.pdf.

Jayasuriya, K. (2003). Embedded mercantilism and open regionalism: The crisis of a regional political project. *Third World Quarterly*, *24*(2), 339–355.

Jessop, B. (1994). Post-Fordism and the state. In A. Amin (Ed.). *Post-Fordism: A Reader*. Oxford: Blackwell, pp. 251–279.

Jonas, A. (2006). Pro scale: Further reflections on the "scale debate" in human geography. *Transactions of the Institute of British Geographers*, *31*, 399–406.

Jonas, A. E. G. (2013). Place and region III. *Progress in Human Geography*, *37*(6), 822–828.

Jones, M., & MacLeod, G. (2004). Regional spaces, spaces of regionalism: Territory, insurgent politics, and the English question. *Transactions of the Institute of British Geographers*, *29*, 433–452.

Keating, M. (1998). *The New Regionalism In Western Europe: Territorial Restructuring And Political Change*. Cheltenham: Edward Elgar.

Keating, M., & Wilson, A. (2014). Regions with regionalism? The rescaling of interest groups in six European states. *European Journal Political Research*, *53*, 840–857.

Lagendijk, A. (1997). Will the new regionalism survive? Tracing dominant concepts in economic geography. Mimeograph, CURDS, University of Newcastle-Upon-Tyne, 1–33.

Lovering, J. (1999). Theory led by policy: The inadequacies of the "new regionalism" (illustrated from the case of Wales). *International Journal of Urban and Regional Research*, *23*(3), 379–395.

Lubell, M., Schneider, M., Scholz, J., & Mete, M. (2002). Watershed partnerships and the emergence of collective action institutions. *American Journal of Political Science*, *46*(1), 148–163.

MacLeod, G. (2001). New regionalism reconsidered: Globalization and the remaking of political economic space. *International Journal of Urban and Regional Research*, *25*(4), 804–829.

Mahon, R., & Johnson, R. (2005). NAFTA, the redesign, and rescaling of Canada's welfare state. *Studies in Political Economy*, *76*, 7–30.

Makoni, E. N., Meiklejohn, C. L., & Coetzee, M. J. (2008). Distilling a "new regionalist" planning agenda for South Africa: Is the provincial growth and development strategy (PGDS) measuring up? *Planning Africa Conference 14–16 April 2008*. Johannesburg, Sandton Convention Centre.

Mansfield, E., & Milner, H. V. (1999). The new wave of regionalism. *International Organization*, *53*, 589–627.

Markey, S. (2010). Primer on place-based development. Working Document CRD – 2 for the project, Canadian Regional Development: A Critical Review of Theory, Practice, and Potentials. Corner Brook, NL.

Markey, S. (2011). A primer on new regionalism. Working Document CRD – 4 for the project, Canadian Regional Development: A Critical Review of Theory, Practice, and Potentials. Corner Brook, NL.

Markey, S., Breen, S., Vodden, K., & Daniels, J. (2015). Evidence of place: Becoming a region in rural Canada. *International Journal of Urban and Regional Research*, *39*(5), 874–891.

Markey, S., Halseth, G., & Manson, D. (2008). Challenging the inevitability of rural decline: Advancing the policy of place in Northern British Columbia. *Journal of Rural Studies*, *24*(4), 409–421.

Markey, S., Halseth, G., & Manson, D. (2012). *Investing in place: Economic renewal in Northern British Columbia*. Vancouver: UBC Press.

Markey, S., & Heisler, K. (2011). Getting a fair share: Regional development in a rapid boom-bust rural setting. *Canadian Journal of Regional Science*, *33*(3), 49–62.

Maxwell, S. (Ed.). (2008). *The Business Of Water A Concise Overview Of Challenges And Opportunities In The Water Market (A Compilation Of Recent Articles From Journal AWWA)*. Denver: American Water Works Association.

McGuirk, P. (2007). The political construction of the city-region: Notes from Sydney. *International Journal of Urban and Regional Research*, *31*, 179–187.

Mitchell, B. (2005). Integrated water resource management, institutional arrangements, and land-use planning. *Environment and Planning A*, *37*(8), 1335–1352.

Mitchell, M. (2013). From organisational learning to social learning: A tale of two organisations in the Murray-Darling Basin. *Rural Society*, *22*(3), 230–241.

Morgan, K. (1997). The learning region: Institutions, innovation and regional renewal. *Regional Studies*, *31*(3), 401–503.

Morgan, K. (2004). Sustainable regions: Governance, innovation and scale. *European Planning Studies*, *12*(6), 871–889.

Muys, J. C. (2000). Innovations in water management. *Water International*, *25*(4), 526–533.

Nelles, J. (2009). Civic capital and the dynamics of intermunicipal cooperation for regional economic development. PhD Dissertation. University of Toronto.

Nelson, J. (2002). New regionalism and planning: A conversation with Ethan Seltzer. *Critical Planning*, *9*(Summer), 47–53.

OECD. (2010). *OECD Rural Policy Reviews: Québec, Canada 2010*. Paris: OECD Publishing.

Ortiz-Guerrero, C. E. (2013). The new regionalism: Policy implications for rural regions. *Cuadernos de Desarrollo Rural*, *10*(70), 47–67.

Overbeek, G. (2009). Opportunities for rural–urban relationships to enhance the rural landscape. *Journal of Environmental Policy & Planning*, *11*(1), 61–68. doi:10.1080/15239080902775058.

Paasi, A. (2004). Place and region: Looking through the prism of scale. *Progress in Human Geography*, *28*(4), 536–546.

Paasi, A. (2013). Regional planning and the mobilization of "regional identity": From bounded spaces to relational complexity. *Regional Studies*, *47*(8), 1206–1219.

Pahl-Wostl, C., Gupta, J., & Petry, D. (2008). Governance and the global water system: A theoretical exploration. *Global Governance: A Review*, *14*, 419–435.

Perrin, T. (2012). New regionalism and cultural policies: Distinctive and distinguishing strategies, from local to global. *Journal of Contemporary European Studies*, *20*(4), 459–475.

Peterson, A., McAlpine, C. A., Ward, D., & Rayner, S. (2007). New regionalism and nature conservation: Lessons from South East Queensland, Australia. *Landscape and Urban Planning*, *82*, 132–144.

Peterson, A., Walker, M., Maher, M., Hoverman, S., & Eberhard, R. (2010). New regionalism and planning for water quality improvement in the great barrier reef, Australia. *Geographical Research, 48*(3), 297–313.

Pezzoli, K., Marciano, R. J., & Zaslavsky, I. (2001). Transborder city-regions and the quest for integrated regional planning. Contribution to Track 15: Transnational Planning.

Pitschel, D., & Bauer, M. W. (2009). Subnational governance approaches on the rise – Reviewing a decade of Eastern European regionalization research. *Regional & Federal Studies, 19*(3), 327–347.

Polèse, M. (1999). From regional development to local development: On the life, death, and rebirth(?) of regional science as a policy relevant science. *Canadian Journal of Regional Science, 22*(3), 299–314.

Prytherch, D. (2006). Narrating the landscapes of entrepreneurial regionalism: Rescaling regionalism and the planned remaking of València, Spain. *Space & Polity, 10*, 203–227.

Rainnie, A. (2004). New regionalism in Australia. *Sustaining Regions, 4*(2), 13–18.

Rainnie, A., & Grobbelaar, M. (Eds.). (2005). *New Regionalism in Australia*. Burlington: Ashgate.

Rast, J. (2006). Environmental Justice and the new regionalism. *Journal of Planning Education and Research, 25*(3), 249–263.

Reimer, B. (2005). *A rural perspective on linkages among communities.* Prepared for building, connecting and sharing knowledge: A dialogue on linkages between communities. Montreal: Concordia University.

Reimer, B., Vodden, K., & Brett, M. (2011). *Reflections on rural-urban interdependence.* Retrieved from http://cdnregdev.ruralresilience.ca/?page_id=155.

Reimer, W. (2006). The rural context of community in Canada. *Journal of Rural and Community Development, 1*, 155–175.

Reimer, W., & Markey, S. (2008). *Place Based Policy: A Rural Perspective.* Human Resources and Social Development Canada. Retrieved from http://billreimer.ca/research/files/ReimerMarkeyRuralPlaceBasedPolicySummaryPaper20081107.pdf.

Rhodes, R. (1996). The new governance: Governing without government. *Political Studies, 44*, 652–667.

Ridley, T., Yee-Cheong, L., & Juma, C. (2006). Infrastructure, innovation and development. *International Journal of Technology and Globalisation, 2*(3/4), 268–278.

Riggirozzi, P. (2010). Region, regionness and regionalism in Latin America: Towards a new synthesis. *New Political Economy, 17*(4), 421–443.

Robinson, J., Berkhout, T., Burch, S., Davis, E. J., Dusyk, N., & Shaw, A. (2008). *Infrastructure & Communities: The Path To Sustainable communities.* Victoria, British Columbia: Pacific Institute for Climate Solutions.

Rodríguez-Pose, A. (2008). The rise of the "city-region" concept and its development policy implications. *European Planning Studies, 16*(8), 1025–1046.

Rogerson, C. M. (2001). Spatial development initiatives in Southern Africa: The Maputo development corridor. *Tijdschrift voor economische en sociale geografie, 92*, 324–346.

Rothwell, N. (2006). Canada's watersheds: The demographic basis for an urban-rural dialogue. *Rural and Small Town Canada Analysis Bulletin No. 6.* Ottawa. https://www150.statcan.gc.ca/n1/en/pub/21-006-x/21-006-x2005006-eng.pdf?st=wgZ0xvqm.

Sancton, A. (2001). Canadian cities and the new regionalism University of Western Ontario. *Journal of Urban Affairs, 23*(5), 543–555.

Savitch, H. V., & Vogel, R. K. (2000). Introduction: Paths to new regionalism. *State & Local Government Review, 32*(3), 158–168.

Scott, A. J. (1998). *Regions and The World Economy: The Coming Shape Of Global Production, Competition, And Political Order.* Oxford: Oxford University Press.

Scott, J. W. (2007). Smart growth as urban reform: A pragmatic "recoding" of the new regionalism. *Urban Studies, 44*(1), 15–35.

Scott, J. W. (Ed.). (2016). *De-coding New Regionalism: Shifting Socio-Political Contexts in Central Europe and Latin America.* New York, NY: Routledge.

Shearmur, R. (2010). Space, place and innovation: A distance-based approach. *Canadian Geographer/Le Géographe Canadien, 54*(1), 46–67.

Stoker, G. (1998). *Governance As Theory: Five Propositions.* Blackwell, OK and Oxford: UNESCO.

Storper, M. (1997). *The Regional World: Territorial Development In A Global Economy.* New York, NY: Guilford Press.

Tacoli, C. (1998). Beyond the rural-urban divide. *Environment and Urbanization, 10*(1), 3–4.

Tomaney, J. (2010). *Place-Based Trends And Approaches To Regional Development: Global Australian Implications.* Sydney: Australian Business Foundation.

Townsend, A. (2005). Multi-level governance in England. Background paper prepared by the International Centre for Regional Regeneration and Development Studies, Durham University. Retrieved from www.dur.ac.uk/resources/cscr/odpm/Multilevel.pdf.

Tsukamoto, T. (2011). Devolution, new regionalism and economic revitalization in Japan: Emerging urban political economy and politics of scale in Osaka-Kansai. *Cities, 28*(4), 281–289.

Väyrynen, R. (2003). Regionalism: Old and new. *International Studies Review, 5*, 25–51.

Vodden, K. (2015). Results of a critical examination of new regionalism in the Canadian context. *Canadian Rural Revitalization/North Atlantic Forum Annual Conference.* Summerside, Prince Edward Island.

Vodden, K., Carter, K., & White, K. (2013). *A primer on innovation, learning, and knowledge flows.* St. John's, NL: Memorial University of Newfoundland. Retrieved from http://cdnregdev.ruralresilience.ca/wp-content/uploads/2013/08/Primer-on-innovation-Aug12.pdf.

Vogel, R. K., & Nezelkewicz, N. (2002). Metropolitan planning organizations and the new regionalism: The case of Louisville. *Publius: The Journal of Federalism, 32*(1), 107.

Wallis, A. (2002).The new regionalism: Inventing governance structures for the early twenty-first century. Retrieved from www.miregions.org/Strengthening%20the%20Role/The%20New%20Regionalism%20Paper%20by%20Wallis%20at%20CUD.pdf

Ward, K., & Jonas, A. E. G. (2004). Competitive city-regionalism as a politics of space: A critical reinterpretation of the new regionalism. *Environment and Planning A, 36*(12), 2119–2139.

Wheeler, S. (2002). The new regionalism: Key characteristics of an emerging movement. *Journal of the American Planning Association, 68*(3), 267–278.

Windsheimer, D. (2007). New regionalism and metropolitan governance in practice: A major smart growth construction project in the Waterloo region – The light rapid transport project. *International Research in Metropolitan Studies, 51*, 1–147.

Wolfe, D. A. (2010). The strategic management of core cities: Path dependence and economic adjustment in resilient regions. *Cambridge Journal of Regions, Economy and Society, 3*(1), 139–152.

Wolfe, D. A. (2011). Regional resilience and place-based development policy: Implications for Canada. *Canadian Political Science Association Annual Meeting.* Waterloo, ON, Wilfred Laurier University.

Wolfe, J. M. (2003). Globalization, governance and the new regionalism: Planning responses in Montreal, Canada. *39th ISoCaRP Congress.*

Young, N. (2010). Business networks, collaboration and embeddedness in local and extra-local spaces: The case of Port Hardy, Canada. *Sociologia Ruralis, 50,* 392–408.

Zimmerbauer, K., & Paasi, A.. (2013). When old and new regionalism collide: Deinstitutionalization of regions and resistance identity in municipality amalgamations. *Journal of Rural Studies, 30,* 31–40.

Zirul, C., Halseth, G., Markey, S., & Ryser, L. (2015). Struggling with new regionalism: Government trumps governance in Northern British Columbia, Canada. *Journal of Rural and Community Development, 10*(2), 136–165.

4 Project approach

Critical reflections on methodology and process

Sarah-Patricia Breen and Kelly Vodden

1 Introduction

The focus of this chapter is on the research approach of the project. The chapter is divided into two sections. The first section, research methods, identifies and discusses the approach taken by the research team, including an overview of the mixed method case study approach, the structure of the research team, an overview of the case study regions, and the details of data collection and analysis. The second is a reflection of the experiences of the research team, including the strengths and challenges associated with large, cross-country, case study projects, and how the research team approached challenges encountered. Overall, we provide insights into the planning and execution of a multi-level, team-based, interdisciplinary research studies across a large geography over a multi-year time frame, a form of research that has become increasingly common as researchers and their institutions strive to address the significant and complex challenges of current times (Mauser et al., 2013). Despite growing recognition of the importance of interdisciplinary and even transdisciplinary approaches, progress in moving in this direction has been slow (Apgar et al., 2016; Pahl-Wostl et al., 2012). Our hope, therefore, is that the lessons from the project presented below will have value for others engaged in similar research endeavours.

2 Research methods

2.1 Case study approach

The research team adopted a multi-year, mixed methods case study approach for this project. We took a constructivist perspective in the research design, where the results of the analysis were based on the revealed perspectives and interpretations from targeted semi-structured interviews, combined with literature reviews, observations, and experiences of the research team – along with participant feedback on emerging findings (Vodden et al., 2015).

We selected four provinces, each with one case study region. With supplementary funding and identified local interest, we added a second region in Newfoundland and Labrador (NL) with the aim of providing further insights on two particular project themes (governance and innovation). This brought the total case study regions to five (see Map 4.1).

The experience, relationships, and location of the co-investigators were important considerations in case study selection. In each case a clearly delineated region could be identified, but each site is complex and contains multiple over-lapping jurisdictions and sub-regions with existing regional structures and/or planning initiatives. A range of case study regions were selected, with variations in population and demographic trends, rural–urban dynamics (e.g., including and/or with varying proximity to major urban centres), presence, form and sta-bility of regional governance institutions, physical geographies, and historical economic profiles (see Table 4.1). All case study regions selected, however, included communities and areas or "sub-regions" that were considered typical of rural Canada, including one or more of the following characteristics:

- Remote locations relative to major decision-making centres, without major urban influences;
- Relatively low density and sparse population settlements; and
- Similar development histories, particularly a historical reliance on natural resource industries.

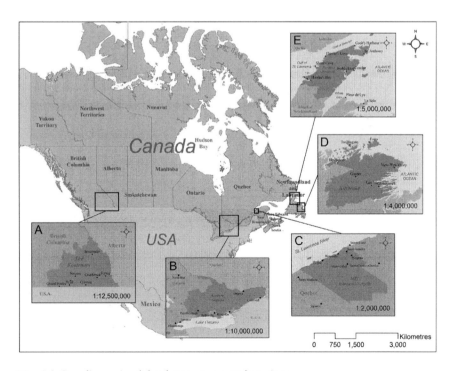

Map 4.1 Canadian regional development case study regions

The differences among the provinces (e.g., governance organization, as described in Chapter 2) worked to ensure that case study regions were varied in terms of size, industry dependence, organizational frameworks, and development experiences while also sharing common characteristics. Despite these differences, it was possible to conduct a robust cross-case analysis. Additionally, the range of case study regions helped support generalization of the findings to other rural regions across Canada.

2.2 The research team

The interdisciplinary research team included four co-investigators, one post-doctoral researcher, and 14 undergraduate and graduate research assistants, from faculties of geography, planning, sociology, and resource management. A survey of team members revealed that the majority had past research experience in mixed-methods research. The most valued qualities of good research identified by the research team include the relevance of the research, the inclusion of a robust theoretical framework, and ensuring the appropriate and reliable measurement of concepts and variables.

The research team worked collaboratively on the overarching research questions, but was also divided into smaller teams for data collection (by case study region) and analysis (by new regionalism theme). Lead investigators were assigned to each province, with the leads based at universities within each province, and to each of the five identified themes of new regionalism and their respective "theme teams". The research team worked collaboratively to plan, discuss, and execute the project. Team meetings were held via conference calls, typically on a quarterly basis, although there were periods of greater frequency during times of high activity (e.g., data collection). Team meetings were supplemented by email discussions, as well as the use of Basecamp – an online platform for organization, file sharing, calendar, and task-tracking. The research team met in person at the annual conference of the Canadian Rural Revitalization Foundation (see http://crrf.ca), using the conference as an opportunity to meet, as well as to present to a broader national and international audience on the progress and findings of the project. This national network (CRRF) became a collaborator in the knowledge mobilization aspects of the research.

2.3 Case study regions

A regional profile was created for each region as part of the literature review stage of the project. These profiles remain available online at http://cdnreg dev.ruralresilience.ca. The following provides a brief overview of each of the case study regions with information drawn from these profiles. Table 4.1 summarizes some basic regional characteristics.

Table 4.1 Case study region overview

	Kootenay Development Region, BC	Eastern Ontario, ON	Rimouski-Neigette MRC, QC	Kittiwake, NL	Northern Peninsula, NL
Region type	Provincially designated economic region	Voluntary – region of the Eastern Ontario Warden's Caucus	Provincially designated land use, planning, and development region	Provincially designated economic zone/region[1]	Provincially designated Rural Secretariat region
Population (2016)	151,403	2,080,505	56,650	46,110	11,290
Largest urban centre (2016)	Cranbrook 20,047	Ottawa 934,243	Rimouski 48,664	Gander 11,688	St. Anthony 2,258
# of communities of 10,000+	2	8	1	1	0
Physical size	57,787 km^2	49,000 km^2	2,700 km^2	14,000 km^2	17,483 km^2
Population density (pop/km^2)	2.62	42.46	20.98	3.29	0.65
Economic base	Historically natural resource development (mining, forestry); recent tourism, amenity, and technology sector growth, majority of employment in the services sector	Historically agriculture, milling, forestry, and mining; post war growth of manufacturing and services sector, including tourism, public service, and technology	Historically agriculture and natural resource sectors. The majority of employment is in tertiary sectors (health care, retail, education); continuing pockets of dependence on natural resource sectors	Historically and continued areas of fishing dependence but largest sectors are retail, health and social services, and manufacturing/construction; forestry also important and increasingly tourism	Historically tied to natural resources; fishing and forestry continue to be economic mainstays; also sales and service, construction and related industry, and manufacturing

(Source: Regional profile documents, Statistics Canada, 2016)

2.3.1 Kootenay Development Region, British Columbia

The Kootenay Development Region (the Kootenays – the region) is located in the south-east corner of British Columbia (BC) (see Map 4.2). The Kootenays are bordered by the province of Alberta to the east, the Canadian/American border to the south, and the Thompson-Okanagan Development Region to the west and north.

The region contains three regional districts, a form of local government in BC consisting of incorporated municipalities and multiple electoral areas that govern the unincorporated communities (Bish & Clemens, 2008; Breen, 2016b). As shown in Map 4.2, the Regional Districts of Kootenay Boundary, Central Kootenay, and East Kootenays make up the Kootenay Development Region. The region also has multiple other jurisdictions, including school boards, local health areas, college areas, and more.

The mountainous terrain isolates the region from the outside, as well as fragmenting it internally. The region is water rich, home to the majority of the Canadian portion of the headwaters of the Columbia River system, and has a high level of biodiversity. The region's geology includes rich mineral deposits, pockets of productive agriculture, and geothermal resources (Stevenson et al., 2011).

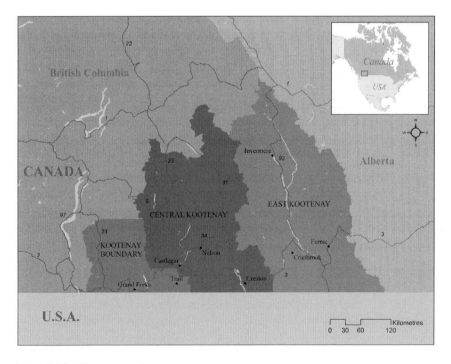

Map 4.2 The Kootenay region

While the region is large physically (6.2% of the BC landmass), the population contains only 3.3% of the provincial population (BC Stats, 2012; Statistics Canada, 2017). The closest urban centres (100,000+) are outside the region (e.g., Kelowna – approximately 80 km from the region, Spokane – 187 km, Calgary – 265 km, Vancouver – 430 km). The majority of communities, incorporated and unincorporated, are home to less than 5,000 people (Statistics Canada, 2017). Demographic trends are stable or showing slight growth, as well as an aging population, with variations across the region (Columbia Basin Regional Development Institute, 2017).

Multiple Indigenous peoples moved and lived throughout the region for over 10,000 years (Parks Canada, 2009). In the early 1800s, European contact came with explorers and fur traders, who were followed by prospectors and miners and then by railway construction, community settlement, agriculture, and logging (Stevenson et al., 2011). In the 1960s and 1970s, dams were installed in the region for power generation and flood control, altering the landscape and flooding communities (Columbia Basin Trust, 2012).

While the region's history and present are rooted in natural resource development, there has been economic diversification related to tourism, amenity migrants, and a growing technology sector (Breen, 2016a). The majority of employment is in the services sector and while there has been recovery since the 2008/2009 economic crash, unemployment in the region remains higher than pre-recession levels and higher than provincial and national rates (Breen, 2016a). There are multiple actors related to regional development across the Kootenays, including, but not limited to: the Columbia Basin Trust, three Community Futures Development Corporations, Selkirk College, College of the Rockies, the Kootenay Association for Science and Technology, and Kootenay Rockies Tourism.

2.3.2 Eastern Ontario, Ontario

Eastern Ontario (the region) stretches from the border of Ontario and Québec to the north-east, the St. Lawrence River and Lake Ontario to the south, the Greater Toronto Area to the south-west, and Algonquin Park to the north-west (see Map 4.3).

The Eastern Ontario Warden's Caucus (EOWC) is a voluntary collective of wardens and mayors of counties and municipalities, whose purpose is to work collaboratively to "enhance recognition for municipalities as an order of government through meaningful communication and representation with the federal and provincial governments, and each other" (Eastern Ontario Wardens Caucus, 2017). Map 4.3 shows the region as divided by counties, or the "upper tier" governments that provide services such as arterial roads, health and social services, and land use planning.

The region accounts for 4.5% of Ontario's landmass (Eastern Ontario Wardens Caucus, 2017) and 15.5% of the population (Statistics Canada, 2017). The region is diverse, including rural agricultural areas, cottage country, mid-sized cities

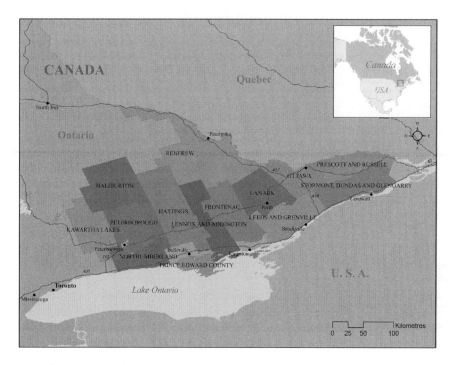

Map 4.3 Eastern Ontario

(e.g., Kingston, Brockville), the City of Ottawa, and a mix of English and francophone communities. Population growth is common across the region, but the rate and patterns vary. The region has a notably aging labour force, similar to Ontario as a whole, as well as youth out-migration and an influx of retired baby boomers (Eastern Ontario Wardens Caucus, 2017). Beyond the EOWC, the region is also home to 15 Community Futures Development Corporations, 12 Conservation Authorities, three tourism regions, regional offices for various provincial ministries, the federal Eastern Ontario Development Program, and various other actors.

The region is one of the most biologically diverse areas of Ontario, including portions of the Canadian Shield, Lake Ontario lakeshore, and Ottawa Valley, with both Great Lakes St. Lawrence and deciduous forests (Lanark County, 2012). Differences in climate and soil contribute to a region that is well suited to agriculture in the south and forested in the north (Agriculture and Agri-Food Canada, 2016; Eastern Ontario Wardens Caucus, 2017). Thousands of rivers and lakes stretch across the region, as do multiple provincial parks (Lanark County, 2012; Ontario Parks, 2012).

Pre-European contact, there were multiple Indigenous peoples within the region (KNET, 2012). European contact, via explorers and fur traders, occurred as early at 1600 (Canada History, 2012). The legacy of French explorers and settlements continues to be seen today in the francophone areas, with language adding a unique element to this region. During the American Revolution, many British Loyalists moved north to Eastern Ontario (Kingston Historical Society, 2003; Watson, 2011) and Scottish and Irish immigrants followed during the War of 1812 (Lanark County, 2012).

Historically the region's economy was focused on agriculture, milling, forestry, and mining (Statistics Canada, 2006b). However, economic changes following World Wars I (WWI) and II (WWII), with economic busts followed by a boom, the growth of manufacturing (e.g., branch plant economy), and the construction of Highway 401 (Kingston Historical Society, 2003; Ontario Government, 2011). Following WWII there was also a population boom – a combination of natural birth and immigration – which altered the demography of the region with not only rapid population growth, but urbanization (Kingston Historical Society, 2003; Ontario Government, 2011). While natural resources (e.g., agriculture and forestry) remain important, there has also been a shift to and growth in the services sector, including tourism, the public service, and the technology sector, as well as growth in educational opportunities (e.g., colleges and universities in region), which have changed the dynamics of the labour force. In 2009, Eastern Ontario's unemployment rate of 6.9% was less than the provincial rate of 9% (MTCU, 2009). A recent decline in labour-force growth rates shows a decline in people participating in the labour force (MTCU, 2009).

2.3.3 Municipalities Regionale de Comte Rimouski-Neigette, Québec

The regional county municipality (i.e., Municipalities Regionale de Comte – MRC) of Rimouski-Neigette (the region) is located on the southern peninsula of the St. Lawrence River within the Bas-Saint-Laurent (BSL) administrative and economic region in the province of Québec (Gouvernement du Québec, 2014; MRC de Rimouski-Neigette, 2015a) (see Map 4.4). The region is 300 km east of Québec City, has the St. Lawrence River to the north, New Brunswick to the south, MRC La Mitis to the east, and the MRC of Basques to the west.

The MRC de Rimouski-Neigette is one of 86 such regions in the province. It includes one unorganized territory and nine municipalities (OECD, 2010). MRCs are led by a council of mayors from within the region (OECD, 2010) and are primarily responsible for spatial planning; waste, fire, and civil protection planning; management of watercourses; evaluation of local municipalities; and local economic development (OECD, 2010). Apart from the MRC, additional regional actors include the BSL, La Société d'aide au développement de la collectivité (SADC) de la Neigette (La Société d'aide au développement de la collectivité de la Neigette, 2015), Centre Local de Development Rimouski-Neigette (MRC de Rimouski-Neigette, 2015a), and the Université du Québec à Rimouski (Université du Québec à Rimouski, 2015).

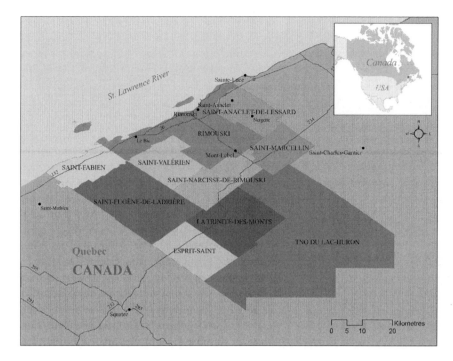

Map 4.4 MRC de Rimouski-Neigette

The region is physically smaller than the other case study regions, totaling 0.2% of Québec's total land mass and 0.7% of Québec's total population (Statistics Canada, 2012, 2017). The region's glacial history has resulted in high-quality soil, and consequently high-quality agricultural land (MRC de Rimouski-Neigette, 2015b). Beyond agriculture, the region has mixed land types, including the lowlands of the Gulf of St. Lawrence, Appalachian, islands, tidal flats, and terraces (MRC de Rimouski-Neigette, 2015a). The region is also home to the Bic National Park, as well as other parks and reserves. The MRC media considers the population to be stable (MRC de Rimouski-Neigette, 2015a), although 2.8% growth was seen between the 2016 and 2011 censuses (Statistics Canada, 2017). The majority in the region are French speaking.

Prior to European contact, several Indigenous peoples lived and moved throughout the region. While multiple European explorers and fur traders crossed the region, there were no permanent European settlements until 1694, when the regional population grew alongside increased trade, industry, and railway access (MRC de Rimouski-Neigette, 2008). Economically, the majority of people are employed in tertiary sectors (e.g., health care, retail, education). Employment in the secondary sectors (e.g., manufacturing, construction, utilities) is estimated at about 10%, and primary sector employment is estimated at about 5%, with continuing pockets of dependence on natural resource sectors such as agriculture, forestry, hunting, fishing, and mining (MRC de Rimouski-Neigette, 2015a). According to the last National Household Survey, the region's unemployment rate was 6.8% (Statistics Canada, 2011).

2.3.4 Kittiwake Region, Newfoundland and Labrador

The Kittiwake Region (Kittiwake – the region) is located on the north-east coast of the island of Newfoundland. It corresponds with the jurisdiction of the Kittiwake Economic Development Corporation, one of the province's former Regional Economic Development Zone Boards, and with the provincially designated Economic Zone 14 (see Map 4.5). The region is bordered by the Atlantic Ocean to the north and east, and Economic Zones (12, 13, 15) to the west, south, and south-east respectively.

Physically, the region is part of the boreal shield ecozone, with similar vegetation and a continental climate characterized by long, cold winters and short, warm summers (Bell, 2002; Vodden, 2009). In terms of biodiversity,

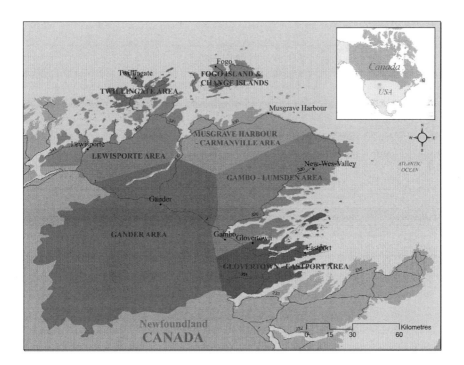

Map 4.5 Kittiwake region

there are a range of mammals in the region (e.g., black bear, lynx, woodland caribou), as well as multiple bird and fish species, including the once abundant Atlantic cod, which drew settlers to the region (Bell, 2002).

Across the region there are approximately 120 communities, including incorporated municipalities, local service districts, unincorporated communities, and two Mi'kmaq bands. There are three inhabited islands that are accessible only via ferry: Fogo Island, Change Islands, and St. Brendan's. There have been a number of shifts and iterations of governance within the region, including amalgamations, joint municipal councils, and regional councils. Beyond local governments there are a number of other regional actors, including Rural/Regional Development Associations (RDAs), tourism, business, and community-based associations, alongside many others.

The region accounts for 3.4% of the NL land mass and 8.8% of the province's population (Kittiwake Economic Development Corporation, 2009). Of the 120 communities in the region, only six have populations over 2,000, with Gander being the largest (11,688) and the primary service location within the region (Kittiwake Economic Development Corporation, 2006; Statistics Canada, 2017). The major urban and decision-making centres in NL are outside the region (e.g., St. John's – 250 km, Corner Brook – 320 km).

Kittiwake has a long history, both Indigenous and settler. Indigenous communities have been dated to 5,000 years ago (Pastore, 1999). European settlement includes a range of European settlers (English and French), dating into the 1600s, with a substantial history reflecting trading routes, as well as different cultures and religions (Explore Newfoundland and Labrador, 2010). More recently the area also experienced re-settlement from outports (small settlement in coves and inlets along the coast) to more centralized communities (Handcock, 2002).

The Kittiwake region's economy remains strongly influenced by fisheries, primarily shrimp and crab fisheries since the ground fish moratoria of the 1990s. In 2006, there were 19 communities in the region with fish processing facilities (Kittiwake Economic Development Corporation, 2009). However, despite the importance of fishing, the largest sectors in the region are retail, health and social services, and manufacturing/construction (Kittiwake Economic Development Corporation, 2009). Forestry-related activities are also important to the economy, as is, increasingly, tourism. Shortages of skilled labour have emerged as a pressing concern within the region.

2.3.5 *Northern Peninsula, Newfoundland and Labrador*

The Great Northern Peninsula of Newfoundland (the Northern Peninsula – the region) is the largest peninsula on the island and the northern-most region, which includes three former Regional Economic Development Boards (see Map 4.6). The borders align with the former Rural Secretariat Regional Council of St. Anthony-Port aux Choix area, on the tip of the Northern Peninsula. It is bordered to the west, north, and east by the Strait

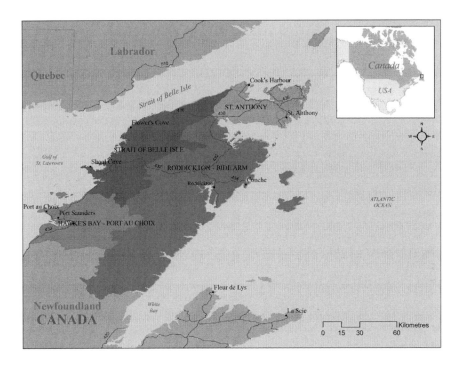

Map 4.6 Northern Peninsula

of Belle Isle and the Atlantic Ocean, and the Corner Brook-Rocky Harbour Rural Secretariat region in the south. The Northern Peninsula provided additional insights, data, and information, particularly related to innovation and governance themes (see for example Carter & Vodden, 2017; Gibson, 2014). It was not a core case study region, however, and thus does not appear in some of the detailed analysis and results of the research.

Today there are 51 communities on the peninsula and a mix of governance structures, including incorporated municipalities, local service districts, and unincorporated communities. Similar to the Kittiwake region, there are a number of important regional actors including the RDAs, the Community Business Development Corporations (CBDCs), and formerly the Rural Secretariat Regional Council and the Northern Peninsula Regional Collaboration Pilot Initiative, among others.

Physically the region includes barren hills, marshy plains, rock outcrops, fjords, and mountains. The Long Range Mountains (about 800 m in height) are the dominant physical feature (Simms, 1986). While many mineral deposits have been identified (e.g., uranium, zinc, copper), only zinc has been commercially mined (Ryan, 1983). The region is unique both in terms of its vegetation and climate, as compared to the rest of the island (Government of Newfoundland

and Labrador, 2012). The waters surrounding the region include a range of fish species (Government of Newfoundland and Labrador, 2012).

The peninsula accounts for 4.3% of the provincial land mass and is home to about 2.5% of the NL population (Statistics Canada, 2006a). The largest centre is St. Anthony (2,258), followed by Roddickton–Bide Arm (999), with nearly all communities being under 1,000 people (Statistics Canada, 2017). The region is located approximately 250 km from the City of Corner Brook and over 800 km from the provincial capital city and only population centre of more than 100,000 in NL (St. John's Census Metropolitan Area (CMA)). The region's population has seen both continued decline and aging at greater rates than the provincial averages.

Settlement in the region dates over the past 4,500 years and includes multiple Indigenous cultures (e.g., Archiac Indians, Dorset Palaeoeskimo culture), Vikings, Norse, and various European cultures, including the colonial influences of the French and British (Nydal, 1989; Reader, 1998). Natural resources (e.g., fishing) were the driving influence of settlement. Permanent settlement of the region did not occur until the late 18th century, and even then St. Anthony was the first incorporated municipality in 1945 (Simms, 1986).

As with the other case study regions, the economic history of the region is tied to natural resource development, primarily the fishing that drew so many cultures to the region. Today fishing and forestry continue to be important economic mainstays for the region. The natural resource sectors account for approximately a quarter of regional employment (including related manufacturing) (Community Accounts, 2018). Health care and social services, retail, and construction industries are also major employers. When compared to the rest of the province, the region has both a higher unemployment rate and lower incomes (Community Accounts, 2018).

2.4 Data collection

Across these case study regions, the primary source of data for this project was targeted semi-structured interviews both at the regional and provincial level in the four provinces. This included interviews with representatives of organizations working at the regional, provincial, and federal scales. We conducted interviews between 2011 and 2014 and explored regional development efforts within each of the specific case study regions. We developed a standardized data collection schedule and protocol to ensure that each provincial team took a similar approach, while affording the flexibility to tailor methods to unique situations as the need arose within each of the regions.

Prior to conducting the interviews, we developed regional profiles, drawing from an extensive literature review (these profiles remain available online at http://cdnregdev.ruralresilience.ca). These profiles familiarized team members with the regions and helped to identify potential interview participants.

Using internet searches and regional documents, a list of potential contacts was created for each region, which included representatives from: federal, provincial, regional, and municipal governments; development agencies; and non-governmental organizations. We also sought to ensure coverage of three arenas within regional development (i.e., economic development, recreation, and water management), as well as geographic coverage of each region, including different sizes and types of communities. Additionally, a "snowball" approach was used to identify additional interview participants. The makeup of interview participants varied for each region reflecting differences in context.

Each interview followed the same topic guide, but with flexibility allocated for place-specific questions and follow-ups. The theme teams clarified the scope and definition of each theme and developed a set of indicators for the presence (or absence) of each theme within development policy and practice. This led to the production of a set of theme-based "primers" or working papers as well as the interview guide. Theme primers and the interview guide are available at http://cdnregdev.ruralresilience.ca. As a result of the flexibility afforded by the semi-structured and place-based approach, there were differences between how questions were asked by different provincial teams and in different types of interview participants. We recorded the interviews[2] and notes throughout. Complete transcripts were made of each interview. Interview participants were also asked for relevant documents (e.g., strategic plans, annual reports), which were reviewed to add context to the interviews. We created a database of interview participants, with one master interview sheet kept for the entire project, affording comparison between the projects and regions. We conducted a total of 133 interviews with 136 organizations and 162 individuals (see Table 4.2).

Researchers kept field journals during visits to the case study regions to record observational data, including details of interviews (e.g., body language, tone) and general reflections of the region itself, including observations of individual communities and organizations, and relationships among interview participants and agencies. We also took photographs of physical, economic,

Table 4.2 Interview participant summary

	British Columbia	Ontario	Québec	Newfoundland	TOTAL
Provincial Interviews	10	4	11	6	31
Regional Interviews	22 (27 individuals, 23 organizations)	33 (57 individuals, 35 organizations)	19 (19 individuals and organizations)	28 (28 individuals and organizations)	102 (162 individuals, 136 organizations)
Total Interviews	32	37	30	34	133

and cultural landscapes. Finally, we kept all email communications, alongside post-interview notes. All research materials were shared among the research team with respondent identification limited to team members conducting the data collection. Identification numbers were used for data analysis and pseudonyms for materials used beyond team members.

2.5 Data analysis

The sample selection procedures and the number of interviews in each region do not support quantitative needs for statistical inference to a broader population. However, we feel that the systematic and broad scope of our framework and respondent selection procedures ensures a reasonable basis for generalizations to the regions considered. Not only were we conscientious about seeking a range of representatives for the topics, themes, organizations, and positions of importance to new regionalism, but we have subjected their responses to cross-checking with local documents, respondents from a variety of networks and organizations, and feedback from other knowledgeable informants from the regions.

Comparative analysis using this type of information collection is fraught with special challenges since common themes and issues must be identified and addressed even as the unique conditions of each location are respected. In order to manage these conflicting objectives, we took several approaches to our analysis. The first was to use the interview transcripts and summaries as data for content analysis. This analysis was conducted with respect to the five key themes of new regionalism in order to assess the extent and nature of their occurrence in the interview responses (see Chapters 1 and 3).

We transcribed the interview responses (or notes in the case of Ontario) into electronic form and conducted analysis using QSR NVivo qualitative analysis software. All data was stored, coded, and analysed using one NVivo file that was kept on a shared computer and remotely accessed by the entire team. Using NVivo ensured that all analysis was conducted on the same data set. Teams assigned to each province and theme completed all coding and analysis, with analysis undertaken by theme (e.g., place-based development) and geography (e.g., findings for the Kootenay Region). Similarly to the data collection, the same overall approach was taken to data analysis across the teams, but with the flexibility to slightly modify the foci according to theme and location-specific interests. We analyzed provincial-level interviews with regional development practitioners and policy-makers separately in order to provide supplementary insights and context to the narrative for each theme and study region.

We used a broad analytical framework to allow for multiple lines of inquiry across the same data sets, with both overarching and theme-specific protocols. An overarching protocol document for analysis and coding was developed to provide consistency across the case study regions, themes of new regionalism, and arenas of regional development. Throughout the project, we produced multiple papers focusing on specific elements of the data collected, each using slight variations in the conceptual frameworks and approaches to examine the themes in detail.

Each theme team assigned coders to conduct the NVivo analysis. The overarching protocol included explicit instructions on accessing the data to ensure only one coder was working with the data set at any time. Each coder read the regional profiles and relevant documents prior to beginning, in order to help them better understand the context surrounding each region. Theme leaders worked with coders to develop and clarify the codes used for each theme, drawing from a list of indicators for the presence or absence of each theme developed prior to data collection.

To help verify the interpretations of the theme coders, provincial team members who were familiar with the region and, therefore, held important contextual knowledge, coded their interviews with two overarching codes ("arena" and "theme") – noting sections throughout each interview that related generally to each of the five themes and each of the three arenas. This allowed the theme team coders to check the data they were assigning to a particular theme against that assigned by the provincial team. All coders took notes throughout this process, recording their impressions of the interviews, the agencies and documents mentioned, explanations for coding of certain sections, and other relevant comments. "Memos" were added in NVivo allowing interviewers and coders to add relevant notes (e.g., notes from interviewers on interview-participant body language and tone) and review those of others. Theme-based coders could then also review the provincial team's coding notes, for example, checking against their own for insights and to ensure that this material had been included in the theme team's coding and subsequent analysis.

We completed multiple iterations of analysis. The aim was to determine: 1) whether there was evidence of the relevant new regionalism theme or subthemes in regional planning, design, and practice in Canada; 2) to assess the extent to which the theme or sub-theme was present within the case study regions; and 3) how it was manifested. The first pass identified interview data related to the respective themes through coding, while the second allowed for additional clarification and detail to be added and for the generation of additional codes where needed – based on identified patterns. For each theme, the first round of frequency analysis focused on whether there was discussion of the topic within each transcript. Each theme was identified by a code. Each code was then used to compute the frequency with which the theme arose within the interviews using the "matrix coding" query on NVivo (for all regions except the Northern Peninsula, as noted above). One mention of "Place Branding" (see Chapter 6), for example, was sufficient to identify the respondent as sensitive to this concept. A calculation of the percentage of total interviews where the respondent mentioned a particular theme or concept at least once then became the primary basis for initial comparison across indicators and regions, as presented in the tables in Chapters 5 to 9. To view the full set of indicators and related frequency calculations, please see the project's website: http://cdnregdev.ruralresilience.ca.

The second round of analysis allowed the coders to examine whether discussion of an indicator was indicating the presence or absence of the topic in development policy and practice. For the purposes of the theme chapters in this book (Chapters 5 to 9), only positive data (i.e., presence) are displayed. To access the complete tables for each theme (including presence, absence, and overall mention data) with specific percentage values, please see the project's website: http://cdnregdev.ruralresilience.ca. In some cases, theme teams also calculated the total number of mentions of a particular concept (within each interview and across the data set), considering that there was likely to be some significance in the difference between a respondent who mentioned, for example, "water" many times within the interview in relation to rural–urban interaction and one who only mentioned it once or twice.

Coders also ran specific queries as needed by team members, for example, looking for particular terms, people, or groups. Some themes and indicators lent themselves better to numerical representation than others. For some, a pattern searching technique was considered more appropriate and was used more heavily. For all themes and indicators, we conducted further qualitative analysis to explore meanings and practices within the study regions associated with topics highlighted by this initial analysis. Once the initial coding was completed, the coders and other researchers met both as theme teams and as a larger group to cross-check findings and discuss implications and directions for further investigation.

For comparative purposes, we required a standardization procedure to compare results from the four regions in a way which respected the different number of interviews in each. Since the number of interviews in each region was relatively small (see Table 4.2), to avoid distorting the statistical quality of the data through the direct comparison of percentages or proportions we adopted an ordinal representation of the results. This meant collapsing the proportions into four values: those where no mention of the concept was made in the interviews being considered (N), those where 1% to 33% of the interview participants mentioned the concept at least once (L – low prevalence within the data set), those where 34% to 67% of the interview participants mentioned it at least once (M – medium), and those where 68% to 100% of the relevant interview participants mentioned it at least once (H – high). We used the similarities and differences among these four categories across codes, overall themes, and regions to identify potential similarities, differences, or important issues for further analysis. The team did not consider this frequency analysis as providing a strong indicator for drawing conclusions but as a starting point or guide to identify likely avenues for further analysis. This analysis was then conducted using the wide variety of data and information at our disposal.

2.6 Report back and knowledge mobilization

Following this initial process of coding and analysis, team members brought their findings to study regions and interview participants both in order to report back and solicit feedback. We secured an additional grant from Canada's Social

Sciences and Humanities Research Council with the assistance of provincial, national, and international collaborating knowledge networks such as CRRF and the Rural Policy Learning Commons (RPLC) to support knowledge mobilization activities in 2016–17. Throughout the course of the project, the research team made over 22 international presentations and webinars, 62 national workshops and presentations, and seven presentations and workshops used specifically for knowledge mobilization in the project case study regions. These included two final regional workshops held in the Northern Peninsula, NL and in the Kootenays, BC and a national workshop held in Guelph, Ontario in conjunction with the CRRF's annual conference (co-hosted by the RPLC). We have also created project reports and working papers, vignettes profiling lessons learned on explored new regionalist themes from the case study regions, and academic articles. For more information on knowledge mobilization activities and project resources please see the project's website: http://cdnregdev.ruralresilience.ca.

3 Reflections

3.1 Reflections on methods

Upon the successful completion of the research, there were project elements worthy of critical reflection. As described above, there were differences in both data collection and analysis between the case study regions and across theme teams. While these differences reduced consistency, we feel they were justified given: i) the contextual differences among the regions and provinces, and ii) the differences among themes, with a level of independence afforded to each theme team that allowed each to be guided by theme-specific literature, as well as the overarching new regionalism literature. While this made comparisons difficult at times, the reverse approach would have resulted in a failure to account for important differences between regions and themes as well as the differing skills, experiences, connections, and disciplinary traditions of the investigators.

This project was conducted over five years. While this allowed for observation over time, a strength of the research, the length of the study also created challenges. Unlike controlled experiments, case studies are a snapshot of a complex, dynamic reality. Changes to situations (e.g., change in government, staff, funding, or economic conditions) can occur rapidly. Data collection occurred over different time periods (within a matter of months) across the teams due to researcher availability, including timing of student thesis research and other logistical constraints. This meant there were changes in contextual factors among the time periods, data collection and analysis, and various writing projects. Team members attempted to track such changes through monitoring documents, interview participant feedback on research products, and building relationships with key individuals within the study regions who were also able to review products and provide feedback. When products were in progress, we made revisions to account for such changes;

however, revisions were not made retroactively – meaning completed products are a snapshot of that moment in time.

Lastly, the project was both complex and ambitious. Given the breadth of the core concepts of regional development and new regionalism along with the size and diverse nature of the country across which the research took place, it was challenging to contain the project within a reasonable scope, as well as to coordinate a large research team spread across geography and time. Issues and challenges naturally arose as the project progressed, however the experience, diversity, and depth brought to the project by each team member resulted in a project rich in detail, containing many important insights, and, we hope, transferable lessons.

3.2 Lessons learned

After the completion of the research and prior to writing this volume, we conducted a 16-question survey of research team members, exploring the strategies and results of the research. The majority of team members felt that the main goals of the project centred around a common theme (the explorations of regional development in present-day Canada), remained consistent throughout the project period. All interview participants felt that the data collection and analysis methods were appropriate and that the project goals were met.

Meeting minutes also provided a source of reflection on the project and lessons learned, demonstrating the volume of in-depth conversations and discussions that helped to shape the project. Overall the perception and feedback seen within meeting minutes and the survey were positive. Reflections from team members demonstrate the acknowledgement of the positive outcomes of the project, while also identifying lessons learned. For example, records of team meetings indicate that select differences in methods and approaches, while justifiable, also posed some challenges. For example, the decision not to record and transcribe the interviews carried out in Ontario resulted in fewer available details to code and made comparisons between the Ontario data set and others more challenging. The minutes also reflect the team's efforts to grapple with the complexity of regional development across a diverse country. A simplified or more focused goal and approach would have decreased the challenges and time required, but may not have been sensitive to the nuances among themes and places, or resulted in the same robustness of the study.

The team felt that in some ways the approach to knowledge mobilization could have been improved, particularly for providing public information. This is a common challenge for all academic research endeavours. One possible solution identified in our post-project review would be to develop more structured partnerships with regional organizations, which could then serve to guide knowledge mobilization for practitioner and policy audiences. Such an approach would most likely mean important trade-offs, however, between pressures for addressing local, current issues and the more long-term interests of academic researchers.

It was felt that we worked effectively as a team and that the differences in age, experience, familiarity with technology, and other elements provided many opportunities for peer learning and mentoring. Overall, team members felt that the mix of experience on the team was positive and useful, bringing a range of perspectives. It was noted that incorporating additional expertise from economic, political, or quantitative fields would have brought additional skills and perspectives to the project.

Communication was facilitated through a variety of tools, however none of these tools were noted as being an adequate replacement for (often costly) in-person meetings when dealing with the more conceptual-, design-, and strategy-related discussions required. This underscores the logistical challenges of working across a country the size of Canada. Though a project of this size and scope is not easy, the resulting relationships and networks from this project were immense, with many project team members continuing to work together, as well as with organizations they connected with during this project, on related and new projects through national and international networks and connections that were both utilized and strengthened through this research.

Notes

1 Economic zone and Rural Secretariat boundaries no longer represent regions with relating governance organizations (as discussed in Chapter 2) but they continue to be used in the province for statistical purposes (see https://nl.communi tyaccounts.ca).
2 All interviews were audio-recorded, except in Ontario, where interviews were not recorded but detailed notes were taken. Québec interviews were conducted in French and translated to English for data analysis.

References

Agriculture and Agri-Food Canada. (2016). Canada Land Inventory (CLI). Retrieved August 13, 2017, from http://sis.agr.gc.ca/cansis/nsdb/cli/index.html.

Apgar, J.M. et al. (2016). Moving beyond co-construction of knowledge to enable self-determination. *IDS Bulletin*, [S.l.], 47(6). Retrieved January 8, 2013, from http://bulletin.ids.ac.uk/idsbo/article/view/2830.

BC Stats. (2012). *Development Region 4 – Kootenay Socio-Economic Profile*. Retrieved from http://www.bcstats.gov.bc.ca/Files/43de13e5-50be-4c8a-87b4-e0ff26ce6364/Socio-EconomicProfile-DevelopmentRegion4.pdf.

Bell, T. (2002). Boreal shield ecozone. Retrieved January 14, 2013, from www.heritage.nf.ca/environment/boreal_shield.html.

Bish, R., & Clemens, E. (2008). *Local Government in British Columbia* (Fourth). Richmond: Union of British Columbia Municipalities.

Breen, S.-P. (2016a). *Economy Trends Analysis*. Castlegar. Retrieved from http://data cat.cbrdi.ca/sites/default/files/attachments/TA_Economy_2016.pdf.

Breen, S.-P. (2016b). *From Staples Theory to New Regionalism: Managing Drinking Water for Regional Resilience in Rural British Columbia.* Burnaby BC: Simon Fraser University.

Canada History. (2012). *Samuel De Champlain.* Retrieved August 1, 2012, from www.canadahistory.com/sections/eras/2worldsmeet/champlain/champlain.htm.

Carter, K. L., & Vodden, K. (2017). Applicability of territorial innovation models to declining resource-based regions: Lessons from the Northern Peninsula of Newfoundland. *The Journal of Rural and Community Development, 12*(2/3), 74–92.

Columbia Basin Regional Development Institute. (2017). *Columbia Basin-Boundary Population Update.* Castlegar. Retrieved from http://datacat.cbrdi.ca/sites/default/files/attachments/PopulationUpdate-FinalApril242017.pdf.

Columbia Basin Trust. (2012). *Columbia River Basin: Dams and Hydroelectricity.* Retrieved from https://thebasin.ourtrust.org/wp-content/uploads/delightful-downloads/HydroPowerDams_Final_web.pdf.

Community Accounts. (2018). *St. Anthony – Port au Choix Rural Secretariat Regional Profiles.* Retrieved January 19, 2012, from http://nl.communityaccounts.ca/profiles.asp?_=vb7En4WVgbWy0nI_.

Eastern Ontario Wardens Caucus. (2017). *About EOWC.* Retrieved August 11, 2017, from www.eowc.org/en/.

Explore Newfoundland and Labrador. (2010). *The Kittiwake Coast.* Retrieved April 18, 2013, from www.explorenewfoundlandandlabrador.com/scenic–routes–central–region/the–kittiwake–coast.htm.

Gibson, R. (2014). Collaborative governance in rural regions: An examination of Ireland and Newfoundland and Labrador. Doctoral (PhD) thesis, Memorial University of Newfoundland.

Gouvernement du Québec. (2014). *Rimouski-Neigette.Rimouski-Neigette.* Retrieved January 7, 2015, from translate.googleusercontent.com/translate_c?depth=1&hl=en&prev=search&rurl=translate.google.ca&sl=fr&u=www.toponymie.gouv.qc.ca/ct/ToposWeb/fiche.aspx?no_seq=141044&usg=ALkJrhiyoo0ftsfXP8Y6pxjUSwDZqEndng.

Government of Newfoundland and Labrador. (2012). Northern Peninsula Subregions. Retrieved January 19, 2012, from www.nr.gov.nl.ca/nr/forestry/maps/npeninsula_eco.html.

Handcock, G. (2002). Family and community origins on the Eastport Peninsula. In *Society, Economy and Culture.* Retrieved April 18, 2013, from www.heritage.nf.ca/society/eastport.htm.

Kingston Historical Society. (2003). *Chronology of the History of Kingston.* Retrieved August 1, 2012, from http://kingstonhistoricalsociety.ca/chronology.html.

Kittiwake Economic Development Corporation. (2006). *Analysis of Zone 14 Transportation Infrastructure.* Retrieved from www.kittiwake.nf.ca/documents/transportation.pdf.

Kittiwake Economic Development Corporation. (2009). *Strategic Economic Plan 2009–2011.* Gander, Newfoundland and Labrador, Canada: Kittiwake Economic Development Corporation.

KNET. (2012). *First Nation Communities in Ontario.* Retrieved August 1, 2012, from www.communities.knet.ca.

Lanark County. (2012). *County History.* Retrieved August 13, 2017, from www.lanarkcounty.ca/Page1894.aspx.

La Société d'aide au développement de la collectivité de la Neigette. (2015). *Mission.* Retrieved January 14, 2101, from www.sadcneigette.ca/index.php?option=com_content&view=article&id=155&Itemid=470.

Mauser, W., Klepper, G., Rice, M., Schmalzbauer, B.S., Hackmann, H., Leemans, R., & Moore, H. (2013). Transdisciplinary global change research: The co-creation of knowledge for sustainability. *Current Opinion in Environmental Sustainability*, *5*(3), 420–431.

MRC de Rimouski-Neigette. (2008). *La diversite culturelle, une richesse a partager!* Retrieved from www.mrcrimouskineigette.qc.ca/service/culture/immigration/politique_accueil.pdf.

MRC de Rimouski-Neigette. (2015a). *MRC de Rimouski-Neigette.* Retrieved January 7, 2015, from www.mrcrimouskineigette.qc.ca.

MRC de Rimouski-Neigette. (2015b). *MRC de Rimouski-Neigette.* Retrieved January 7, 2015, from www.mrcrimouskineigette.qc.ca/.

Nydal, R. (1989). A critical review of radiocarbon dating of a Norse settlement at l'Anse aux Meadows, Newfoundland Canada. *Radiocarbon*, *31*(3), 976–985.

OECD. (2010). *OECD Rural Policy Reviews Québec, Canada.* OECD Publishing. Retrieved from https://read.oecd-ilibrary.org/urban-rural-and-regional-development/oecd-rural-policy-reviews-quebec-canada-2010_9789264082151-en#page15.

Ontario Government. (2011). *History of Ontario - World Wars.* Retrieved August 21, 2012, from www.ontario.ca/en/about_ontario/004527.html?openNav=history.

Ontario Ministry of Training Colleges and Universities (MTCU). (2009). *Employment Ontario Eastern Region 2009 Annual Labour Market Report.* Retrieved August 27, 2012, from www.tcu.gov.on.ca/eng/labourmarket/currenttrends/docs/regional/2009east.pdf.

Ontario Parks. (2012). *Signature Landscapes.* Retrieved February 12, 2017, from http://ontariooutdoor.com/landscapes.aspx?language=en.

Pahl-Wostl, C., Giupponi, C., Richards, K., Binder, C., de Sherbinin, A., Sprinz, D., Toonen, T., & van Bers, C. (2012). Transition towards a new global change science: Requirements for methodologies, methods, data and knowledge. *Environmental Science and Policy*, *28*, 36–47. Doi:10.1016/j.envsci.2012.11.009.

Parks Canada. (2009). *Kootenay National Park of Canada History of the Park.* Retrieved May 9, 2012, from www.pc.gc.ca/pn–np/bc/kootenay/natcul/natcul10.aspx.

Pastore, R. T. (1999). The Boyd's Cove Beothuk Site. Retrieved January 26, 2013, from www.heritage.nf.ca/aboriginal/beo_boydscove.html.

Reader, D. (1998). *The 1997 Archaeological Survey of the Bird Cove Area, Northwestern Northern Peninsula Newfoundland.* St. John's: Government of Newfoundland and Labrador.

Ryan, A. (1983). Geology of the west coast of Newfoundland. *Newfoundland Journal of Geological Education*, *7*(2).

Simms, D. (1986). *Rural Development in Newfoundland: "A Legitimation Crisis" (Background report to the Royal Commission on Employment and Unemployment).* St. John's. Retrieved from https://www.library.yorku.ca/find/Record/275398

Statistics Canada. (2006a). *2006 Community Profiles – 2006 Census.* Ottawa.

Statistics Canada. (2006b). *Community Information Database.* Retrieved February 8, 2012, from www.cid-bdc.ca/home.

Statistics Canada. (2011). *National Household Survey (NHS) Profile, 2011.* Retrieved October 1, 2016, from www12.statcan.gc.ca/nhs-enm/2011/dp-pd/prof/index.cfm?Lang=E.

Statistics Canada. (2012). *Rimouski-Neigette, Québec (Code 2410) and Québec (Code 24) (table) 2011 Census* (Census Profile No. 98–316–XWE). Ottawa.

Statistics Canada. (2017). *2016 Census.* Retrieved April 3, 2017, from www12.statcan.gc.ca/census-recensement/2016/dp-pd/prof/index.cfm?Lang=E.

Stevenson, S. K., Armleader, H. M., Arsenault, A., Coxson, D., DeLong, S. C., & Jull, M. (2011). *British Columbia's Inland Rainforest*. Vancouver: UBC Press.

Université du Québec à Rimouski. (2015). The University. Retrieved January 15, 2015, from www.uqar.ca/english/.

Vodden, K. (2009). *New Spaces, Ancient Places: Collaborative Governance and Sustainable Development in Canada's Coastal Regions*. Burnaby BC: Simon Fraser University.

Vodden, K., Markey, S., Douglas, D., & Reimer, B. (2015). Canadian regional development: A critical review of theory, practice and potentials. Retrieved March 27, 2017, from http://cdnregdev.ruralresilience.ca/.

Watson, K. (2011). *United Empire Loyalists*. Retrieved August 12, 2017, from www.rideau-info.com/canal/history/loyalists.htm.

5 Searching for multi-level collaborative governance

Ryan Gibson

1 Governance and new regionalism: an introduction

Governance is a central tenet of new regionalism, with Wallis (2002) noting "new regionalism is all about governance" (p. 2). As noted in Chapter 3, governance is about empowerment, linkages, flexibility, partnerships, and information sharing. It should be clearly understood that governance is not synonymous with government. In fact, a critical focus of governance in new regionalism is the movement away from reliance only on government and toward new forms of governing. These new forms of governing, each built on the place-specific attributes of the region, seek innovative mechanisms for advancing regional development, revitalization, and sustainability. Our collective understanding of how the transition from government to governance plays out in rural regions is not robust, such that Reimer (2004) suggested it was the revolution that no one noticed.

The emergence of governance materialized out of a recognition that the current opportunities and challenges facing society and communities are wicked, reaching beyond the capacity or mandate of any one-level government, the private sector, or voluntary and non-profit organizations. As a result, new forms of collective decision-making are required that engage traditional and non-traditional actors. Governance manifests itself in a number of different models. Throughout the various approaches to regional governance, the key characteristics are that it involves a process, the involvement of regional actors, collective decision-making, and new methods of engagement. This research builds on two major models of multi-level and collaborative governance. These models offer conceptual overlaps and a unique platform to identify and understand the manifestation of governance in rural regions in Canada.

Understanding the catalysts leading to the emergence of new forms of governing is the starting point for this chapter. New forms of governing, including multi-level collaborative governance, emerged from criticisms of the Westminster model of government and its inability to address regional opportunities and challenges. The key characteristics of multi-level collaborative governance as presented from the literature-informed data collection in each of the regions of this research. In all, we used a series of 19 indicators to evaluate the presence of multi-level collaborative governance.

The findings identify some components of multi-level collaborative governance taking place in rural Canada. How multi-level collaborative governance was applied varied, from water governance arrangements to new service provision associations. When present, the empirical evidence from the interviews is in line with the theoretical understanding of multi-level collaborative governance. Key themes emerging from the governance analysis include the blurring of responsibilities, barriers to multi-level collaborative governance, and lack of human and financial resources for implementation. Reflections from the empirical evidence suggest areas that require further attention, such as macro-level influences, the implications of the Truth and Reconciliation Commission (2015) recommendations within the Canadian context, and issues of human resource burn-out.

Multi-level collaborative governance is taking place in some elements of the rural landscape of Canada; however, it is far from universal in its application and in many cases falls short of the key criteria for multi-level collaborative governance. The form and function of these governance initiatives vary greatly, largely building on place-based dynamics. Understanding the details of multi-level collaborative governance and the barriers hindering new forms of governing are important for anticipating the future of rural regions and regional development in Canada.

2 Emergence and evolution of governance[1]

The term "governance" is used to describe a wide range of processes, structures, institutions, and activities. The term is regularly used, and variously defined, in policy documents, academic writing, private sector strategic plans, community-based literatures, and throughout the media. However, all too often these multiple definitions of "governance" are not synonymous, resulting in confusion. In some cases they are used to refer to government policy and institutions alone, in others they include non-government organizations – but all of these maintain a focus on public policy issues. The most general approaches include governance in any form of organization, from informal clubs and networks to government organizations. In each case, the analysis considers the ways in which the activities of the organizations are organized, constrained, facilitated, coordinated, determined, and managed – at both formal and informal levels (Coase, 1937; Weber, 1947). The tools for such control and governance will vary by the type of organization (Salamon, 2002).

In order to focus the discussion, our analysis of governance and new regionalism centres on public policy, participation and collaboration, democracy, and processes in government organizations at federal, provincial, regional, and municipal levels along with non-government organizations engaged explicitly with regional and community development-related issues (Bevir, 2009). The transition from government to governance is of particular concern for this chapter. This section provides a brief assessment of this evolution and emergence of governance studies starting from the Westminster model of government, then examines the key characteristics of governance, to explore the transition from government to governance in the context of rural regional development in Canada.

2.1 Evolution of governance studies

Understanding the Westminster model of government is an important starting point from which to distinguish the emergence of governance (Rhodes, 1997). From this position, the influences of the New Public Management and polycentrism facilitate an understanding of the movement from government to governance.

The Westminster model of government, such as that currently utilized in Canada and the United Kingdom, is based on the assertion that there is a singular centre of power. This centre of power consists of a series of institutions and organizations, with dedicated personnel and a monopoly of power within a bounded territory (Hay, Lister, & Marsh, 2006). The singular head of power is often the sovereign, a prime minister, or a house of parliament. The power wielded by the centre is often powerful and resilient (Bevir & Rhodes, 2011; Rhodes, 1997). The Westminster model of government can easily be seen throughout Canada, whether the centre of power is in Ottawa or the provincial or territorial capitals.

The Westminster model of government is challenged by frameworks proposing centreless societies or polycentrism. In polycentric societies there are multiple centres of power, such as at the family level, community level, organizational level, provincial level, national level, or supranational level (Luhmann, 1982; Morgan, 2007). Within polycentrism, the engagement of a mixture of government(s), networks, and markets is viewed as ideal for public policy creation and implementation. Propositions regarding multiple centres of power and the engagement of multiple actors in decision-making challenge the traditional tenets of the Westminster model of government.

Further challenging the Westminster model is the rise of New Public Management (Osborne & Gaebler, 1992). New Public Management theories and public sector reforms in the 1980s and 1990s introduced marketization and corporate management into government. Through these efforts, governments attempted to create cross-linked networks or partnerships among government, private sector, and non-governmental actors to overcome fragmentation and downsizing of the public service (Bevir, 2009). The New Public Management created a decreased role for central governments and an increased role for new policy actors (Adshead, 2002).

Governance emerged from the criticism of large central governments' inabilities to accommodate the preferences of diverse communities or regions, multi-sectoral opportunities, and transboundary issues (Hooghe & Marks, 2002; Newman, Barnes, Sullivan, & Knops, 2004; Rosenau, 1997). In the movement from government to governance, Woods and Goodwin (2003) identify five key transformations: (i) reduction of the government's role, (ii) transfer of responsibilities to the local level by governments, (iii) government initiatives seeking to harmonize policy delivery through partnerships, (iv) the reorganization of local institutions to address regional issues, and (v) the introduction of amendments to increase the power, responsibilities, and finances of local government. The shift from government to governance can be at least be partially witnessed in all sectors and all regions.

2.2 Characteristics of governance

Governance studies are increasingly interdisciplinary. Contributions to governance studies emerge from disciplines such as public policy, political science, geography, economics, sociology, and environmental studies. More broadly, advancements in our understanding of governance emerge from studies focused on health, natural sciences, and social sciences. This interest in governance from multiple disciplines results in what Jessop (1995) describes as an eclectic and disjointed discourse. The criticisms of these disjointed ideas emerge from the lack of conceptual clarity and disciplines sometimes acting in isolation (Bevir, 2011).

Despite this critique, four common elements emerged: process, collaboration, collective decision-making, and engagement of actors beyond only government. The first common element is that governance is a process. All governance arrangements engage in a process, or processes, that may be either formal or informal. Formal processes may involve legal agreements among partners, informal processes may involve simply a verbal or tacit commitment by stakeholders to work together. Second, governance requires collaborations with multiple actors, such as local residents, community or regional-serving organizations, civil society, the public sector, and the private sector. Third, governance requires collective decision-making among stakeholders. Many governance studies suggest the process of decision-making under a governance model should strive for consensus decision-making. It is also recognized that consensus decision-making may not always be attainable, in which case alternative decision-making models should be utilized. Finally, governance represents a new way of engagement that extends beyond simply the activities of government (i.e., the public sector). The governance process is also characterized by a local or regional level emphasis with the engagement of stakeholders, such as civil society actors, community leaders, and the business sector, in an autonomous and legitimate organization.

Rhodes (1996) provides a frequently quoted definition of governance as "a change in the meaning of government, referring to a new process of governing; or a changed condition of ordered rule; or the new method by which society is governed" (pp. 652–653). Three themes emerge from Rhodes' description of governance: the movement away from government, use of new processes, and change of ordered rule. These three themes emerge in most definitions of governance (cf. Abrams, Borrini-Feyerabend, Gardner, &

Heylings, 2003; Keohane & Nye, 2002; Kooiman, 1993; Vodden, Ommer, & Schneider, 2006). In Rhodes' definition of governance, he stresses that governance is not a synonym for government. Rather, governance is a more inclusive and participatory phenomenon or set of processes. Fundamentally, governance requires a change in how government operates through new processes and methods (Rhodes, 1997). This perspective is echoed by Rosenau (1992), who notes that governance requires government to engage non-governmental organizations in discussions and decision-making. Kooiman (1993) extends this understanding by stating that no single actor, whether public or private, has the required knowledge, experience, and power to solve the complex problems confronting communities and regions – thereby leading to the emphasis on collaboration.

To further the understanding of governance, Stoker (1998, p. 18) made the following five propositions illustrating the breadth of its characteristics:

1. Governance refers to a set of institutions and actors that are drawn from but also beyond government.
2. Governance identifies the blurring of boundaries and responsibilities for tackling social and economic issues.
3. Governance analysis identifies the power dependence involved in the relations between institutions involved in collective action.
4. Governance is about autonomous self-governing networks of actors.
5. Governance emphasizes the capacity to get things done, which does not rest on the power of government to command or use its authority. It sees government as able to use new tools and techniques to steer and guide.

These five propositions support and build on the work of Rhodes, Bevir, and Kooiman. They provide key areas for investigation and a platform for investigating and assessing governance initiatives in rural areas.

2.3 Multi-level collaborative governance

The literature identifies and describes multiple forms or types of governance. Each model of governance proposes a slightly different emphasis, which makes the models more or less appropriate depending on the local context and the issues being addressed. These models range from good governance (Leftwich, 1994; Weiss, 2000), interactive governance (Kooiman, Bavinck, Chuenpagdee, & Mahon, 2008), partnerships (Ansell, 2000; Bache, 2000), policy networks (Bogason & Toonen, 1998; Lowndes & Skelcher, 1998), network governance (Provan & Kenis, 2007), and contemporary governance (Magnette, 2003). Our research focuses on multi-level collaborative governance to examine new regionalism in Canada.

The primary focus of multi-level collaborative governance is found in two literature streams: multi-level governance and collaborative governance.

Multi-level governance focuses on the dispersion of governance across multiple jurisdictions (Hooghe & Marks, 2002; Marks, Hooghe, & Blank, 1996). In multi-level governance, decision-making is shared among multiple actors at different levels. The dispersion of authority can be vertical: to actors located at other levels, or horizontal: to non-government actors (Bache & Flinders, 2005). This model of governance builds particularly on Stoker's propositions regarding the engagement of non-government actors, the sharing of power and responsibilities, and the blurring of boundaries. Central to multi-level governance is the recognition and application of polycentrism (Benz & Eberlein, 1999; Conzelmann, 1998). Multi-level governance focuses on multiple centres of power and the relationships to non-traditional public policy actors, such as local government, voluntary or nonprofit organizations, or the business community occurring on multiple levels or scales.

Collaborative governance, building on the work of multi-level governance, focuses on how groups of actors share power and, often, share resources to create and/or enhance public policy and programs. Emphasis is placed on cooperation, collaboration, and consensus building among actors (Bevir, 2009; Eberlein & Kerwer, 2004). In particular, collaborative governance takes into consideration the starting conditions, the collaborative processes (trust, commitment to process, face-to-face dialogue, and shared understanding), institutional design (ground rules, transparency), facilitated leadership, and outcomes of a given governance arrangement (Ansell & Gash, 2007). The engagement of diverse actors in a consensus environment can lead to restored relationships among community leaders, community-/regional-based organizations, and traditional decision-makers (Van Buuren & Edelenbos, 2007).

Together these two forms of governance – multi-level and collaborative – provide a useful lens with which to examine the experiences and narratives of interview participants across the case study communities. Multi-level collaborative governance offers a number of potential benefits. First, this form of governance is focused on engaging non-traditional actors in decision-making processes (Ansell & Gash, 2007). Expanding the network of actors involved in decision-making facilitates participation, trust, and a heightened examination of policies. Second, the co-construction of policy through governance initiatives enables enhanced accountability and empowerment (Bevir, 2009). Third, given the diversity of actors and their local/regional knowledge, governance is able to generate regionally relevant and appropriate solutions to the challenges and opportunities confronting a given region (Van Buuren & Edelenbos, 2007).

3 Key multi-level collaborative governance themes

As indicated above, the research team developed a series of indicators to examine multi-level collaborative governance across the case study regions. These indicators were developed from key literature on multi-level collaborative governance, the government to governance transition, and the key characteristics of governance. They refer to the existence, purpose, and characteristics of multi-level collaborative governance arrangements as experienced by local and regional actors.

When examining the multi-level collaborative governance interviews across each of the five case study regions, a series of five key themes were identified. We subsequently classified these themes through content analysis of the interviews and assignment of appropriate codes. Each of the themes suggest factors that either facilitated or hindered the development of multi-level collaborative governance initiatives. The key themes emerging from the analysis included: (i) the wide diversity of experiences with components of multi-level collaborative governance, (ii) a governance conundrum in which communities recognized the value of collaboration but chose not to engage in multi-level collaborative governance initiatives, (iii) increased responsibilities without an increase in financial resources, (iv) institutional challenges related to volunteer burnout, past experiences in collaboration, and unequal power dynamics between rural and urban communities, and (v) active public engagement.

3.1 Diversity of experiences with multi-level collaborative governance

Each of the case study regions illustrate initiatives that held at least some characteristics of multi-level collaborative governance initiatives. There was great diversity in these initiatives. Some initiatives were formalized with agreements or memoranda of understanding, while others were informal arrangements. Other multi-level collaborative governance initiatives had many years of history to their credit, while others were brand new. Across the initiatives that might be characterized as multi-level collaborative governance, some are growing while others are stagnant.

Comparisons across the country suggested important differences between the experiences of multi-level collaborative governance, particularly when it comes to the diversity of actors engaged. Initiatives in British Columbia (BC) and Québec (QC) were more likely to be described as positive experiences compared to Ontario (ON) and Newfoundland and Labrador (NL) (see Table 5.1). The interviewees described a variety of mandates for governance initiatives; however, only an environmental mandate in BC ranked above a low score. In terms of collaborating partners in governance activities, the level of engagement of actors from within their region ranked high in BC, QC, and NL and medium in Ontario. A low level of engagement from actors outside the region was reported in all provinces, except NL where a medium engagement was rated.

The composition of actors engaged in governance activities was equally diverse. In all instances, interview participants identified actors beyond government – a key characteristic of governance arrangements. Participants in these collaborations varied by region (see Table 5.2.). In BC there was strong engagement between municipal governments and community-based organizations. In NL there were only moderate levels of engagement with

Table 5.1 Evidence of the presence of multi-level collaborative governance from interview data: positive experiences, mandates, and partners

Indicators	BC (n=22)	ON (n=33)	QC (n=19)	NL (n=28)
Positive experiences from collaboration	M	L	M	L
Mandate				
Environmental	M	L	L	L
Economic	L	L	L	L
Social and community	L	L	L	L
Collaboration partners				
In the community	M	M	L	M
In the region	H	M	H	H
Outside the region	L	L	L	M

L (Low) = 1% to 33% of the interviews indicated that the concept was present; M (Medium) = 34% to 67% of the interviews indicated the concept was present; H (High) = 68% to 100% of the interviews indicated the concept was present.

Table 5.2 Evidence of the presence of engagement of actors in multi-level collaborative governance from interview data

Indicators	BC (n=22)	ON (n=33)	QC (n=19)	NL (n=28)
Community/regional-based organizations	H	M	L	M
Municipal government	H	M	L	M
Indigenous involvement	L	L	L	L
Regional government	L	L	L	M
Provincial government	L	L	L	M
Federal government	L	L	L	L
Private sector	L	L	L	L

L (Low) = 1% to 33% of the interviews indicated that the concept was present; M (Medium) = 34% to 67% of the interviews indicated the concept was present; H (High) = 68% to 100% of the interviews indicated the concept was present.

these local-level participants – equal to the engagement with municipal governments at the regional and provincial levels. Engagement with Indigenous communities, federal government, and the private sector were low in all case study regions despite the importance of regional development funders and the presence of regional development agencies (see Chapter 6). Case Study 5.1 illustrates the diversity of actors engaged in the multi-level collaborative governance.

Case Study 5.1 Conseil des bassins versants du Nord Est du Bas Saint Laurent (Québec)

The *Conseil des bassins versants du Nord Est du Bas Saint Laurent*, from the *municipalité régionale de comté de Rimouski-Neigette* region, demonstrates the many of key components of multi-level collaborative governance. The *Conseil* has a mandate to implement integrated watershed management with the aim of providing long-term protection to regional water resources. It created a round table forum bringing together local landowners, fishers, farmers, environmental organizations, regional municipal governments, provincial government departments, and private businesses to discuss and implement water protection activities, programs, and policies. The *Conseil* oversees a watershed area of approximately 8,154 km^2.

The *Conseil* was established in 2009 when the Government of Québec re-distributed the responsibility for water protection to regional organizations. This multi-level collaborative governance initiative embodies the five key propositions presented by Stoker (1998). It is clear from the devolution of responsibilities from the government of Québec to the *Conseil* that there is a blurring of boundaries and no reliance on government to get things done. The *Conseil* also engages a wide variety of actors and demonstrates power interdependence among the actors.

Experiences similar to the *Conseil* were observed throughout the country. It should be stressed, however, that homogeneity was not observed among all experiences of multi-level collaborative governance. The experience of the *Conseil* is not representative of all multi-level collaborative governance initiatives described. In many instances, governance activities embodied a selection of Stoker's (1998) propositions, but not all of them. This often led to confusion or challenges, many of which will be discussed below.

Further information on *Conseil des bassins versants du Nord Est du Bas Saint Laurent* can be found at http://obv.nordestbsl.org.

Multi-level collaborative governance initiatives across the project regions focused on a number of different scales of policies (see Table 5.3). Interview participants in QC were notable in that they placed a relatively high level of emphasis on provincial policies. Along with NL they also placed a moderate level of emphasis on municipal levels of policy (see Case Study 5.2). NL and ON focused a moderate level of attention on provincial and federal government levels. The focus of multi-level collaborative governance initiatives in BC was spread across all levels but at relatively low levels for all.

Table 5.3 Evidence of the presence of a focus of multi-level collaborative governance influence from interview data

Indicators	BC (n=22)	ON (n=33)	QC (n=19)	NL (n=28)
Municipal policies	L	L	M	M
Regional policies	L	L	L	L
Indigenous policies	L	L	L	L
Provincial policies	L	M	H	M
Federal policies	L	M	L	M

L (Low) = 1% to 33% of the interviews indicated that the concept was present; M (Medium) = 34% to
67% of the interviews indicated the concept was present; H (High) = 68% to 100% of the interviews
indicated the concept was present.

3.2 The governance conundrum

Although there were illustrations of multi-level collaborative governance in
all regions, this does not mean they lack challenges. A high (H) level of
respondents from BC and QC mentioned such challenges and medium (M)
levels were expressed in ON and NL. These challenges ranged from the lack
of human and financial resources, to challenges with divesting power and
responsibilities from a level of government.

A critical challenge identified by participants in all regions was the "governance conundrum" – a recognition of the potential of collaborating,
matched with an inability or unwillingness to do so. Community leaders,
community-based organizations, and private sector representatives often
expressed a willingness to engage in multi-level collaborative governance
initiatives since they recognized the potential benefits that could be
achieved through collaborative approaches. At the same time, however,
many of them did not participate in any multi-level collaborative governance initiatives. The governance conundrum was expressed by eight communities, with at least one in each of the four case study regions
indicating that they have been unable to find ways to engage in multi-
level collaborative governance. We identified a number of reasons for the
lack of multi-level collaborative governance, ranging from the lack of
human capacity to participate, limited levels of trust, and a dearth of
common interests between regional actors. This apparent dissonance paral-
lels that found in certain aspects of the theme of integrated development
(Chapter 7). Comments from interview participants illustrating this governance conundrum include the following:

> The day-to-day issues and practices prevented officials from engaging in
> collaborative development plans.
>
> [Municipal government, ON]

Willingness to collaborate is there, just nothing has come up that people will collaborate on.

[Community-/regional-based organization, BC]

There is a lack of trust between communities, cities' negligence to rural areas, and the lack of willingness of surrounding communities prevent collaboration.

[Municipal government, QC]

We hardly ever collaborate. We never have and it is hard as hell to collaborate on even a local level with anybody. It is hard to get three villages together to do anything. It is nearly impossible to get the district together to do anything.

[Municipal government, BC]

… it is pretty hard to collaborate with limited finances to do a whole lot more than just the basics.

[Municipal government, ON]

3.3 Increased responsibilities without increased resources

The transition from government to governance involves the transferring of responsibilities, such as shared decision-making, from central governments to local and regional actors. This transferring process often causes a blurring of the boundaries between government and local actors, as noted earlier by Stoker (1998). The transferring of responsibilities is not always accompanied with a transfer of financial and/or human resources. Interview participants in all regions noted substantial challenges associated with the lack of necessary resources to facilitate multi-level collaborative governance and the associated responsibilities (see Case Study 5.3).

As shown in Table 5.4, governance activities included moderate (M) levels of change in decision-making, increased responsibilities, reorganization of local actors, and regional planning. However, there were only low (L) levels of increases in financial resources, power, or clarity mentioned. One of the key motivations for multi-level collaborative governance is the ability to deliver relevant and responsive services and programs in a cost-effective manner. One interview participant, for example, claimed that, "attitudes towards working together change if it involves cost savings" [Municipal government, ON]. The ability to work together with a variety of regional actors to ensure programming and policies are relevant to their communities is compromised if the multi-level collaborative governance initiative does not have the necessary funds to meet, plan, and implement activities. Interview participants noted that most local organizations do not have sufficient existing financial resources to pick up new activities and expenses. Many organizations are struggling to meet their current financial needs.

Table 5.4 Evidence of the presence of multi-level collaborative governance characteristics from interview data

Indicators	BC (n=22)	ON (n=33)	QC (n=19)	NL (n=28)
Collaborative decision-making processes	M	L	M	M
Increased finances	L	L	L	L
Increased local power	L	L	L	L
Increased responsibilities	L	L	L	M
Increased clarity of the responsibilities of different actors	L	L	L	L
Reorganization of local actors	L	L	M	L
Involved in regional planning	L	L	M	L

L (Low) = 1% to 33% of the interviews indicated that the concept was present; M (Medium) = 34% to 67% of the interviews indicated the concept was present; H (High) = 68% to 100% of the interviews indicated the concept was present.

Many local level actors in our survey expressed an expectation that provincial and federal governments would provide adequate funding to facilitate multi-level collaborative governance. This would include funding for both facilitation of discussions among governance actors and the implementation of recommendations and priorities. In QC, one interview participant noted a unique challenge. Their multi-level collaborative governance initiative receives core funding from the provincial government to ensure all actors can meet, communicate, and identify regional priorities. However, once regional priorities are identified, the multi-level collaborative governance initiative has no financial resources to implement their priorities. Their financial resources are allocated for operational expenses and cannot be utilized for programming or human resources to support the programming. This experience generated frustration among all the participants in the governance initiative, jeopardizing their long-term commitment to the multi-level collaborative governance initiative.

The lack of financial and/or human resources to facilitate multi-level collaborative governance is a critical challenge that impedes successful collaboration. It compromises the momentum and long-term potential of multi-level collaborative governance initiatives.

3.4 Overcoming institutional challenges

Multi-level collaborative governance often diverges from the current political and bureaucratic styles of government. The movement toward governance requires transformations in processes and programs for both senior government and local-level actors. These transformations to facilitate a multi-level collaborative governance arrangement often create requirements for new or revised institutional processes. All stakeholders need to recognize these requirements and be prepared to make the necessary investments while acknowledging potential opportunities and risks. Experiences from across the case study regions identified four key institutional challenges that hindered multi-level collaborative governance: past histories of amalgamation, volunteer burnout, an unclear understanding of governance within government, and unequal power dynamics between rural and urban communities.

At the local level, multi-level collaborative governance is hindered by animosity among key leaders and local organizations from previous amalgamations and local government re-organizations. Interview participants in both ON and NL indicated that the negative experiences with past amalgamations served to as a hindrance to meaningful multi-level collaborative governance in their region. Past experiences with amalgamation left an ill-will towards collaboration and governance, often expressed towards the provincial government and sometimes neighbouring communities. One municipal interview participant in ON expressed frustration that members of their region, for example, "still have hard feelings from the 1990s amalgamations", which is preventing effective multi-level collaborative governance from taking place.

Case Study 5.2 Northern Peninsula Regional Collaboration Pilot Initiative (Newfoundland and Labrador)

The 2009 Speech from the Throne announced a fundamental shift in how the government of Newfoundland and Labrador would work with communities regarding collaboration and governance. John Crosbie, then lieutenant governor of Newfoundland and Labrador, announced that "[through] a bold new Regional Collaboration Pilot Project, my Government will work with regional leaders to explore collaborative forms of governance that advance regional sustainability" (Government of Newfoundland and Labrador, 2009). From that announcement, the government of Newfoundland and Labrador created the Northern Peninsula Regional Collaboration Pilot Initiative (NPRCPI) to explore how to do collaboration and governance differently in the province.

The region

Regional collaboration and governance were not new to the communities of the Northern Peninsula when the Speech from the Throne was read. In fact, communities throughout the region have long participated in inter-community activities and worked in various ways with all levels of government, as shown through regional cooperatives, regional development agencies, regional waste management association, a regional tourism agency, and a joint municipal council (Vodden, Hall, & Freshwater, 2013). The NPRCPI represented a new opportunity to explore alternative ways for communities, non-profit organizations, and businesses to work with the provincial government while building on past regional collaborations.

The Northern Peninsula region, as discussed in Chapter 4 (see Map 4.6), represents a total of 51 communities, including 16 incorporated communities, 18 local service districts, and 17 unincorporated areas. The region has a total population of approximately 12,241, with general population declines being witnessed since 1981 (Government of Newfoundland and Labrador, 2012). The Northern Peninsula has often been marked as a region of marginality, high unemployment, underdeveloped economy, and high dependence on transfer payments (Simms & Ward, 2016; Sinclair & Felt, 1993).

The new governance arrangement

The three primary purposes of the newly created NPRCPI were: (i) to provide advice to government decision-makers; (ii) to create an inclusive forum in the region for discussions of challenges and opportunities, and (iii) to provide advice on how government can develop and support innovative regional collaboration. The membership of the initiative consisted of 12 individuals identified from three regional groups and five provincial government departments. The 12 regional members were identified from the Joint Mayors Council, the two regional economic development boards, and the St. Anthony – Port au Choix Regional Council of the Rural Secretariat. Each of these organizations identified three individuals to join the Northern Peninsula Regional Collaboration Pilot Initiative. The five government departments invited to participate were Innovation, Trade and Rural Development; Municipal Affairs; Rural Secretariat; Tourism, Culture, and Recreation; and Transportation and Government Works.[2] The Rural Secretariat was the lead government partner, providing facilitation and organizational and secretarial support to the initiative (Gibson, 2015).

The NPRCPI did not formally have any rules for their engagement. It operated without a formal leadership structure throughout its entire mandate. The work of the initiative was guided by the three primary purposes and a commitment to exploring enhanced ways of collaborating as a region. Throughout the course of the NPRCPI, decisions were made through consensus. The initiative members met face-to-face approximately three to four times per year. The calling of meetings, agenda setting, and chairing of the meetings was delivered by the Rural Secretariat staff. Each meeting, usually one to two days in duration, often focused on one specific regional theme, such as transportation or tourism.

Outputs and outcomes

Over the four years of the NPRCPI, the representatives crafted detailed advice to provincial departments on regional priorities and how to most effectively invest money into the region. In particular, the initiative spent considerable time working with two government departments to craft regionally specific advice for future funding and programming: Municipal Affairs and Government Transportation and Works. In both instances, the NPRCPI members were provided with access to substantial information on how these departments make decisions and what information is available to guide decision making. With this information in hand, the initiative was then challenged to think regionally for the Northern Peninsula. Recommendations emerging from the NPRCPI were not universally accepted when received by government. This proved to be a setback for members, often deflating their momentum to bring change in regional approaches to the Northern Peninsula. At the same time, the setback served as a catalyst for members to re-group and continue their work to advance regional thinking and decision-making.

Over the course of four years, the NPRCPI undertook a number of applied research initiatives. These initiatives focused on enhancing understandings of the fishery and forestry industries and social networking among actors in the Northern Peninsula region.

The members of the NPRCPI noted three key outcomes from their experiences. First, enhanced relationships among stakeholders in the Northern Peninsula and the provincial government emerged. The initiative allowed for new relationships and the enhancement of existing relationships. Second, it increased trust among key actors in the Northern Peninsula region and representatives of the provincial government. The ability to meet on a regular basis and engage in meaningful and difficult discussions in a respectful environment promoted the sense of trust among all participants. Finally, it improved understanding of the Northern Peninsula region among provincial governments participating in the NPRCPI (Gibson, 2015).

Reflections on the governance experience

The NPRCPI was initially created to concluded in March 2012. The government of Newfoundland and Labrador continued the initiative for approximately one additional year before it was discontinued. The NPRCPI was an experiment by the government of Newfoundland and Labrador. This experiment explored regional collaboration and governance in a manner unseen before in the province.

The NPRCPI meets many of the key characteristics of governance. It was an initiative with membership that extended beyond government. The initiative engaged municipal leaders, economic development stakeholders, and members of the St Anthony – Port au Choix Regional Council of the Rural Secretariat. The initiative also blurred the lines regarding responsibility for tackling regional issues and recognized that the capacity to get things done was not the mandate of the government. Where the NPRCPI deviated from Stoker's (1998) propositions is that it did not constitute an autonomous self-governing network. Without a leadership structure and clear mandate, the initiative was largely driven by government.

Although the NPRCPI is no longer active, it has provided a wealth of information on regional collaboration and regional governance. These insights hold substantial transferability to other jurisdictions, in both Canada and beyond.

A critical institutional challenge for many local actors is the ability to provide sufficient human resources to multi-level collaborative governance initiatives. The quintessential characteristics of rurality – primarily large distances between communities and low population densities (Reimer & Bollman, 2010) – compound these institutional challenges. For many local actors, participation in multi-level collaborative governance requires volunteers to attend meetings. Community-based organizations in each region of the country expressed concern about volunteer burnout and how it would impact potential engagement, or lack of engagement, with multi-level collaborative governance initiatives. The rural demographic trends of aging communities and out-migration created further concern among interview participants that volunteer burnout issues would not be resolved in the short term. The issue of volunteer burnout may prevent some organizations from participating in multi-level collaborative governance.

New multi-level collaborative governance initiatives often require new processes and new understanding by all actors involved. The ability for provincial and federal governments to recognize and accommodate these processes was highlighted as a challenge. Interview participants often noted that provincial and federal government employees working with multi-level collaborative governance initiatives understood the new design and the differences from previous government–community relationships. Unfortunately, other government employees often struggled to understand the differences and nuances of multi-level collaborative governance when compared to more traditional hierarchical governance structures. As a result, those involved in governance often discovered a challenge in working with the broader provincial and federal government outside of the actors involved in the governance initiative. A municipal government interviewee from NL noted, "the folks in the provincial capital simply do not understand what we are doing – they think our collaboration is no different than how the government worked with communities previously".

Finally, the relationships between rural and urban communities was emphasized as a challenge to multi-level collaborative governance. Often these communities have a long history of collaboration, including positive and negative experiences. In ON and QC interview participants noted concern that urban communities wielded more power than rural ones (see Chapter 8 for further discussion of rural–urban interactions). In some instances, this concern emerged from the governance design whereby urban communities had more votes in decision-making, such as in the Municipalités Régionales de Comté (MRCs). In other instances, urban communities were accused of using their power or finances to influence collective decisions. The design of multi-level collaborative governance initiatives can serve as a limitation for participation, especially for rural communities. In the process of transforming from government to governance, rural–urban dynamics need to be identified and addressed.

3.5 Active public engagement

Throughout the governance literature, a common concern is whether the general public is informed enough or inclined to be active in public policy. Given that multi-level collaborative governance initiatives operate in a fundamentally different manner than those of government, the public may assume that governance lacks legitimacy or authority.

Actors involved in multi-level collaborative governance initiatives from across the country echoed these academic concerns. Many interview participants noted that public participation is not common beyond the direct members of the multi-level collaborative governance initiative: "[there is] no strategic choice to involve the public in decision making" [Community-/regional-based organization, BC]. Other interview participants acknowledged that "participatory processes are not strong" [Community-/regional-based organization, ON] and "public participation [is] not common" [Municipal government, NL]. See Chapter 7 where public participation is discussed as being a minority practice in Eastern Ontario from the perspective of integrated development policy and planning.

The lack of public engagement is not universal among the case study regions. Interview participants in QC acknowledged their organization had a key role in restoring communication between the public and municipalities. In ON, an interview participant noted that a change in leadership had facilitated increased public engagement. What is clear is that there is no common approach to public engagement with multi-level collaborative governance.

Case Study 5.3 Yukon Regional Round Table

In 2006, a unique multi-level collaborative governance institution was created among Indigenous communities, incorporated and unincorporated communities, and various levels of government in the Yukon. Initially, eight rural communities and Indigenous peoples came together since there was no forum for multi-community collaboration discussions in the territory (Annis & Beattie, 2008; Gibson, Annis, & Dobson, 2007). Over the next two years, the Yukon Regional Round Table's (YRRT) membership grew to include 14 communities and First Nations, three territorial government departments, and four federal government departments. The mandate of the round table focuses on collaborative economic development, networking among communities, healthy and respectful relationships, and shared promotion of community events (Gibson, Annis, & Dobson, 2007).

The governance of the YRRT consists of two bodies: the round table and the advisory council. Each community and First Nation appointed two representatives to the round table. This body was responsible for setting collective directions, decision-making, and the implementation of activities. The round table members decided to make all decisions by consensus. As one mayor stated, "the binding agent of the group is good will – that is the only authority the group has" (Gibson, Annis, & Dobson, 2007, p. 9). The advisory council consists of representatives of territorial government departments, federal government departments, and territorial serving organizations. The advisory council serves as a bridge to share information to the round table, convey information from the round table to government departments, and support the round table. The relationship between the Yukon Regional Round Table and the Advisory Committee is illustrated in Figure 5.1.

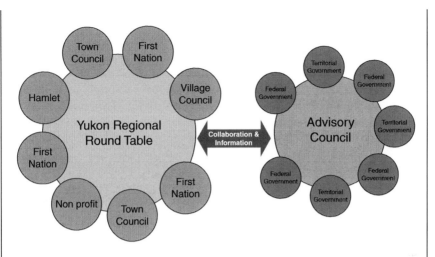

Figure 5.1 Governance model of the Yukon Regional Round Table

As a collaborative forum, the YRRT tackled a number of regional opportunities related to collaborative community economic development; accountability and credibility; healthy, respectful relations; networking; coordinated promotion; and social development initiatives. The round table implemented a series of regional initiatives focused on asset mapping, collaborative tourism-marketing partnerships, and network capacity development (Wirth, 2008).

The YRRT was a successful new governance model. It was not without its challenges, such as limited human resources (both human and financial) and maintaining interest of stakeholders over long periods of time. The group was quickly recognized by community and First Nation leaders as the only non-political forum of communities (both incorporated and unincorporated), First Nations, territorial government, and federal government representatives.

4 Reflections and future directions

Similar to new regionalism more broadly, the application of multi-level collaborative governance in the case study regions is generally nascent at best. The theoretical underpinnings of multi-level collaborative governance suggest this model is well suited to the new challenges and opportunities being encountered by rural regions. These models encourage a networked approach by engaging non-traditional actors in collective decision-making, knowledge sharing, resource sharing, and governing processes. The empirical evidence from across Canada suggests multi-level collaborative governance is taking place, in some instances with significant challenges, but not universally across the case studies.

The empirical findings from rural regions in Canada parallel many of the key themes identified in the broad literature on multi-level collaborative governance. The empirical findings demonstrate the "blurring of lines" among actors is present. Regional interviews identified that the transfer of responsibilities among actors in the multi-level collaborative governance initiatives can be hindered by institutional barriers. Further, interview participants highlighted concerns about increasing responsibilities through multi-level collaborative governance without a corresponding increase in either financial or human resources. This experience of heightened engagement with no shifts in power, responsibility, or resources is problematic. Stoker (1998) and Ansell and Gash (2007) clearly state a transfer of power is required for a process to be considered governance. Without this shift in power and/or responsibility, we are witnessing advanced mechanisms of engagement by government, not governance.

The evidence from our investigation also demonstrates there is still much to be understood. Three particular areas requiring further attention include the role of macro-level events, the implementation of the Truth and Reconciliation Commission recommendations, and the challenges associated with volunteer burnout. Our investigation primarily focused on regional actors, processes, and outputs. This analysis does not tackle the influence of macro-level events on regional initiatives. For example, how does the role of economic recessions such as the 2008 economic crisis or financial austerity from higher levels of government impact multi-level collaborative governance? How are rural areas influenced by Indigenous planning initiatives?

The implementation of the Truth and Reconciliation Commission recommendations will have substantial implications for multi-level collaborative governance in rural regions. From a purely spatial perspective, there is considerable overlap in Indigenous territories and rural regions in Canada. Interview participants alluded to new collaborations with Indigenous communities, businesses, and organizations as part of their governance arrangements. It is anticipated that multi-level collaborative governance initiatives will continue to increase the engagement of Indigenous actors, which to date has been limited in the case study regions.

The success of multi-level collaborative governance initiatives, as described in the literature, are attributed to many factors, including meaningful engagement of regional actors. For small organizations and businesses, the commitment of time and energy to actively participate in multi-level collaborative governance arrangements are significant. For voluntary and non-profit organizations, the investment of time and energy rests solely on volunteers. The ability for all regional actors to commit the necessary time is a challenge for successful multi-level collaborative governance. The risk of burnout among all actors is a pressing concern and one that requires further examination.

Some narratives of multi-level collaborative governance initiatives from the case studies embody Wallis' (2002) new regionalism characteristics of networks, openness, collaboration, empowerment, and trust. Although multi-level collaborative governance initiatives can take different forms and functions, such as the Yukon Regional Round Table or the Northern Peninsula Regional Collaboration Pilot Initiative, they are an important phenomenon being experienced by communities, voluntary and nonprofit organizations, private sector, and all levels of government. Multi-level collaborative governance is also critical to advancing the principles and practices of new regionalism.

Notes

1 This section is an excerpt from the project's Collaborative Multi-Level Governance primer, found on the project's website: http://cdnregdev.ruralresilience.ca
2 The names of many government departments have changed since the Northern Peninsula Regional Collaboration Pilot Initiative began in 2009.

References

Abrams, P., Borrini-Feyerabend, G., Gardner, J., & Heylings, P. (2003). *Evaluating Governance: A Handbook To Accompany A Participatory Process For A Protected Area*. Ottawa: Parks Canada and TILCEPA.

Adshead, M. (2002). *Developing European Regions: Comparative Governance, Policy Networks, and European Integration*. Burlington: Ashgate.

Annis, R. C., & Beattie, M. (2008). *The Community Collaboration Story*. Brandon: Rural Development Institute, Brandon University.

Ansell, C. (2000). The networked polity: Regional development in Western Europe. *Governance, 13*(3), 303–333.

Ansell, C., & Gash, A. (2007). Collaborative governance in theory and practice. *Journal of Public Administration Research and Theory, 18*(4), 543–571.

Bache, I. (2000). Government within governance: Network steering in Yorkshire and the Humber. *Public Administration, 78*(3), 575–592.

Bache, I., & Flinders, M. (2005). *Multi-Level Governance*. Toronto: Oxford University Press.

Benz, A., & Eberlein, B. (1999). The Europeanization of regional policies: Patterns of multi-level governance. *Journal of European Public Policy, 6*(2), 329–348.

Bevir, M. (2009). *Key Concepts in Governance*. London: Sage.

Bevir, M. (2011). Governance as theory, practice, and dilemma. In M. Bevir (Ed.), *The SAGE Handbook of Governance* (pp. 1–16). Thousand Oaks, CA: Sage.

Bevir, M., & Rhodes, R. (2011). The stateless state. In M. Bevir (Ed.), *The SAGE Handbook of Governance* (pp. 203–217). Thousand Oaks, CA: Sage.

Bogason, P., & Toonen, T. (1998). Networks in public administration. *Public Administration, 76*(2), 204–227.

Coase, R. H. (1937). The nature of the firm. *Economica, 4*(16), 386–405. Doi:10.1111/j.1468-0335.1937.tb00002.x.

Conzelmann, T. (1998). "Europeanisation" of regional development policies? Linking the multi-level collaborative governance approach with theories of policy learning and policy change. *European Integration Online Papers, 2*(4), 1–23.

Eberlein, B., & Kerwer, D. (2004). New governance in the European Union: A theoretical perspective. *Journal of Common Market Studies, 42*(1), 121–142.

Gibson, R. (2015). *Collaborative Governance In Rural Regions: An Examination of Ireland and Newfoundland and Labrador* (PhD Dissertation). Memorial University of Newfoundland.

Gibson, R., Annis, R. C., & Dobson, J. (2007). *Collaborative Evaluation Of The Yukon Regional Round Table and the Yukon Advisory Group*. Brandon: Rural Development Institute, Brandon University.

Government of Newfoundland and Labrador. (2009). *Speech from the throne 2009: Delivered at the opening of the second session of the forty-sixth general assembly of the province of Newfoundland and Labrador*. Retrieved January 19, 2012, from www.exec.gov.nl.ca/thronespeech/2009/speech2009.htm.

Government of Newfoundland and Labrador. (2012). *Annual Activity Report 2011–12: St. Anthony – Port au Choix Regional Council of the Rural Secretariat Executive Council*. St John's: Government of Newfoundland and Labrador.

Hay, C., Lister, M., & Marsh, D. (Eds.). (2006). *The State: Theory and Issues*. Houndmills: Palgrave Macmillan.

Hooghe, L., & Marks, G. (2002). Types of multi-level governance. *Cahiers Européens de Sciences Po, 3*, 1–30.

Jessop, B. (1995). The regulation approach and governance theory: Alternative perspectives on economic and political change. *Economy and Society, 24*(3), 307–333.

Keohane, R., & Nye, J. (2002). Governance in a globalizing world. In R. Keohane (Ed.), *Power and Governance in A Partially Globalized World* (pp. 1–41). London: Routledge.

Kooiman, J. (Ed.). (1993). *Modern Governance: New Government-Society Interactions*. London: Sage.

Kooiman, J., Bavinck, M., Chuenpagdee, R., & Mahon, R. (2008). Interactive governance and governability: An introduction. *The Journal of Transdisciplinary Environmental Studies, 7*(1), 1–11.

Leftwich, A. (1994). Governance, the state and the politics of development. *Development and Change, 25*(2), 363–386.

Lowndes, V., & Skelcher, C. (1998). The dynamics of multi-organizational partnerships: An analysis of changing modes of governance. *Public Administration, 76*(2), 313–333.

Luhmann, N. (1982). *The Differentiation Of Society*. New York, NY: Columbia University Press.

Magnette, P. (2003). European governance and civic participation: Beyond elitist citizenship? *Political Studies, 51*(3), 144–160.

Marks, G., Hooghe, L., & Blank, K. (1996). European integration from the 1980s: State-centric v. multi-level governance. *Journal of Common Market Studies, 34*(3), 341–378.

Morgan, K. (2007). The polycentric state: New spaces of empowerment and engagement? *Regional Studies, 41*(9), 1237–1251.

Newman, J., Barnes, M., Sullivan, H., & Knops, A. (2004). Public participation and collaborative governance. *Journal of Social Policy, 33*(2), 203–223.

Osborne, D., & Gaebler, T. (1992). *Reinventing Government*. New York, NY: Penguin Press.

Provan, K., & Kenis, P. (2007). Modes of network governance: Structure, management, and effectiveness. *Journal of Public Administration Research and Theory, 18*(2), 229–252.

Reimer, B. (2004). Foreword. In R. Annis, F. Racher, & M. Beattie (Eds.), *Rural Communtiy Health And Well-Being: A Guide To Action* (p. 1). Brandon: Rural Development Institute, Brandon University.

Reimer, B., & Bollman, R. (2010). Understanding rural Canada: Implications for rural development policy and rural development planning. In D. Douglas (Ed.), *Rural Planning And Development in Canada* (pp. 10–52). Toronto: Nelson Education.

Rhodes, R. (1996). The new governance: Governing without government. *Political Studies, 44*(4), 652–667.

Rhodes, R. (1997). *Understanding Governance: Policy Networks, Governance, Reflexivity And Accountability.* Buckingham: Open University Press.

Rosenau, J. (1992). Citizenship in a changing global order. In J. Rosenau & E.-O. Czempiel (Eds.), *Governance Without Government: Order And Change In World Politics* (pp. 272–295). Cambridge: Cambridge University Press.

Rosenau, J. (1997). *Along The Domestic-Foreign Frontier: Exploring Governance In A Turbulent World.* Cambridge: Cambridge University Press.

Salamon, L. M. (2002). *The Tools Of Government: A Guide To The New Governance.* Toronto: Oxford University Press.

Simms, A., & Ward, J. (2016). *Regional Population Projections for Labrador and the Northern Peninsula, 2016–2036.* St John's: Harris Centre of Regional Policy and Development, Memorial University.

Sinclair, P., & Felt, L. (1993). Coming back: Return migration to Newfoundland's Great Northern Peninsula. *Newfoundland Studies, 9*(1), 1–25.

Stoker, G. (1998). Governance as theory: Five propositions. *International Social Science Journal, 50*(155), 17–28.

Truth and Reconciliation Commission of Canada. (2015). *Honouring the truth, reconciling for the future: Summary of the final report of the truth and reconciliation commission of Canada.* Retrieved June 5, 2018, from www.trc.ca/websites/trcinstitution/index.php?p=890.

Van Buuren, A., & Edelenbos, J. (2007). Collaborative governance. In M. Bevir (Ed.), *Encyclopedia of Governance* (pp. 105–107). Thousand Oaks, CA: Sage.

Vodden, K., Hall, H., & Freshwater, D. (2013). *Understanding Regional Governance In Newfoundland And Labrador: A Survey Of Regional Development Organizations.* St John's: Harris Centre for Regional Policy and Development, Memorial University.

Vodden, K., Ommer, R., & Schneider, D. (2006). A comparative analysis of three models of collaborative learning in fisheries governance: Hierarchy, networks, and community. In T. Gray (Ed.), *Participation in Fisheries Governance* (pp. 291–306). Dordrecht: Springer.

Wallis, A. (2002). *The new regionalism: Inventing governance structures for the early twenty-first century.* Retrieved August 23, 2011, from www.miregions.org/Strengthening%20the%20Role/The%20New%20Regionalism%20Paper%20by%20Wallis%20at%20CUD.pdf.

Weber, M. (1947). *The Theory Of Social And Economic Organization.* New York: The Free Press.

Weiss, T. (2000). Governance, good governance and global governance: Conceptual and actual challenges. *Third World Quarterly, 21*(5), 795–814.

Wirth, W. (2008). Yukon Regional Round Table: Community leaders sharing ideas and creating change. Presented at Rural Matters! Forging Healthy Canadian Communities, Edmonton, Alberta.

Woods, M., & Goodwin, M. (2003). Applying the rural: Governance and policy in rural areas. In P. Cloke (Ed.), *Country Visions* (pp. 245–262). London: Pearson.

Yukon Regional Round Table. (2008). Yukon Regional Round Table June 2008 newsletter. Whitehorse: Yukon Regional Round Table.

6 Identity and commitment to place

How regions "become" in rural Canada

Sean Markey, Sarah-Patricia Breen, Kelly Vodden, and Jen Daniels

1 Introduction

Canada has long been described as a country of regions. This is not unexpected, given the scale of the Canadian geopolitical space and a historical reliance on a staples-based economy shaped by core–periphery dynamics in different parts of the country. As a result, Canada has been divided into myriad regions using factors such as climate, physical features, politics, and economic activities.

While regional development disparities in Canada were recognized in the early 1900s, prior to the 1950s Canada lacked an articulated public policy and any formal program for addressing the structural problems associated with uneven regional development (Beaumier, 1998; Fairbairn, 1998; Polèse, 1999). It was only during the immediate post-WWII period that the federal government began to adopt explicit regional development policies (Weaver & Gunton, 1982; Savoie, 1992, 2003; Beaumier, 1998).

As in other industrialized parts of the world, Canadian regional development evolved using an underlying if implicit theoretical framework with a goal to facilitate economic growth within spatially defined areas. Space here is understood using simple Cartesian logic—connecting various locations to somewhere else on an "isotropic plane". As described in standard business and economic geography texts, locational and investment decision-making are based on balancing three location-focused points:

1. the location of the raw material inputs to the production process;
2. the location of the target market; and
3. the location of the production facility.

This balance requires consideration of the costs of moving raw materials versus finished products (usually based on the bulk transport costs of each) against other key inputs such as the cost and skills of the labour force, regulation or taxation costs, power and energy costs and availability, and the market value of the product.

The Canadian economy relies heavily on natural resources—both directly and indirectly. Governments have chosen policies that treat these resources as commodities in relatively unprocessed forms. This means the creation of an economic and social infrastructure that is fundamentally organized to move raw natural resources across great distances, through trade, to more advanced industrial economies where they are refined, processed, and sold in transformed states. The returns on these commodities serve as a basis for importing consumer items, machinery, and electronics and a great variety of personal and commercial services (Reimer, 2014).

The regional investment process during the post-WWII period was driven by the need to reconcile local staple assets with distance and topography, in addition to geopolitical boundaries such as tariff and non-tariff barriers. The result was the creation of resource-dependent regional economies, connected via roads, rail lines, and port facilities that supported the movement of extracted resources from rural to urban spaces. In western and northern Canada, governments established policies for the development of resource frontiers to overcome the costs of space in order to access remote resource sites, facilitate harvesting and production, and transport resources to markets for the benefit of the local, regional, and provincial economies. This approach is exemplified by the "roads to resources" policies initiated at the national level under Prime Minister Diefenbaker, in power from 1957 to 1963, or provincial counterparts, such as the province-building era under BC Premier WAC Bennett, in power from 1952 to 1972. It was via those roads developed under the policies of Diefenbaker and his contemporaries that the vast resource reserve of distant rural spaces was accessed for provincial and national benefit (Mitchell, 1983).

However, in a globalized economy where geographic space (i.e., raw distance, measured in terms of time or financial transfer costs) is declining in importance and the capacity of federal and provincial governments is eroding, we find that the simplistic spatial model that has guided Canadian regional development policy for 60 years is fragmenting. Researchers have articulated this transition in development theory, policy, and practice as the shift from space-based to place-based development (Portugali, 2006; Markey et al., 2012). Decisions around the location (and retention) of labour and capital are now driven by a much more complex set of variables. The characteristics of places in terms of regulations, connectivity to the world economy, available labour supply, supportive industries and skills, quality-of-life services and amenities, natural environment, safety, political stability, and a host of other inputs to the production and decision-making systems mean that a composite of factors differentiating places now guide the investment decisions of capital, as against the previously simple balance of costs of labour, resources, and transportation. In other words, as space is becoming less important in the global economy, place is becoming more important (Douglas, 2005).

This raises the question of whether place is emerging in practice as a critical dimension in the development of Canadian rural regions. Recently, Jones and Paasi (2013) set as an assignment for regional researchers: the task to better understand how regions "become". There is symmetry to the timing of this question in Canada. We have a decent understanding of how regional development, using a space-based approach, was constructed in the 30-year period between the 1950s and the early 1980s: a period known as the "long boom" of staples-dependent expansion (Hayter, 2000) or as the "Intervention Period" in Chapter 2. Following the recession of the early 1980s, we have also garnered a reasonable consensus regarding the restructuring principles and processes, driven by a neoliberal agenda, that have been dismantling much of that hard and soft regional development infrastructure for the past 30 years (Beaumier, 1996, 1998; Polèse, 1999; Savoie, 2003). This now leaves us with the question of what next? Will rural regions in Canada continue to fray under the pressures of political and economic restructuring, or will they re-group, drawing upon new (or revisited) principles and processes to identify opportunities and new ways of being? This is the essence and uncertainty surrounding the incoherent negotiation period articulated in Chapter 2 (see Chapter 2, Figure 2.1).

Regional development has been making a comeback, even though many countries throughout the industrialized world have been steadily dismantling (in policy and investment) the development infrastructure associated with the first wave of post-war regionalism. New regionalism has emerged as a prominent, if highly contested approach—including the reconceptualization of the spatial entity of the region—for addressing the complexity of territorial development and mitigating the negative impacts associated with both political and industrial restructuring (Barnes & Gertler, 1999; Storper, 1999; Scott, 2000, 2004). As senior governments and large industries have withdrawn from direct development responsibility, regions promise both enough scale and capacity to construct and invest in new trajectories of development. New regionalism thus occupies an intermediate position, within a dynamic tension between the abandonment of traditional patterns of top-down stewardship and the appeal of local control and place-sensitive intervention.

Within the concept of place and place-based development is the interpretation of *identity* as a mobilizing and organizing force for regionalism. As Bristow (2010) states, place is a "holistic concept that bridges the analysis of people, institutions, and economies with the context-specific natural resources on which they ultimately depend" (p. 155). New regionalism demands a more active regional participation and engagement in the development process, which may include individual or co-construction action with any level or type of government. New regionalism, in incorporating governance as one of its dimensions, allows for government if and when required (Amin, 1999; Hettne et al., 2000; Heisler, 2012). Thus, in answering Jones and Paasi's (2013) question of how regions become, it seems a critical answer involves the recognition and mobilization of regionalism by regional actors. Regardless of the theoretical transition from space to place, in practice these regional actors, particularly in the face of declining senior government or industrial stewardship of regions, must essentially choose to be a region—and to act accordingly in their planning and development decisions and activities.

2 Understanding place

Place-based development is an holistic and targeted intervention that reveals, utilizes, and enhances the unique natural, physical, and/or human capacity endowments of a particular location for the development of the in-situ community and/or its biophysical environment. Place, within the context of rural development, is reflected in Massey's (1984) work, which recognizes that combinations of assets, populations, histories, and circumstances mean that general processes are always modified by the conditions of place. This contextual turn is found in a variety of ongoing rural research themes, including post-productivism; conceptualizations of the role of competitiveness, as opposed to comparativeness; and the adoption of a territorial, rather than sector-based, orientation to rural policy development (Massey, 1984, 1995; Barnes et al., 2000, Kitson et al., 2004).

Post-productivism refers to the transformation, in values and economic activity, associated with a de-emphasis on primary resource production and extraction in favour of more diversified economic activities (Reed & Gill, 1997). Places function differently now than they did a decade or more ago. Mather et al. (2006) indicate that in rural debates, the tendency is to present post-productivism in terms of dimensions, rather than specific definitions. These dimensions include the nature and type of production (from commodity to non-commodity outputs), the multidimensionality of objectives associated with landscape and resources (including environmental, amenity, and ecosystem service values), and the importance of governance and representation (involving a greater diversity of actors and institutions) in land-use and other decision-making. In each of these dimensions, place is considered to be a more dynamic factor in processes of social and economic development. Niche products that are more dependent on location and local capacity compete for attention with generic and "placeless" commodity products (Filion, 1998; Dawe, 2004). Natural resources in general are viewed as one set of many, as opposed to the only local assets that may be used as vehicles for economic diversification, for valuation, and for representation. Place becomes operational and drives agency in the development process, rather than being a passive platform upon which development takes place (Douglas, 2005).

In the following vignette, Case Study 6.1, we see how the village of Cap-à-l'Aigle, in Québec, re-imagined and combined their place-based assets to create new development pathways for the community and region. The story serves as a powerful illustration of place-based development in the new rural economy, serving to animate many of the ideas and practices outlined in this chapter.

Case Study 6.1 Place-based vignette—Cap-à-l'Aigle (provided by Bill Reimer)

The citizens of Cap-à-l'Aigle, Québec turned to their place-based assets when looking for community development options. The conjuncture of geoclimatic conditions, a vibrant horticultural legacy, tourism enterprises, proximity to aquatic life, personal connections, and regional collaboration allowed them to develop their settlement of less than 1,000 people into a village with international recognition.

Cap-à-l'Aigle is a small village in the Charlevoix region of Québec, about 150 km east of Québec City. It lies in a microclimatic region that is very favorable to heavy snowfalls, horticulture, and especially lilacs. When the municipal leaders were looking for development opportunities in the early 1990s, they turned to local assets that had emerged over the years. One was the many lilacs that had been planted by their citizens and the associated network of enthusiasts who had expanded their knowledge, experience, and information as they pursued this interest. As a result of these activities, the village became well known for the burst of colour and fragrance that emerged each spring, branding itself as the "Village des Lilas" (Village of Lilacs).

Over the years, the local lilac enthusiasts had established international networks through conferences, meetings, festivals, and associations such as The International Lilac Society. These networks not only attracted a wide variety of people to the region but in 1997, led to the donation of hundreds of lilac varieties from a German ornithologist. Thanks to the efforts of a local journalist (Denis Gautier) and the mayor (Bruno Simard) this donation provided the basis for the Jardins Cap-à-l'Aigle (Gardens of Cap-à-l'Aigle)—with one of the largest varieties of lilacs in the world (www.tourisme-charlevoix .com/en/attractions/les-jardins-du-cap-a-laigle/).

It was also a village that had developed an extensive network of tourist accommodations—primarily based on small bed-and-breakfast establishments and chalets that were well known by both Québecers and American visitors. By integrating this network with that of the lilac enthusiasts, encouraging the development of a world-class food culture, building a local marina (Port de refuge), and expanding collaboration with nearby villages, Cap-à-l'Aigle has been able to attract whale-watchers, boating enthusiasts, food connoisseurs, hikers, golfers, cyclists, and even skiers who visit the Charlevoix region.

These initiatives, in turn, encouraged additional contributions—such as Les Jardins de Quatre-Vents (Gardens of the Four Winds). This 15-hectare garden near the village was maintained for over 50 years by New York philanthropist and village descendent, Francis H. Cabot. It is now world-renowned as one of the "best private gardens of our times" (http://cepas.qc.ca/jardins-de-quatre-vents/).

The Cap-à-l'Aigle story is very much about place-based assets: geo-climatic, physical, and social. By combining these assets in new ways and marketing them provincially, nationally, and internationally, they have been able to develop an economic and social base that promises sustainability over the long term. Their willingness to collaborate with other centres in the region has not only opened up additional local opportunities but added their own attractions to those of others— making the Malbaie region a destination for international guests who would otherwise not have taken notice of the area (www.tourisme-charlevoix.com/en/sectors/la-malbaie/).

Conceptualizations of competitiveness within the "new" economy are also significant to place-based development. This includes the resource orientation of post-productivism, but extends beyond it. Turok (2004) identifies how the concept of competitiveness remains a poorly understood and deployed term. However, despite this, debates around economic restructuring and the transition from Fordism to post-Fordist production have paid considerable attention to the shift away from the importance of comparative advantage in favour of considerations of competitive advantage (Kitson et al., 2004). Comparative advantage is determined more narrowly by the fixed existence and quality of resources (Gunton, 2003). By comparison, competitive advantage is more complex. It is dependent not only on the inherent assets of a particular place to attract and retain capital and workers that have become much more mobile, but *the actions* needed to capitalize on those assets, much as we see in the Cap-à-l'Aigle story (Kitson et al., 2004). As a result, competitive advantage requires places and policy-makers to consider a wider variety of both quantitative (e.g., physical infrastructure, production, location) and qualitative (e.g., social capital, innovation, institutions) variables in economic development planning (MacLeod, 2001).

2.1 Identity and commitment to place

Important to our understanding of rural place-based development is the sense of identity that may bond people to a particular location. Place-based development draws upon residents' sense of place and place identity, which is fundamentally rooted in people's individual and collective commitment to the places they inhabit. Discussion of identity emerged within the place literature parallel to the tensions between capital and the lived experiences brought about via the ideological triumph of neoliberalism (e.g. Hough,

1990; Massey, 1994; Harvey, 1996; Paasi, 2004). The question of *regional identity* has continued to be a significant part of this discussion.

With a long history of debate surrounding the definition and delineation of "regions" the question of regional identity is particularly contentious, as is the complexity of mobilizing regional identity for the purpose of regional and place-based development strategies (Douglas, 2005; Paasi, 2013). One reason for this challenge is the implied assumption that regional identity is a pre-existing phenomenon within a given area, which can be analyzed using specific research materials and instruments, such as survey data or material artifacts that somehow capture or represent the region (Paasi, 2003). Second, Paasi (2013) identifies the ambiguous and fuzzy boundaries of regional identity and notes that it is a social construct "produced and reproduced in discourse", (p. 1208) that is both plural and contextual. Third, a related assumption leveled at queries of regional identity, and regionalism as a whole, is that territorial and relational conceptions of place are in conflict—such that the existence of an increasingly interconnected (relational) world has eroded grounded notions of place (territory)—or, seriously undermined the efficacy of territorial approaches in understanding the region. However, a critical, empirically driven, approach to questions of regional identity reveals not only a materially "rooted" global phenomena, but regional politics that are simultaneously relational and territorial (Massey, 2004; Escobar, 2008; Jonas, 2012).

With due diligence, we need to ask what people mean when they speak of place identity, because our understanding of what identity means in each case should be "a result of conceptualization and an actual research process, rather than a point of departure" (Paasi, 2003, p. 481). In other words, regions are not discrete, preordained units into which the earth is divided; rather, they are messy, overlapping, and defined by factors that are geographically, culturally, politically, institutionally, and historically contingent as well as socially relevant. Thus, in development research and practice, we must explore the connections of people to their environs, their life in various spaces, and their daily practices. From here is it possible to consider how the notion of identity is germinated and actualized, the spatial extent at which it operates, and, in turn, if and how region and identity are mobilized in place-based development.

Sense of identity and commitment to place are critical features for mobilizing sites of resistance (to, for example, negatively perceived development proposals or policy) or enabling collaborative responses that may activate the positive, proactive dimensions of regional development. Paasi (2003) suggests it is often difficult to determine how regional identity is made, as well as how it affects collective action and politics. He suggests such identity is enacted through two intertwined processes, from above and from below (Paasi, 2003). From above, regional identity is more about territorial control by government, whereas from below, it is a form of identification with a territory and is associated with resistance (Paasi, 2003). In linking sense of place with identity, we are searching for a catalytic response whereby identity and sense of place are transformed into commitment to regionalism—and regional action. We appreciate Paasi's (2003) suggestion that our efforts would be better spent not trying to assign an explanatory role to the concept of regional identity, but rather by explaining how regions emerge and change.

3 Searching for place

Establishing indicators as a guide for the analysis of our research data related to place and place-based development, along with other themes, served a number of purposes. First, this forced us to clearly define what we meant by place, and how we were going to investigate it in our case regions. Second, the indicators served to enhance the consistency of our inquiry across our case study regions, an important concern given that the work was being done by different people at different times. And, finally, they helped to guide our analysis. We designed the indicator table (Table 6.1) based upon our literature review work on place-based development, using a team meeting to workshop and select the final indicator list.

As noted in Chapter 4, the initial operational step was to examine the data related to each of the place-focused concepts within the field data from our case study regions (see Table 6.1 or http://cdnregdev.ruralresilience.ca for more detailed frequency analysis). This served as an indication of attention to place-based approaches to regional development within the regions and helped to guide our investigations toward the larger narrative around the emergence and expression of identity presented below. Table 6.1 represents the attention given to place-based issues by our respondents. By examining the relative frequency of interviews in which these issues are mentioned, we see that social topics are most often addressed in this category (see the number of H, or high, frequencies).

For example, the issue of *identity* is most consistently mentioned across our field sites, with *social infrastructure* and *community cohesion* being relatively high as well. Economic issues are more mixed, with *access to capital* being most important across field site interviews while issues such as *economic diversity, transportation infrastructure, economic infrastructure*, and *built infrastructure* all show high levels in some places, but lower levels in others. A similar pattern of diversity by field sites is found with the environmental indicators, although BC stands out as a region where most environmental indicators are relatively higher than the others.

These indicators are exploratory. We have used them to identify significant themes or outliers, to identify differences (and similarities) among cases, and to focus our more in-depth coding and analysis of interview transcripts. As shown in Table 6.1, the issue of *identity* stands out as the most consistently and frequently mentioned topic in our interviews, whereas other topics show mixed assessments about the extent to which development approaches are supporting these important aspects of healthy communities and regions. Following this lead, our focus in this chapter is on identity—an overarching theme across interview participant responses and a foundation of place-based development.

Table 6.1 Evidence of the presence of place-based considerations and approaches from interview data

Indicator	BC (n=22)	ON (n=33)	QC (n=19)	NL (n=28)
Economic				
Place Branding	M	M	M	M
Economic Diversity	H	L	M	M
Informal Economy	M	N	N	L
Transportation Infrastructure	M	M	M	H
Economic Infrastructure	H	M	M	M
Built Infrastructure	H	L	L	M
Transient Workforce	L	L	L	H
Local Entrepreneurs	M	L	L	L
Access to Capital	H	M	H	H
Health of Local Business Sector	M	L	M	M
Presence of Buy-local Campaign	M	M	L	L
Environment				
Community-based Management	M	M	M	M
Sustainability Initiatives	M	M	M	L
Integrated Planning	H	L	L	L
Territorial/Land Use Planning	M	L	L	L
Ecosystem Management Plan	H	L	L	L
Environmental Infrastructure	M	L	L	M
Social				
Inclusion in Planning Process	H	M	H	M
Community Associations	H	M	L	M
Identity	H	H	H	H
Social Infrastructure	H	H	M	H
Level of Transience	M	L	L	M
Equity with Community	M	L	L	M
Community Cohesion	H	M	H	H

N = no mention of the concept was made in the interviews being considered; L (Low) = 1% to 33% of
the interviews indicated that the concept was present; M (Medium) = 34% to 67% of the interviews
indicated the concept was present; H (High) = 68% to 100% of the interviews indicated the concept was
present.

Our particular investigation of place uses a three-part interconnected
framework intended to better understand how regions become established:

1. Identify regional affiliation and sense of place;
2. Inquire about levels of regional participation and engagement with regional
    planning; and

3. Seek examples where regional actors have mobilized to exert influence and construct regionalist structures and initiatives (see Figure 6.1).

We acknowledge the inherent complexity of community and regional development processes and are using this framework as an heuristic device to inform our inquiry of regional emergence.

4 Place emergence in rural Canada

Four themes emerged in our analysis of the case study regions. These include: 1) the significance of regional identity, 2) the structure of regional governance, 3) community versus regional initiatives, and 4) regionalism as regionalization. In terms of links to our conceptual framework, the first theme relates primarily to issues of identity and regional identity formation; the next three themes relate to the participation and mobilization of regional development activities. For each theme, we refer to general case findings and highlight a particular example within each case region. It is within these themes that we will gauge the state of place emergence as part of regionalism across our case locations in rural Canada.

4.1 Regional identity

Questions related to regional identity are at the core of our place-based inquiry. As noted above, the conceptual framework suggests that a sense of regional identity is important for both activating efforts of resistance against the negative forces of restructuring and enabling the emergence of collaborative structures and initiatives to facilitate regional interaction. Our findings suggest that regional identity expressed in our case study interviews is weak. There are a number of possible reasons for this outcome.

First, despite being distinctive features on the Canadian map, in reality the case study regions each exist as multiple, overlapping boundaries of functional

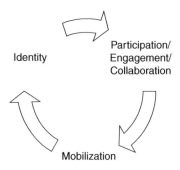

Figure 6.1 Conceptual framework

and political regionalism. Within and across the case study regions, regional governments, education regions, health regions, geographical regions, and environmental regions do not align along the same boundaries. This multitude of regionalisms may have impacted how, based upon their regional affiliation, interview participants identified with their area. For example, interview participants from Kittiwake, Newfoundland, provided a range of different answers when asked to define the region in which they live. Regional definitions are further complicated by the repetitive re-drawing of administrative regional boundaries by senior governments to serve different departmental functions.

Second, people remain strongly attached to their sub-regional community identities (as reflected by our interview participants). Community in this case is not strictly delineated by official local government boundaries, but includes sub-regional areas of incorporated or unincorporated communities, or multiple communities and their surrounding areas. This is not necessarily a negative influence on regional identity, since organized communities are a necessary ingredient for effective regional collaboration (Markey et al., 2012); however, it may become an obstacle to regional identity development and action by the absence of regional institutional structures, as we will discuss below. Our community interview participants spoke of their capacity to unite against external threats, but remained largely internally divided otherwise.

The Columbia Basin Rural Development Institute (RDI) is an example of rural regional innovation (see Case Study 6.2). It plays an important role in supporting the multiple identities within the Kootenays, while developing an overarching regional identity. By conducting applied regional research and producing regional-scale information, the RDI presents valuable information to citizens and decision-makers. This focus on the regional scale, linking together several subregions, helps to build a sense of an overarching regional identity, as well as facilitating evidence-based decision making and policy development. The work also plays an important role in helping to shape regional narratives about the Kootenays, thereby reinforcing a place-identity and sense of place in the region.

Case Study 6.2 Columbia Basin Rural Development Institute

The Columbia Basin Rural Development Institute (RDI) was formed in 2010 through an eight-year funding partnership between the Columbia Basin Trust and Selkirk College (CBRDI, 2018). The RDI evolved from two key initiatives: the Columbia Basin Trust's *State of the Basin* and Selkirk College's *Regional Innovation Chair*. The *State of the Basin*, launched in 2008, was a regional indicator report (Columbia Basin Trust, 2008). The Regional Innovation Chair is an endowed research position established in 2006 that focuses on rural economic development

(Selkirk College, n.d.). The RDI brought these two initiatives together and built on this foundation. Today, the RDI's signature programs include the *State of the Basin*, the work of the *Regional Innovation Chair*, and the *Kootenay Workforce Development Initiative*, as well as a number of applied research projects (CBRDI, 2018).

As this original partnership ends, the RDI is now supported by a variety of funding sources (CBRDI, 2018). The purpose of the RDI is to promote and support informed decision-making and build capacity within the Columbia Basin-Boundary region (CBRDI, 2018). This includes monitoring economic, social, cultural, and environmental indicators and reporting on trends, responding to support requests, and conducting applied research on a variety of topics impacting the region (CBRDI, 2018). The region includes the Kootenay Development Region (i.e., the Regional Districts of East Kootenay, Central Kootenay, Kootenay Boundary), as well as Revelstoke, Golden, Valemount, and Columbia Shuswap Regional District Areas A and B (Columbia Basin Rural Development Institute, 2012).

RDI's knowledge mobilization focuses on producing accessible, plain language documents including summaries of literature (knowledge briefs) and research (research briefs), as well as community profiles. Short "E-Focus" newsletters draw attention to news, activities, and successes within the region. Additionally, the RDI facilitates and supports collaborative partnerships within the region involving local governments, community organizations and networks, business and industry, and other post-secondary institutions.

The RDI illustrates a potential role for academic institutions within regions as close partners serving to benefit the region.

Visit the RDI website for further information and resources: www.cbrdi.ca/.

Finally, following community identity, interview participants spoke about identifying with "rural" as opposed to regional entities. In Newfoundland, for example, very strong patterns of community emerged, but were followed by provincial (e.g., Newfoundlander) and rural Newfoundlander identification before any sense of regional affiliation. The "rural" identification poses an interesting challenge and opportunity for regional development policy-makers. On one hand, it may encourage the continued focus of senior government on policy that is too blunt and contextually naïve to be effective. On the other, it offers an opportunity to construct a more coherent and cohesive rural framework for policy to support wide-scale regional development.

4.2 Regional governance structures

Regionalist structures exist along a government-to-governance continuum that can produce significantly different structures for decision-making (Douglas, 2005). At one end of the continuum, imposed structures of political and service boundaries may mandate some and facilitate other regional interaction within those boundaries. This may then spawn other forms of regional collaboration that begin to supersede the original mandates of the initial structure and assume other characteristics that are identified with new regionalism. Conversely, Peterson et al. (2010) point to the governance end of the continuum as the organic formation of regions within the new regionalist perspective such that:

> [R]egions have the potential to become significant functional spaces for the implementation of governance structures (Keating, 1998; MacLeod, 2001; Dredge, 2005), which can drive the cooperation of government agencies, the market, and civil society (Shaw, 2000; Wolfe, 2003; Scott, 2008), rather than the creation of a new layer of government at the regional level.
>
> (p. 298)

Organic, or bottom-up forms of regional collaboration were present in our case regions. However, they lacked institutional capacity and seemed fragile by depending on key individuals and/or external forces (Markey et al., 2005). However, the informality of these structures may also give them some dexterity and flexibility to respond appropriately to local challenges and opportunities. These informal networks also aligned more closely with how interview participants defined their regions, rather than the imposed boundaries of formal regional institutions (Reimer et al., 2008).

Because of the rural setting, a number of interview participants commented that the relationships and modes of communication among actors did not need to be highly structured and formalized. It was clear, however, that they were not highly robust associations, both in terms of the level of trust in the associations by senior governments and citizens, as well as the lack of capacity required to play larger regional development roles. There was also limited evidence that these regional coalitions were particularly effective in creating substantive regional development outcomes.

The most robust form of regional development structure studied within the project exists in Québec: the *municipalités régionales de comté* (MRCs or regional county municipalities). These serve as an example of top-down regional structure. During the early 1990s, Québec established 86 MRCs and 18 *territoires équivalents à une MRC* (TEs or "territories equivalent to an MRC"). The boards provide a forum where municipal representatives meet to debate and make decisions about development issues, including social programs, territorial planning, economic development, and employment assistance. As Reimer (2010) notes:

Over the 20 or so years of their operation within this new regime, local municipalities have learned how to use the regional structures to voice their concerns, debate, negotiate, compromise, and collaborate with other municipalities. As well, they have learned to negotiate with the provincial government on behalf of their region and village or town. In turn, the provincial government has discovered the value in subsidiarity. It now allocates responsibility to the regional boards for a wide range of economic and social policy and programs, and (most importantly) it shows its confidence in the decisions and accountability of the MRCs.

(p. 269)

MRCs are clearly the most advanced form of regional development in Canada in terms of both structure and capacity. Even so, our case research suggests that attaining the new regionalist ideal of co-constructed and collaborative regional governance sets a high standard. Interview participants in our Québec case study region spoke about the important role of the MRC, but also noted that it too suffered from top-down tendencies and tensions between urban and rural areas. In addition, the designated boundaries of the MRCs only occasionally aligned with local perceptions of the region.

The response of some interview participants to the MRC approach illustrates one of the potential challenges with new regionalism: an increase in the variability of government and governance standards. This may lead to more uneven development across provincial and national space. It has taken Québec 20 years to build the capacity for subsidiarity, but the Rimouski case illustrates that it is an ongoing process. Again, as Reimer (2010) states:

> The particular form of regional government found in Québec may not be satisfactory for all provinces, but the value of the principles remains. Local participation and influence are critical to reflect the unique circumstances of each location. At the same time, such bottom-up development needs an institutional context of strong regional governance to make it work. The inevitable conflicts of interest that emerge among municipalities require multiple venues for the expression, negotiation, and compromise that must take place before action is possible. Accountability and representation are necessary ingredients for establishing an adequate level of trust that will allow the system to work. All of this requires the development of a common language and understanding for collaboration.
>
> (p. 270)

4.3 Community versus region

Within each region we witnessed considerable tension among the development ambitions and efforts of different communities (including both single incorporated municipalities or unincorporated town sites). There are existing patterns of regional collaboration, such as the sharing and use of critical infrastructure and service delivery. However, while full of potential to facilitate broader regional discussions and collaborations, these existing patterns remain relatively passive in terms of scaling-up toward more substantive and diversified regional action. As one interview participant stated, communities within the region exist in a state of "reluctant cohesion", which is clearly not conducive to fostering a new regional sense of place.

Competitiveness continues to be perceived as a zero-sum game within most regions, emulating traditional local economic development patterns of inter-community competition (Markey et al., 2005). Harvey (1996) argues that there is an inherent tension in place construction through political economic frameworks. This is attributed to the promotion of a place's assets, often argued as a component of what makes a place unique, by entrepreneurs and local economic development actors in an attempt to ensure a continuation of place. The problem arises since over the past few decades, capital has become increasingly mobile and there have been intensified efforts at the local level to "sell a place", as in the fashionable practice of "branding". This can pit one place against another in an unsustainable mode of zero-sum competition. Such strategies of trying to "differentiate [places] as marketable entities ends up creating a kind of serial replication of homogeneity" (Harvey, 1996, p. 298).

In the Kootenays, communities within the region have no ingrained history of cooperation. They lack a legacy of collective action because there was simply no need to cooperate in the past. Instead of seeing themselves collectively, the strength of the resource economy, and the belief that resource booms would follow natural bust cycles, instilled a culture of individualism across the region—a behavioural response exacerbated by the physical geography. As described by Bradbury (1987), the resource economy structure also reinforced bilateral linkages between individual hinterland communities, the provincial metropolitan core (for public policy and management functions), and the headquarters of the resource industry (for employment and economic functions). Such a structure truncated the development of, and indeed the need for, inter-community dialogue and cooperation across the province.

Despite the inter-community tensions and parochial tendencies that continue to persist in rural regions, interview participants spoke about how the lack of regional collaboration serves both as a competitive disadvantage and an impediment to senior government engagement. If rural new regionalism in Canada is not at a highly evolved state, perhaps at least there is the recognition of what effective regionalism could contribute to development prospects.

4.4 Regionalism as regionalization

The fourth barrier to place-based regional affiliation is associated with the political administrative restructuring policies of senior governments. Regionalization is more often than not imposed and implemented as the creation of

regional municipalities by senior governments, rather than regional development in a participatory manner. Over the past 30 years, this has included
considerable removal and forced amalgamation of services at the rural regional
level (Douglas, 2005). Under these conditions, regionalism is most consistently identified with a negative experience in terms of quality of life and
infrastructure for rural and small towns. There is a fear that simply engaging
in regional dialogue and planning may ultimately serve to spur further or new
amalgamations—of communities and services. The regionalism agenda is seen
to be someone else's, driven by putative administrative efficiencies, cost cutting, downloading of services and other responsibilities, and a commitment to
fewer and larger-scale local governments.

Interview participants spoke to us about how forced regionalization of government and services exacerbated zero-sum competition between communities and created false boundaries. The local political process also plays a role
here, since local mayors and councils are judged by their constituents with
respect to what they deliver—or lose—for their communities.

The location of key infrastructure represents the largest challenge to the
realization of tenets of new regionalism in the case study regions. Traditional
approaches have treated infrastructure as an issue of individual communities
or regions—often reinforcing a competitive approach to inter-community
development. From a new regionalism point of view, however, regional
approaches to infrastructure should be seen as a complement, rather than
competitor, to community development. This is where the various components of new regionalism need to be operating simultaneously, by linking
place-based development with integrated planning and effective models of
governance.

The case and impact of forced amalgamation in Eastern Ontario emerged
as a good example of the implications for regional development. These amalgamations were initiated from the top down, coming from the Harris provincial government in the 1990s. The intention of the amalgamations was to
reduce the number of municipalities, thereby improving efficiencies and
saving money. There was little consultation involved in this process and the
resulting amalgamations often saw mergers among communities divided along
rural/urban, or English/French culture and language lines. In stark contrast to
this is the endogenously created and managed Wardens Caucus, a made-in-
Eastern-Ontario multi-municipal organization that collaborates across the
entire region and represents the region in annual negotiations with the Province of Ontario.

Amalgamation forces communities to work together, and in some cases,
there is more cooperation as a result. However, considerable mistrust and tension remains, particularly in areas with strong pre-amalgamation divisions. In
these cases, where it is possible to work separately (e.g., community festivals,
recreation activities), interests are focused at the pre-amalgamation community scale since hard feelings remain between the populations that were
forced together. Fortunately, these divisions have been slowly reduced with

time and the influx of new residents without knowledge of this history. The English/French divisions, however, remain strong. As a result of the legacy of these forced amalgamations, any discussion on regional action is generally viewed negatively since "region" has become synonymous with "amalgamation" as opposed to voluntary, functional collaboration.

5 Fragile place-based regionalism

Our research suggests that despite recognition of the importance of place, there are considerable barriers to achieving place-based regional development in rural Canada. Our framework, inspired in part by Paasi's (2003) suggestion that we study manifestations of identity, and Jones and Paasi's (2013) question of how regions become established, adopts a more utilitarian, as opposed to theoretical, model for seeking to identify and define regional identity as a foundation for enabling regional organization and initiatives. The evidence nevertheless allows us to reflect on the theoretical role of place-based development within new regionalism in Canada, and contributes to international calls for further regional case research.

The study suggests that identity plays a critical role in fostering regional development processes. First, our case studies suggest that regional identity is a strong motivating force—and a potential binding agent—that underlies (and undermines) various development initiatives. People and organizations are very committed to *their place*—and seek to pursue development activities that both capitalize on and protect the assets of those places. This defined "place" is, in most instances, the local community, even though a wider spatial entity is accorded some recognition. Much work is needed, through transparent, collaborative processes, to sort through overlapping boundaries and development priorities to achieve a sense of regionalism. For the sake of new regionalist enterprises, awkward political regions and forced functional regions impede and confuse the formation of a regional identity. In addition, legacies of community separateness, linked with specialized staples-based community economies, continue to reinforce local conceptualizations and practices of competitiveness. However, people's pride in, and desire to protect, their communities and regions both define and reinforce their sense of identity. Identity can then be drawn upon as an asset in the development process: an asset that is capable of providing common ground upon which to explore varying development pathways. However, based on the empirical evidence from these case studies, regional identity is either too emergent, confused by overlapping boundaries, or associated with negative outcomes to be a significant force for new regionalism in Canada.

Second, given the theoretical importance of identity for defining effective regions, understanding identity is critical for developing effective place-based policy at both local and senior government levels. Generalized development policies are most effective when they are contextualized to the conditions and priorities of place (Reimer & Markey, 2008). This requires the top-down capacity—and willingness—to adapt policy instruments, and the bottom-up capacity to identify and mobilize local assets and priorities as well as represent local identity in an articulate, forceful, and effective manner. Our cases show some nascent evidence of this "co-construction" of regional development policies and programs in Canada. Clearly, however, there is more work to be done—and many ongoing frustrations to sort and channel into productive development process. The MRC structures in Québec come closest to facilitating effective co-construction of regional development, but even in these now mature institutions, the challenges of attaining effective regional governance continue to exert themselves, including boundary tensions and limits to regional identity representation.

Our findings are also heavily influenced by the rural settings of our case regions. Much of the literature on new regionalism maintains an urban bias, focusing on city regions, which require a translation and consideration of relevance when seeking comparative lessons for rural areas. Our research suggests that it is especially important when considering how restructuring may limit the capacity to construct effective place-based development and regional governance in rural areas. Equally, restructuring initiatives have centralized rural infrastructure and service delivery, which cast a shadow over more progressive efforts to foster regional development.

Christopherson et al. (2010) provide a summation of "what factors enable a region to adjust and adapt over time" (p. 6), including: a strong regional system of innovation; a modern productive infrastructure; a skilled, innovative, and entrepreneurial workforce; a supportive financial system providing patient capital; and a diversified economic base, not over-reliant on a single industry. While the ruralization of this list will inevitably produce different variables, it is a particularly daunting set of characteristics for rural and small-town areas across Canada.

If new regionalism holds any potential for enhancing the viability and sustainability of rural regions, regions themselves must overcome tendencies for parochialism and become organized at the regional scale. Better understanding of the reflexive relationship between identity and place-based development holds promise for realizing these dual objectives. As Douglas (2005) states, rural regions as potential victims of restructuring must move away from "case-making" and move toward "place-making". At present, however, we suggest that place-based development is at best an emergent phenomenon at the regional scale within our case study regions in Canada.

References

Amin, A. (1999). An institutionalist perspective on regional economic development. *International Journal of Urban and Regional Research, 23*(2), 365–378.

Barnes, T., Britton, J., Coffey, W., Edgington, D., Gertler, M., & Norcliffe, G. (2000). Canadian economic geography at the millennium. *Canadian Geographer, 44*(1), 4–24.

Barnes, T., & Gertler M. (Eds.). (1999). *The New Industrial Geography: Regions, Regulation And Institutions*. New York, NY: Routledge.

Beaumier, G. (1996). Regional development in Canada. Current issue review *88-13E*, Ottawa.

Beaumier, G. (1998) Regional Development in Canada. Retrieved May 14, 2012, from http://publications.gc.ca/collections/Collection-R/LoPBdP/CIR/8813-e.htm.

Bradbury, J. (1987). British Columbia: metropolis and hinterland in microcosm. In L. D. McCann (Ed.), *Heartland and Hinterland: A Geography of Canada.* Scarborough: Prentice-Hall Canada, 400–441.

Bristow, B. (2010). Resilient regions: re-'place'ing regional competitiveness. *Cambridge Journal of Regions, Economy and Society, 3,* 153–167.

Christopherson, S., Michie, J., & Tyler, P. (2010). Regional resilience: theoretical and empirical perspectives. *Cambridge Journal of Regions, Economy and Society, 3,* 3–10.

Columbia Basin Rural Development Institute. (2012). Columbia Basin Rural Development Institute. Retrieved September 12, 2012, from www.cbrdi.ca/.

Columbia Basin Rural Development Institute (CBRDI). (2018). Columbia Basin Rural Development Institute. Retrieved April 30, 2018, from www.cbrdi.ca/.

Columbia Basin Trust. (2008). *State of the Basin Report.* Retrieved from www.cbt.org/Initiatives/State_of_the_Basin/.

Davenport, M.A., & Anderson, D.H. (2005). Getting from sense of place to place-based management: an interpretative investigation of place meanings and perceptions of landscape change. *Society and Natural Resources, 18,* 625–641.

Dawe, S. (2004). Placing trust and trusting place: creating competitive advantage in peripheral rural areas. In G. Halseth & R. Halseth (Eds.), *Building For Success: Exploration Of Rural Community And Rural Development.* Brandon: Rural Development Institute, 223–250.

Douglas, D. (2005). The restructuring of local governments in rural regions: a rural development perspective. *Journal of Rural Studies, 21*(2), 231–242.

Dredge, D. (2005). Local versus state-driven production of 'the Region': regional tourism policy in the Hunter, New South Wales, Australia. In Rainnie, A. and Grobbelaar, M. (Eds.) *New Regionalism in Australia.* Aldershot: Ashgate, 301–319.

Escobar, A. (2008). *Territories of Difference: Place, Movements, Life, Redes.* Durham, NC: Duke University Press.

Fairbairn, B. (1998). *A Preliminary History Of Rural Development Policy And Programmes In Canada, 1945–1995.* Saskatoon: University of Saskatchewan.

Filion, P. (1998). Potential and limitations of community economic development: individual initiative and collective action in a post-Fordist context. *Environment and Planning A, 30,* 1101–1123.

Gunton, T. (2003). Natural resources and regional development: an assessment of dependency and comparative advantage paradigms. *Economic Geography, 79*(1), 67–94.

Harvey, D. (1996). *Justice, Nature And The Geography Of Difference.* Oxford: Blackwell.

Hayter, R. (2000). *Flexible Crossroads: The Restructuring Of British Columbia's Forest Economy.* Vancouver: UBC Press.

Heisler, K.G. (2012). *Scales Of Benefit And Territories Of Control: A Case Study Of Mineral Exploration And Development In Northwest British Columbia.* PhD Thesis. Burnaby: Simon Fraser University.

Hettne, B., Inotai, A., & Sunkel, O. (Eds.). (2000). *National Perspectives On The New Regionalism In The North.* Vol. 2. Helsinki: United Nations University.

Hough, M. (1990). *Out of Place: Restoring Identity To The Regional Landscape.* New Haven, CT and London: Yale University Press.

Jonas, A.E.G. (2012). Region and place: regionalism in question. *Progress in Human Geography*, *36*(2), 263–272.

Jones, M., Paasi, A., & Sciences, E. (2013). Geography of regions guest editorial: regional world(s): advancing the geography of regions. *Regional Studies*, *47*(1), 1–5.

Keating, M. (1998). *The New Regionalism in Western Europe*. Cheltenham: Edward Elgar.

Kitson, M., Martin, R., & Tyler, P. (2004). Regional competitiveness: an elusive yet key concept. *Regional Studies*, *38*(9), 991–999.

MacLeod, G. (2001). New regionalism reconsidered: globalization and the remaking of political economic space. *International Journal of Urban and Regional Research*, *25*(4), 804–829.

Markey, S., Halseth, G., & Manson, D. (2012). *Investing In Place: Economic Renewal In Northern British Columbia*. Vancouver: UBC Press.

Markey, S., Pierce, J.T., Vodden, K., & Roseland, M. (2005). *Second growth: community economic development in rural British Columbia*. Vancouver: UBC Press.

Massey, D. (1984). Introduction: geography matters. In D. Massey & J. Allen (Eds.), *Geography Matters! A Reader*. Cambridge: Cambridge University Press, 1–11.

Massey, D. (1994). *Space, Place And Gender*. Minneapolis, MN: University of Minnesota Press.

Massey, D. (1995). *Spatial Divisions of Labour*. London: Macmillan.

Massey, D. (2004). The responsibilities of place. *Local Economy*, *19*(2), 97–101.

Mather, A., Hill, G., & Nijnik, M. (2006). Post-productivism and rural land use: cul de sac or challenge for theorization. *Journal of Rural Studies*, *22*, 441–455.

Mitchell, D. (1983). *WAC Bennett And The Rise of British Columbia*. Vancouver: Douglas & MacIntyre.

Paasi, A. (2003). Region and place: regional identity in question. *Progress in Human Geography*, *27*(4), 475–485.

Paasi, A. (2004). Place and region: looking through the prism of scale. *Progress in Human Geography*, *28*(4), 536–546.

Paasi, A. (2013). Regional planning and the mobilization of "regional identity": from bounded spaces to relational complexity. *Regional Studies*, *47*(8), 1206–1219.

Peterson, A., Walker, M., Maher, M., Hoverman, S., & Eberhard, E. (2010). New regionalism and planning for water quality improvement in the Great Barrier Reef, Australia. *Geographical Research*, *48*(3), 297–313.

Polèse, M. (1999). From regional development to local development: on the life, death, and rebirth of regional science as a policy relevant science. *Canadian Journal of Regional Science*, *22*(3), 299–314.

Portugali, J. (2006). Complexity theory as a link between space and place. *Environment and Planning*, *38*, 647–665.

Reed, M., & Gill, A. (1997). Tourism, recreational, and amenity values in land allocation: an analysis of institutional arrangements in the postproductivist era. *Environment and Planning A*, *29*, 2019–2040.

Reimer, B. (2010). Space to place: bridging the gap. In G. Halseth, S. Markey, & D. Bruce (Eds.), *The Next Rural Economies: Constructing Rural Place In Global Economies*. Cambridge, MA: CABI, 263–274.

Reimer, B. (2014). Rural and urban: differences and common ground. In H. Hiller (Ed.), *Urban Canada: Sociological Perspectives* (Third edition, 64–87). Don Mills: Oxford University Press.

Reimer, B., Lyons, T., Ferguson, N., & Polanco, G. (2008). Social capital as social relations: the contribution of normative structures. *Sociological Review*, *56*(2), 256–274.

Reimer, B. & Markey, S. (2008). *Place-Based Policy: A Rural Perspective.* Montreal: Concordia University. Retrieved from http://billreimer.ca/research/files/ReimerMar keyRuralPlaceBasedPolicySummaryPaper20081107.pdf.

Savoie, D. (1992). *Regional Economic Development: Canada's Search For Solutions.* Toronto: University of Toronto Press.

Savoie, D. (2003). *Reviewing Canada's regional development efforts.* Royal Commission on Renewing and Strengthening Our Place in Canada (NL). Retrieved May 16, 2012, from www.gov.nf.ca/publicat/royalcomm/research/Savoie.pdf.

Scott, A.J. (2000). Economic geography: the great half-century. In G. Clark, P. Feldman, & M.S. Gertler (Eds.), *The Oxford Handbook of Economic Geography.* Oxford: Oxford University Press, 18–48.

Scott, M. (2004). Building institutional capacity in rural Northern Ireland: the role of partnership governance in the LEADER II programme. *Journal of Rural Studies, 20,* 49–59.

Scott, J.W. (2008). Introduction. In Scott, J.W. (ed.) *De-coding New Regionalism. Shifting Socio-political Contexts in Central Europe and Latin America.* Farnham: Ashgate, 3–16.

Selkirk College. (n.d.). Regional Innovation Chair. Retrieved May 9, 2012, from http://selkirk.ca/research/ric/.

Shaw, T.M. (2000). New regionalisms in Africa in the new millennium: comparative perspectives on renaissance, realisms and/or regressions. *New Political Economy, 5,* 399–414.

Storper, M. (1999). The resurgence of regional economics: ten years later. In T. J. Barnes, & M.S. Gertler (Eds.), *The New Industrial Geography: Regions, Regulation And Institutions.* New York, NY: Routledge, 23–53.

Turok, I. (2004). Cities, regions and competitiveness. *Regional Studies, 38*(9), 1069–1083.

Weaver, C. & Gunton, T. (1982). From drought assistance to megaprojects: fifty years of regional theory and policy in Canada. *The Canadian Journal of Regional Science, 51,* 5–37.

Wolfe, J.M. (2003). A national urban policy for Canada? Prospects and challenges. *Canadian Journal of Urban Research, 12,* 1–21.

7 "Integrated" regional development policy and planning

David J. A. Douglas

1 Introduction

Our purpose is to examine the presence of new regionalist approaches in a number of Canadian regions. To do so, we focus on one of the five sub-concepts that underpin the conceptual framework: integrated development policies and practices (see Chapter 3). The findings and conclusions are relevant to research, policy, and practice, in Canadian and international contexts, because they suggest little evidence of integrated policy and practice, and by extension, new regionalism. The empirical evidence and analysis suggest, at a minimum, the need for further testing of the role and relevance of this overarching conceptual framework, and perhaps a radical refinement, or even falsification.

First, the selected sub-concept "integrated" from new regionalism will be explored by identifying a number of perspectives in development policy and planning practice associated with an integrated approach. With each perspective, selected indicators and possible measures from the project's extensive field research will be presented. A sample of field research questions will be presented, with a brief note on the field methodology, data management, and analytical protocol. Some of the field data from each research region will be presented with an analysis of 15 perspectives identified as symptomatic of an "integrated" approach to development policy and regional planning practice. More in-depth analysis of one region, Eastern Ontario, will be used to highlight selected patterns in the research findings. This will lead to conclusions regarding the role and relevance of new regionalism in Canadian contexts.

The chapter concludes with a brief exploration of the theoretical and conceptual implications of these findings, and some for policy and practice. These will touch on the case for questioning new regionalism as a relevant explanatory conceptual framework, notwithstanding any case for its validity as a normative framework for policy and practice.

2 The selected sub-concept "integrated" in new regionalism

The concept of "integrated" refers to an approach to development policy and planning that explicitly acknowledges and seeks to address the complexity of phenomena, whether they relate to contextual conditions (e.g., regional economy), normative designs (e.g., environmental remediation targets), or issues of process and practice (e.g., participatory procedures). Integrated perspectives in development policies, programmes, and planning practices typically incorporate such dimensions of reality as systems and sub-systems, linkages, networks, uncertainty, feedback, interconnected levels, or holism, and are associated with interdisciplinary approaches to analysis and prescription (Douglas, 2014b).

Using this as an operational definition, we articulated 15 overlapping perspectives for the concept of "integrated" (Douglas, 2014b). These are summarized in Table 7.1 below.

Table 7.1 Integrated development—overlapping perspectives

Perspective	Summary Commentary
Multi- and interdisciplinary	Addressing the reality of integrated phenomena through several disciplinary perspectives (e.g., economics, ecology, and political science).
Other than "economic"— alternative economics	Adopting the so-called "alternative economics" perspective (e.g., Ekins, 1986; Ekins & Max-Neef, 1992) extending the boundaries of conventional economic analysis.
Levels of government	Addressing integrated phenomena and development processes through multiple governmental interests and perspectives.
Counter "silo"	Seeing integrated development as a practice that purposefully addresses and connects the so-called "silo" phenomenon in public policies and management.
Participation	Addressing the multifaceted nature of development through a variety of participatory processes, expanding development participants, agendas, priorities, and perspectives.
Efficiency and effectiveness	Integrating the policy, planning, and management (implementation) phases of development through explicit attention to means and ends and the input-output logic of the development process, with emphasis on impact evidence through formal evaluation.
Holistic human	Taking a complete view of the development agenda and process: explicitly integrating cultural, psychological, health, ethical, and other perspectives with conventional political and economic ones.
Community development	Using development policy and planning incorporating the relational complexities of communities (e.g., power, norms, capacities), and the multifaceted nature of community development processes.
Comprehensive planning	Adopting the rational comprehensive development planning process of systematic technical analysis, calculation and alternatives assessment, public interest identification, and end state recommendations.

(*Continued*)

Table 7.1 (Cont.)

Perspective	Summary Commentary
Politico-territorial (spatial)	Explicitly recognizing the territorial/spatial dimension of development, the operational implications of location, distance, density, scale, and other facets of spatial relationships, with associated analysis and interpretation of spatial phenomena.
Trans-border territorial	Giving attention to jurisdictional boundary conditions, challenges, opportunities and interrelationships, and the selected integration of common collaborative development agendas (e.g., infrastructure, labour markets).
Operational	Use of a project management perspective of the development policy and planning process, the rational architecture of a "results-based" approach, with formalized methods (e.g., critical path method) to integrate objectives, resources, activities, outputs, and outcomes.
Growth and/or equity	Explicitly paying attention to the challenges of balancing growth and equity (or not), and the contested dichotomies of macroeconomic growth and sectoral economic expansion with welfare, distributional, and related issues of social equity.
Complexity	Giving attention to the innate complexity of territorial realities (e.g., political values, histories), the universality of uncertainty, unknown risks, cumulative outcomes, and other dimensions of complexity.
Systems theoretic	Showing awareness of the presence of systems (e.g., retail markets, faunal corridors), nested sub-systems (e.g., seasonal labour markets), linkages and feedback processes, resilience, "information" transfers, uncertainties, and other characteristics of systems.

The question posed to our selected interview participants, relating to the integrated sub-concept was, *"Is there evidence of these various perspectives in the development policy and practice in the Canadian project's case study regions?"*

3 Integrated in development policy and planning: a note on roots and record

The concept of integration has been with us since the earliest days of development policy, and the implementation and management initiatives which we associate with planning. It has been reified beyond its adjectival or adverbial qualities as something of a standard for appropriate or good practice. Whether through the earliest design of intentional communities (e.g., Bourneville, New Harmony), the late 19th and early 20th centuries forays into regional planning, the post-1945 emergence of international development, or the more recent preoccupation with sustainable development, the idea of taking an integrated approach to policy and practice has been propounded as both pragmatically sensible and professionally desirable. The fact that such espoused theory and theory in use (Argyris & Schön, 1974) very often, and perhaps more often than not, diverged to alarming degrees is simply part of our story, and perhaps our confession.

These integrated approaches have involved a variety of meanings when applied to regional development and planning, with considerable overlap among perspectives. It is generally acknowledged that some perspectives have been more dominant than others, such as the one-time all-pervasive rational comprehensive perspective in planning versus the more arcane systems-theoretic perspective (e.g., Banfield, 1959; Faludi, 1984; Friedmann, 1987). Some perspectives have waxed and waned over the years (e.g., Allmendinger, 2017; Douglas, 2010a; Healey, McDougall, & Thomas, 1982), but they have all been in play one way or another. However, some of these concepts have been more evident in academe and professional discourse, with others more evident in policy and practice. What is important to acknowledge is both the ontological and epistemological differences and similarities that inform each perspective. From this we must be cognizant of the substantial and substantive differences and similarities that have emanated in policy, plan design, development organization, development processes, and outcomes, as a result of the adoption of one or more perspectives, and the concomitant exclusion or minimization of others.

The continuing record of political, popular, professional, and academic discourse on the permissive term "sustainable development" (e.g., Brundtland, 1987; IUCN, 1980; Kates, Parris, & Leiserowitz, 2005) provides a useful example of convergence where, from time to time and with different perspectives in the mix, some blending or integrating has occurred. For example, what we refer to here as the *multi- and interdisciplinary* perspective and the *other than "economic"* perspective are very commonly used together when depicting the requisite integration for sustainable development. They are often implicitly supplemented with the *growth and/or equity* perspective, where the theme of redistribution, social justice, and reducing glaring gaps in income and access to resources is part of the problematic and the prescribed solution. The *systems theoretic* and selected other related perspectives have occasionally been found as ingredients in integrated perspectives that explicitly or implicitly speak to the sustainable development thesis in academic discourse and political rhetoric.

The term "integrated" has been almost entirely absent in the use of other synthetic constructs such as "sustainable livelihoods" (SL), where socio-ecological adaptive and self-organizing systems are at the heart of the concept (e.g., Rennie & Singh, 1996). With core defining attributes of non-linearity, uncertainty, diversity, resilience, co-evolutionary dynamics, and learning, the sustainable livelihoods thesis, either as a statement of real world practice in adaptive behaviours or as a normative guide for poverty alleviation and development, would be expected to highlight principles of integration. But it has not. Notwithstanding this, perspectives such as the *systems theoretic*, the *complexity*, the *holistic human*, and the *participation* have contributed to the formulation of the SL concept in rural and regional development.

On first impressions, the rich practice of, and the available theory in, community development (CD), would seem to proffer an excellent example of a thoroughly integrated set of perspectives (Chekki, 1979; Douglas, 1993, 2010b; Gittell & Vidal, 1998; Nozick, 1992, Roberts, 1979). However, notwithstanding some of the dominant practice roots of this eclectic field, such as public health and social work, and the more general theoretical frameworks provided by sociology, social psychology, and other contributing disciplines, the practice/theory links have been weak and the theoretical foundations remain underdeveloped at best (Douglas, 2010b). A variety of disciplines (e.g., geography, sociology) have facilitated some degree of synthesis and an increased appreciation of the multidimensionality of community development, either as outcome or process. But some professional practices (e.g., planning, architecture) have been less than impressive in integrating the physical, social, political, cultural, economic, and other dimensions of the community reality. So, even in a field that by its very nature is interdisciplinary and eclectic in its analyses of issues, its perspectives and formulations of explanatory concepts (Bhattacharyya, 2004), and its derivation of plans and prescriptions, one is struck by the modest degree of integration achieved.

It might be assumed that in environmental planning (and management), integrated perspectives have been achieved and applied. As with any field attempting to draw together the biophysical sciences, social sciences, and the domains of policy and practice, the record has been very mixed. Are the lofty aspirations or claims of Cicin-Sain and Knecht (1998) justified and borne out both by research methodologies and practice? They define what they call Integrated Coastal and Ocean Management (ICOM) as:

> … a continuous and dynamic process by which decisions are made for the sustainable use, development and protection of coastal and marine areas and resources. First and foremost, the process is designed to overcome the fragmentation inherent in both the sectoral management approach and the splits in jurisdiction among levels of government at the land-water interface.
>
> (Cicin-Sain & Knecht, 1998, p. 39)

This call for harmonization suggests that the perspectives we call *levels of government*, the *comprehensive planning* approach, the *counter "silo"* and others should have contributed to driving increased integration. It is generally accepted that in many jurisdictions, environmental protection and assessment legislation (e.g., Environmental Impact Assessment) and associated regulations and practices have become increasingly multidisciplinary, and perhaps interdisciplinary. So, these integrating perspectives may actively be evident. In Mitchell's view, to reach the ultimate goal of managing and developing resources "integration" will involve "relating resources management to management of other societal concerns ranging from job opportunities to housing and regional transportation" (Mitchell, 1986, p. 4). This brings up the elements one might expect in the *counter "silo"* and *levels of government* perspectives. Depending on what is inferred from the term "relating", one might assume that a *comprehensive planning* perspective is implicitly present here but, far less confidently, a *systems theoretic* perspective.

As noted, public policy in regional development continues to use the term "integrated", albeit with some license. It is *the* central concept underpinning the new *National Planning Framework* in Ireland (Government of Ireland, 2017). Explicit integration of institutional arrangements (e.g., the new independent Office of the Planning Regulator), regional development organizations (i.e., three Regional Assemblies of elected officials), local government reform (2014), the linking of all spatial planning with the new 10-year National Investment Plan, and other explicit commitments provide for a very progressive and ambitious development agenda, all pivoting on the organizing concept of integrated development.

In addition, there is an example from the Province of Ontario, Canada, where, in relation to the development of Northern Ontario under the province's *Places to Grow* legislation (2005), there is an explicit commitment to "an integrated approach to these economic development strategies through the creation of regular five-year economic action plans for Northern Ontario" (Province of Ontario, 2011, p. 10). The term is not defined, although the scope of the plan is said to be "comprehensive" (Province of Ontario, 2011, p. 6). Attracting investment for the purpose of growth and economic diversification includes an "integrated and timely one-window response to investment opportunities" (Province of Ontario, 2011, p. 10). Likewise, "[provincial] policies, programmes, and regulations will integrate approaches to natural resources management to support environmental, social and economic health" (Province of Ontario, 2011, p. 37). There is much in the plan that touches on several of the perspectives identified above (see Table 7.1), including concerns to streamline and make more efficient the entire multi-level public sector in the development of Northern Ontario, and the need to connect environmental, resources exploitation, social development, conservation, tourism development, job creation, and quality of life priorities. Collaboration, coordination, and participation are terms used frequently. A territorial dimension is evident in the defining of Northern Ontario itself, and in the commitment to "identify regional economic planning areas as an inclusive collaborative mechanism for long term economic development, labour market, and infrastructure planning that crosses municipal boundaries" (Province of Ontario, 2011, p. 29). Several of the perspectives one might associate with this sub-concept are used in this particular regional development initiative, albeit without a clear definition of the scope and depth of what an integrated policy or development planning process might entail. Therefore, one cannot ascertain with any certainty whether the Ontario plan seeks to attain the lofty heights suggested by Scott (2008) in defining new regionalism as a development process that "integrates notions of economic dynamism, administrative efficiency, community empowerment, civil society, responsive governance within a spatial framework, the region" (Scott, 2008, p. 4).

The concept of "integrated" approaches to development policy and practice is one of the four foundations of the highly influential European Spatial Development Perspective (EU, 1999). Finally, many of the indicators of an integrated approach to development planning suggested in this chapter are found in definitions of planning itself. One example is from the Association of European Schools of Planning (AESOP, 2012). "Planning is an interdisciplinary activity" (AESOP—Association of European Schools of Planning, 2012, p. 2). It deals with closely "interrelated" fields of knowledge and practice. It is designed to achieve "efficient" solutions through "coordinated" activities. It takes an "holistic approach". As has been the case in the evolution of the profession and discipline of planning (i.e., physical planning for urban and regional contexts), the pursuit has increasingly been understood to be intrinsically integrated.

4 Assessing the sub-concept in practice: approach

The questions posed in the field interviews were generated from a substantial body of research on the diverse literature relating to development and development theory, regional development, planning theory and practice, new regionalism, and related fields (Douglas, 2014a). We developed a set of indicators for each perspective (see Table 7.1), and from these a companion set of candidate measures that might be used to establish the presence or absence of each perspective was identified. Research questions were then formulated for each indicator to make up the field interview template. The field research interview instruments are available on the project's website, http://cdnregdev .ruralresilience.ca.

Table 7.2 presents examples from the research project's field questions for a selection of the 15 overlapping perspectives associated with the concept of integrated in regional development policy and planning practice.

For example, the presence of what has been called a *comprehensive planning* perspective was determined by ascertaining, amongst other things, the investment in a number of studies (e.g., surveys, analysis) to underpin the development planning process, its findings, and conclusions, and the generation of a short-list of alternatives for systematic evaluation. The presence of what was referred to as a *counter "silo"* perspective was determined by establishing whether explicit efforts were made to cross over and link disparate and oftentimes competing interests in the bureaucracy, and elsewhere. An approach that was informed by a commitment to ensure the *operational* efficacy of the development process was identified by establishing how the internal input-output or results chain of the development process itself was secured. A *complexity* perspective was explored by determining whether the

Table 7.2 Integrated perspectives in regional development policy and planning: examples of field research questions

Perspective	Sample Questions
Holistic human	"Do the development policy and/or plan explicitly deal with (a) questions of personal security (e.g., the safety of individuals and families, secure in a healthy environment), (b) the spiritual dimensions of residents' lives, (c) the collective sense of community pride, and/or (d) issues around racial, cultural, socioeconomic, and other forms of discrimination?"
Counter "silo"	"We've all heard of the so-called 'silo' phenomenon in development policy and planning. Has your organization undertaken any tasks or projects to overcome these issues? If so, please provide some examples."
Comprehensive planning	"Is your plan based on a multi-topic analysis of the area, encompassing for example the economy, environment, culture, social, and other dimensions of the area?" "Did your organization undertake or commission formal surveys or studies on any (which ones) of these?"
Operational	"Does your development plan explicitly link the targets you hope to achieve (e.g., river lands protection, visitor volume increases) with the inputs that are required to make this happen (e.g., capital budgets, precompleted projects)?"
Participation	"What role, if any, did the general public (private citizens, not only formally organized interest groups) play in the planning process?" "And in the final selection of the development strategy?"

development practice addressed questions of randomness, probabilities, and uncertainties in ecological, cultural, and other systems. A *community development* perspective, as an integrated perspective, was investigated by determining whether the questions of defining the community and its central characteristics were part of the development planning process, and whether related questions of distributive welfare and social justice were integral to the development policy and planning processes. A perspective informed by convictions around social and political inclusion and access, and one which is sensitive to societal pluralities and power differentials, was referred to as the *participation* perspective. The responses to these questions determine the degree to which the policy and planning processes invested in participatory processes, beyond that mandated by statutory requirements.

5 The sub-concept in practice: overall patterns

Table 7.3 provides a comparative summary of the responses from all research regions in this project. Bearing in mind the constraints on data comparisons (see Chapter 4), it will be evident that while there is considerable variation across all regions, there may be a number of fairly regular patterns of policy and practice.

Table 7.3 Evidence of the presence of integrated approaches from interview data

Indicator	BC (n=22)	ON (n=33)	QC (n=19)	NL (n=28)
An "alternative economics" perspectives and practice	H	M	H	M
Counter-silo initiatives	M	L	M	L
Community development perspectives and practice	M	L	L	M
Comprehensive rational planning	M	H	M	H
Complexity perspectives	H	H	H	H
Efficiency and effectiveness designs and practices	M	M	M	M
Growth and equity perspectives	M	L	L	L
Holistic perspectives	L	L	M	M
Multi-disciplinary perspectives	M	M	H	H
Multi-level perspectives and practices	M	M	M	M
Operational perspectives	H	M	M	M
Political territorial perspectives	M	H	H	H
Participatory perspectives and practice	M	L	M	M
Systems perspectives	M	L	H	M
Transborder interconnectedness	N	L	L	L

N = no mention of the concept was made in the interviews being considered; L (Low) = 1% to 33% of the interviews indicated that the concept was present; M (Medium) = 34% to 67% of the interviews indicated the concept was present; H (High) = 68% to 100% of the interviews indicated the concept was present.

Of the 15 indicators, those we have termed *complexity* perspectives and *political territorial* perspectives appear to have a relatively high number of practitioner interview participants who have these dimensions of practice, with the exception of the BC region with respect to the latter indicator. The *efficiency and effectiveness* indicator is reported across all case study regions at a medium level of frequency. An *alternative economics* perspective was mentioned by a relatively high number of interview participants from field sites in BC and QC, and a medium number of interview participants from the ON and NL case studies. *Comprehensive rational planning* approaches are frequently mentioned by interview participants from Eastern ON and NL case studies, but less so in the other regions. While evident across all regions, *participatory* and *community development* perspectives and practices are mentioned at medium or low levels by the interview participants. The *growth and equity* perspective in regional development planning appears to be something of a rarity across all regions, with the exception of BC where it appears to have a medium level of practice. The *transborder* perspective is also a rarity in all regional responses. As mentioned, there are noticeable exceptions, such as the relatively high presence of what we have called *systems* perspectives in the Rimouski region of QC.

Placing Eastern ON within this diverse pattern of regional development practices suggests that this region is reasonably similar to the other Canadian cases. Where there appears to be a relatively high concentration of interview participants reporting a particular dimension to their practice (e.g., *complexity*), it is mirrored by a similar concentration in all other regions. In two other perspectives (*efficiency and effectiveness* and *multi-level*), Eastern Ontario's medium level of responses is matched across all other regions. In *operational* and *territorial* perspectives, the Eastern Ontario pattern appears to be matched by two other regions. While bearing in mind the nature of the data set (See Chapter 4), Eastern ON may be somewhat atypical in that the responses suggest more policy and practice perspectives with a low rating than do the other case study regions. Notable among these are the *participatory* and the *systems* perspectives in regional development practice.

6 The field evidence from Eastern Ontario

6.1 General

Chapter 4 addresses important qualifiers to be noted in the interpretation of the data presented in this chapter. More detailed reporting of the field interviews and analyses for this region and the Kootenays may be found on the project website: http://cdnregdev.ruralresilience.ca.

The response profile from the 33 interviews (56 interview participants) in Eastern Ontario presented in Table 7.3 suggests that integrated practices are not universal. For example, in development planning practice the *comprehensive, complexity*, and *political territorial* perspectives are frequently mentioned (H) across sites, while seven of the other indicators are relatively low (L). Only one third of the 15 indicators we used to ascertain the presence or absence of an integrated approach to development planning show a medium (M) level presence.

Given the academic and professional literature, and experience, one might have expected a universal presence of at least one or two perspectives. The closest to this in development planning practice in Eastern Ontario is the "High" we assigned to responses indicating the presence of the *political territorial* perspectives. Given that most development planning in Eastern Ontario is couched within officially sanctioned spatial entities (e.g., Townships, Community Futures Development Corporation (CFDC) areas, tourism regions, Conservation Authority watersheds), it is not surprising that the political territorial dimension is frequently mentioned.

What should not be concluded from these relatively high response rates is that spatial development planning, commonly found in Europe for example (e.g., Faludi, 2008; Healey, 2004) is a dominant characteristic of practice in

Ontario. Of course, most development practice is pursued on a geographical basis, but this does not mean that the associated analysis and design of development strategies explicitly take into account the functional spatial dynamics of the geography in question. There was in fact very little evidence of spatial analysis from the field interviews.

What might be surprising is that the conventional approach to development planning, usually referred to as *comprehensive rational planning* (e.g., Banfield, 1959; Faludi, 1984; Kaiser, Godschalk, & Chapin, 1995), was also less than universal. While rated as relatively "High" among the 15 indicators of integrated practice in Ontario, the reported occurrence is at least indicative of its less than universal presence. Given the traditional attention to this approach within integrated planning in third level education and professional training and given the persistence of so-called scientific and rational approaches to development planning in government and elsewhere, one might have expected a near universal incidence. However, the field experience bore out the widespread absence of background surveys, research, database development, the formal generation of development alternatives, and other facets of what is referred to as a comprehensive perspective approach in planning. This is reinforced by the relatively sparse evidence of a multidisciplinary perspective to development practice, estimated as at a "Medium" level in this region.

Somewhat puzzling is the apparently "High" presence of a perspective that we have referred to as the *complexity* perspective in new regionalism. It is matched, as might be expected, by a relatively high reported incidence of a comprehensive approach to development planning. But one might have thought that the awareness of the complexity of social, cultural, ecological, and economic systems in play in the development context would go hand in hand with an holistic (L) and perhaps a systems theoretic (L) approach to plan design and management. The same might be said of a perspective that captured the dialectical processes between economic growth and social equity (L). The interviews clearly demonstrate an acknowledgement of complexity that extends into the political complexities of plan approvals and resources commitments, the intricacies of uncertain ecological processes and outcomes, and the untidiness of multi-stakeholder and interest group politics that increasingly characterize the development dynamic. This was very evident in the field. The data may indicate that tacit knowledge and an appreciative capacity on a particular dimension of development do not necessarily translate into development practice characterized by these same attributes, on all fronts. It should, perhaps, not be too surprising that some dissonance is present in the realities of policy and practice.

Striking, if not jarring, is the apparent paucity of *participatory perspectives and practice*, interpreted as "Low" in this region. While one might not have anticipated substantial commitments to this mode of practice in some of the development organizations and sectors surveyed (e.g., Chambers of Commerce), the significant representation of statutory (e.g., municipal land use planning), recreation, and tourism development planning would be expected to augment this response rate. This suggests that beyond the statutory prescriptions for public meetings and other legal formalities in communications, and beyond some of the more progressive practices in conservation and recreation planning observed in the field, this perspective is under-represented in regional development practice—at least in this field site.

While the low incidence of mentions regarding practices exhibiting *systems* perspectives might not be surprising, the dearth of *community development* perspectives and practice is puzzling. This is especially the case when the formal proposals from professional planning (i.e., physical and land use planning), the informal communications of practitioners in environmental planning and conservation, and the public communications from others in the general development field, all suggest a strong commitment to the fundamentals of community development. These include an explicit attention to community per se, including its structure and dynamics. They also include some deference to issues regarding social justice, distributive welfare and equity, access for minorities, and proactive engagement of community residents. Paralleling the low level of participatory processes, and the relative inattention to the growth and equity perspective that underlies so much of the development discourse, the very modest presence of community development perspectives suggests minimal integrated development planning in most aspects of this practice across Eastern Ontario.

Perhaps suggesting an underlying conservatism in development planning in this part of Canada, the relatively low level of evidence of activities and initiatives addressing the so-called silo syndrome is informative. This might complement the relatively strong formal recognition of political territorial realities and their associated jurisdictions noted earlier in the *political territorial* perspective.

It is perhaps surprising in these times when monitoring and evaluation, value for money audits, political pressures for out-sourcing, and a variety of other forms of public expenditures scrutiny and challenges are in vogue, that the *efficiency and effectiveness* perspective in designing development policies and plans shows relatively little saliency. A significant minority of interview participants in development planning and management in Eastern Ontario accorded little attention to formally linking inputs and outputs, the rigorous monitoring of outputs, outcomes, and impacts, and adopting effectiveness and efficiency measures.

Against the grain of responses that suggest some underlying conservatism in development practice, the "Medium" level of responses relating to what might be called an alternative economics is interesting. Many interview participants indicated that they encompass more than the formal economy in their practice, and comfortably build in environmental, cultural, and other dimensions of the rural context as they deal with economic growth and development issues.

Multidisciplinary perspectives in development planning and implementation practice in Eastern Ontario are reported to have a "Medium" level of presence here. Through this perspective, formal disciplines such as economics, ecology, geography, sociology, and others would likely be brought to bear on the issues and objectives at hand.

Perhaps surprisingly, given the nature of the Canadian context, our interview participants' feedback suggests that a relatively modest proportion of development practitioners in Eastern Ontario pursue their practice through multiple levels of government and governance. A fixed number do so by statute and regulation (e.g., Townships and Counties). Others do so for constitutional reasons (e.g., Parks Canada). So, the operational reality of multi-level perspectives and practices is the norm for many agencies. It is surprising, therefore, that less than a majority or only a small majority of interview participants in economic development, tourism planning, water resources management, and other fields envisage their practice as one functioning through multi-level processes.

Integrated perspectives in development practice can also be reflected in formalized programme and project management methods and protocols, such as the "critical path method" or "programme evaluation and review technique". We have identified these as *operational perspectives* in our analysis. In Eastern Ontario, they are assessed to be reported at a "Medium" level of presence in our interviews.

6.2 Overview

The data presented here, and the additional details on the project website (http://cdnregdev.ruralresilience.ca), suggest a very modest level of integrated development planning in Eastern Ontario. There might be tension between the perception, and professional acknowledgement, that the systems through and in which development planning is taking place are more complex and, in reality, more integrated than the planning practice that attempts to influence them. A dissonance and, more troublingly, a shortfall appears to exist. There are some indications that integrated perspectives are recognized, but they are few and far from universal. It is suggested that the presence of this particular sub-concept of new regionalism is, at best, partial and modest.

A sample of the analysis of development planning practice from the Kootenays (British Columbia) case study is presented in Case Study 7.1 to illustrate the details reflected in the statistical analysis.

Case Study 7.1 Selected details of development practice in the Kootenays, British Columbia

Field research highlights some of the diversity of development planning practice in the Kootenays, British Columbia. A social transition from the former environmental advocacy to a better informed and concerned mainstream of society is now in progress. Now the latter see practical and financial reasons to invest in and support alternative energy initiatives (e.g., micro-hydro, geo-thermal). The political and institutional support for environmental planning and management, notably from the regional districts, is a very important factor in this region. With support from the provincial government this integrates higher-level visions, policies, and strategic priorities with regulations and application at the local level (e.g., LEED building codes, water metres). This has been materially advanced by the federal government's support through a return of gas tax revenues pursuant to the municipality preparing and adopting a plan for environmental sustainability, under the Integrated Community Sustainability Plan (ICSP) programme (www.naturalstep.ca/integrated-community-sustainability-planning).

The environmental ethos is pervasive—"We are a solar city" [municipal government, BC]—and involves a great diversity of municipal, community, business, and other initiatives such as installing air to water heat pumps, heat recovery projects, school demonstration projects, bio-energy and greenhouse projects (e.g., Invermere), public education campaigns, business financial incentives, and integrating environmental and carbon footprint criteria directly into the community economic development (CED) process, as in Nelson. About two-fifths of interview participants here indicated that tangible benefits from the environment were a factor in the shaping of policy and practice. As a result, the well known East Kootenays Columbia Valley Local Conservation Fund was easily supported through a plebiscite, and a new tax was brought in on private lands for public and private environmental benefits.

Somewhat surprisingly, the concept of healthy communities, as an explicit aspect of policy and practice, here is a minority perspective. As with Eastern Ontario, there was no explicit incorporation of the "whole economy", self-reliance, bartering, skills exchange, and home-based business into policies and development planning practices.

As with other research case study regions in Canada, the (rational) comprehensive approach to development policy and practice is far from universal in the Kootenays. For those who had some elements of this approach, the economy and employment were the dominant foci of the research that was commissioned by a minority of interview participants in this region. A respondent from a Community Futures Development Corporation noted the opportunistic nature of development surveys and studies. The emergence and decline of issues (e.g., youth unemployment, laid-off forestry workers) throws up priorities and shifts attention. This tendency, combined with changing political attention (often short term) to various issues and the associated funding allocations, serve to generate a moving roster of information needs and related activities.

Not surprisingly, the biophysical environment was a topic of some attention here, but with a minority of interview participants investing in this in terms of formal analysis. Physical infrastructure surveys and analyses were reported in Grand Forks, in some of the Columbia Basin Trust (CBT) funded projects, through the Central Kootenays Regional District, and others. Fibre optic infrastructure assessment and feasibility studies are not uncommon. Water systems, sewage systems, and waste disposal are underpinned by selected studies. The Interior Health Authority's specifications provide design and operational criteria. As with Eastern Ontario, questions of demography and housing received very little direct attention, as data and studies (e.g., profiles, projections) were likely provided by the provincial government.

The concept of environmental health was the centre-point of any evidence of a more holistic approach to development policy and planning in the Kootenays, with two-thirds of the small number of interview participants citing this as a focus of their attention. Most other dimensions of personal and community development (e.g., happiness, social cohesion, inclusion) and lifestyles (e.g., reciprocity, pride, rural way of life) were not mentioned in describing the policy and planning processes.

Townhall-type public meetings were the dominant approach to public participation in this region. A small proportion of those who appeared to have pursued any participatory process used focus groups. Contrary to the findings of the place-based development responses, most other participatory vehicles (e.g., social media, workshops, community cable TV) were not used.

For more information see: http://cdnregdev.ruralresilience.ca.

7 New regionalism in eastern ontario and other canadian regions—some critical reflection

Though it might precipitate some angst among both theoreticians and practitioners, the degree to which development policy and planning practice in the case study regions is more or less "integrated" is not in itself of much concern here. The question we posed was whether this critical component of the posited new regionalism was more or less evident in the local context. On the basis of the extensive field research results, the primary data suggest that a very modest degree of integrated development planning is evident in these rural regions. While there may be evidence of other dimensions of new regionalism in the development practice in the field sites (e.g., innovation and knowledge transfer—see Markey, Breen, Vodden, & Daniels, 2015), the prevailing finding from this analysis is that this purported "new" or newer approach to development planning is essentially absent in practice.

There is much evidence of development practices informed by multidisciplinarity, an awareness of the complexities of the development milieu, and a sense that conventional economics does not encompass the whole economy—certainly not the variegated ways that people and communities create and maintain livelihoods. Likewise, there are numerous examples where practices attempt to integrate environmental considerations into the dominantly economic construction of the development agenda. In addition, there are perspectives evident that we associate with a more integrated approach to development policy and practice. However, the response from the field clearly indicates that most other dimensions of what might connote an integrated approach to development policy and practice are reported by professionals to be either absent or infrequent occurrences.

Analogous to something of a sub-text, the field experiences of the researchers did reveal a widespread appreciation on the part of practitioners of the realities of the interconnected nature of phenomena in the development milieu, the complexities of multiple interrelationships (e.g., different levels of government, ideological constituencies), the challenges of uncertainties and complexity (e.g., globalization), the urgent need to broaden the compass of conventional economic perspectives, and many more dimensions of the realities of the integrated context within which they practice. But, there is something of a tension between "espoused theory" and "theory in use" (Argyris & Schön, 1974; Friedmann, 1987). This capacity does not translate into a practice reflecting it, thus it remains an accommodated dissonance.

Part of the explanation behind these two worlds might be found in the inherited institutional structures and protocols associated with representative democracy, their associated bureaucracies, and related issues (Brown, 1987). At least four levels of government (i.e., federal, provincial, county or regional district, and township or municipality) can be associated with a great variety of development issues in all regions. While varying degrees of administrative decentralization have taken place, very little devolution has occurred. In all regions, as in other parts of Canada, local governments function with very modest resources and even less authority (Douglas, 2006, 2016, Tindal & Tindal, 2009). The governmental presence is accompanied by a plethora of spatial delineations of various, often overlapping "regions" with their associated discontinuities of mandates and resources. This exacerbates the challenges of coordination, longer-term commitments and associated predictability, and communications. Into the multi-level governmental milieu with its ever-changing coterie of policies, programmes, projects, protocols, procedures, and personalities, one must add a variety of other public agencies (e.g., Conservation Authorities, Community Futures Development Corporations), formidable NGOs (e.g. Columbia Basin Trust), and others. Added to this is a changing roster of issue-related, community-based, and area interest groups whose agendas and resources are applied to a great diversity of concerns ranging from heritage resources, youth welfare, housing, and tourism development, to the arts, pollution abatement, Indigenous issues, and general economic development.

The procedural and other rigidities of diverse bureaucratic overlays not only constrain the development practice, but the spatial administrative and other accoutrements of multiple governments in most instances do not reflect the shifting realities of functional systems (e.g., social networks, journey-to-work zones, trade areas). These and the systemic silo characteristics of many large-scale bureaucratic systems all militate against a development practice that might adopt a more integrated process, and one better reflecting the knowledge and convictions of the practitioner.

While in no way unique to these regions, these considerations may be important factors to entertain in any attempt to further a more integrated approach to policy design and implementation, and the development planning and management practice itself.

If one is interrogating the universality of the concept of new regionalism, the representativeness of the Eastern Ontario or the case study regions in the diverse Canadian context might be raised. As already noted, Table 7.3 provides a summary profile of the responses across all research regions in this project, and the dearth of development practice that might suggest an integrated approach is evidently suggested across all regions.

Another lesson and reminder from the field relates to the multiplicity of other development agents beyond the formal government and government related players. There is some indication that the integration that may not be feasible for a local politician, municipal official, or similar person to attempt, yet alone achieve, is being addressed by the myriad community-based, issue-oriented, and other NGOs that populate these regions. These community service organizations, charities, crisis help centres, food banks, counseling services, United Way organizations, environmental watchdogs, ethnic and cultural support groups, youth drop-in centres, job mentoring networks, social justice activists, and many others span the spectrum of issues that in reality constitute development (e.g., culture, gender, communications, shelter, personal security, livelihood). They cover much of the development landscape that more formal and institutionalized agencies do not address. But in addition, many if not most attempt to address the problems and opportunities in an integrated manner (e.g., homelessness and livelihood, environmental health, and child care). Thus, an unknown but likely significant measure of integrated development may be undertaken by a diverse, disparate, and ever-changing non-governmental sector.

If this is the case, it raises the question of governance in rural contexts, our expectations for this shared power, and context-responsive collaborative mode of development (e.g., Douglas, 2018; Stoker, 1998; Welch, 2002). While far from conclusive, the primary data from the field do not suggest a vibrant environment of multi-level and other types of governance, involving government as one but only one of several partners in the development practice. "New regionalism" as a normative theory of development is proffered as something of a prescription for a more inclusive and engaging approach to regional development, one that addresses the institutional constraints of governments and civil society organizations through opportunistic governance arrangements (Morgan, 1997; Ortiz-Guerrero, 2013). As such it might have some practical application for these Canadian regions.

Summary information on a community development planning process, and its implementation design and management in an Indigenous context in Canada, is presented in Case Study 7.2. This exhibits many salient facets of practice that might be associated with an integrated approach to development planning.

Case Study 7.2 Skidegate comprehensive community plan, 2012–2017

The Haida have lived on Haida Gwaii, a 300-kilometre long 200 island archipelago off the northwest coast of Canada, for thousands of years. They have achieved a high degree of self-government and have an active claim for full title to their unceded lands and waters. The archipelago population of approximately 4,000 is largely concentrated in two northern islands, and includes over 1,600 Haida. Around 2,300 Haida live off-islands. The Indigenous community of Skidegate (Figure 7.1) on the southeast coast of Graham Island has about 700 Haida residents on reserve, and around 1,000 off reserve.

This community undertook a series of community-based planning initiatives in 2012, which led to the formal approval by the Skidegate Band Council of a Community Comprehensive Plan (CCP), or *Gud Ga Is*, and an associated Land Use Plan (LUP), or *HIGaagilda KiIGuhlga*. These interrelated plans are explicitly premised on the Constitution of the Haida Nation and its Guiding Laws. The first sets out, among other things, territorial claims, a commitment to cultural sustainability, and an environmental ethos. The second articulates a set of personal and societal behavioural norms and principles, such as the communal sharing of wealth, the interconnectedness of all things, respect, and a needs-based approach to environmental stewardship and personal sustenance.

Several plans were completed before this intensive community-based initiative, but most were not comprehensive, had little participation, and very little community ownership. This community-based planning process was guided by a Community Advisory Committee and implemented by a dedicated planning team, led by an Indigenous community development facilitator. The advisory committee provided guidance on Haida values, language, knowledge, beliefs, and other cultural matters, and acted as the advocate for the CCP before the Skidegate Band Council. A partnership with the School of Community and Regional Planning (SCARP) at the University of British Columbia was instituted, involving faculty support and a series of student internships. Mentoring was made available from two other Indigenous nations, the Gwa 'sala-'Nakwaxda Nations and the Gitksan Nation.

The development planning process was highly consultative, interactive, and participatory, involving the intensive engagement of most community members and groups through a five-phase process, mirroring the life cycle of the salmon. The process involved outreach initiatives, systematic feedback and reporting processes, surveys, recreation events, community dining, some 23 community meetings, open houses, meetings with youth and elders, with those in health facilities, Band Council, and many others. In addition, the process involved the identification of projects that could be attended to immediately, and an action research approach to integrating the planning process and development implementation. Committing to a "living" plan, the process built in monitoring and evaluation, and ongoing plan refinement, with annual community celebrations of successes.

Visions for the community's development, in general terms and as they relate to the lands and waters (LUP), were articulated and translated into a set of development goals, directions, pathways, and required actions. These were assigned indicators over several time periods from the immediate to longer-term horizons.

The subject matter of both interrelated plans was very comprehensive, ranging from youth welfare, housing, employment, language preservation and instruction, health facilities, energy, life skills, community food gathering, community government and governance, a community policing programme, physical infrastructure, value-added timber processing, tourism development, a new fish processing plant, apprenticeships and trades training, land use and conservation, and inter-tidal and shoreline management, to traditional crafts development, elder care, tsunami protection initiatives, road signage, navigation training, enterprise development, oral knowledge transcription, parks and recreation facilities, bylaw enforcement, land and water protection, waste disposal and recycling, reserve boundary extension, dilapidated buildings, more lands for industrial and commercial uses, and many other topics.

The development planning process successfully brought together two overarching dimensions of planning that in most parts of Canada, and indeed the world, have remained inexplicably separate, in terms of policy, legislation, and notably professional practice. This artificial separation and lack of integration has often been challenged and censured (e.g., Douglas, 2010c). These two dimensions are land use planning, or physical planning as it sometimes called, and general community development planning, encompassing social welfare priorities, heritage, language and culture, public administration development, environmental planning, economic development, and other dimensions of community development. This was a very innovative initiative.

Figure 7.1 Haida Heritage Centre at Ḵay Llnagaay

Varying degrees of integrated development planning evolved through the ongoing community conversations and related participatory process. Needs emerged on different fronts (e.g., youth welfare, shoreline conservation) and candidate development priorities were shared. From there an emerging sense of the input requirements for solutions brought in other perspectives and potential players in any implementation process. Issues and opportunities that initially centred around formal education, for example, brought in the school district as a potential player, but it also could bring in the Haida's Rediscovery Camps and their roles in youth cultural awareness and welfare. Further discussion of the issues and opportunities might then involve Haida Child and Family Services, and others. A recursive process of needs and opportunities identification generated potential players in the emergent implementation agenda, which in turn expanded the diversity of perspectives framing the problem or opportunity. All of this, across a great diversity of topics, enhanced the integration potentials of the development planning process.

For more information see—www.skidegate.ca/documents/ccp/2005CCDP.pdf.

Case Study 7.3 presents the case of the Duhallow area in rural Ireland, where the development practice is characterized by a formidable comprehensiveness of perspectives spanning cultural, economic, political, environmental, social, and other issues and priorities, a vibrant ethos of participatory process, rigorous operational efficiency, and selected other dimensions of development practice that can be associated with an integrated approach.

Case Study 7.3 IRD Duhallow, Ireland—a case study in integrated development

IRD (Integrated Resource Development) Duhallow in rural Ireland provides a concrete example of development that is not only comprehensive in its reach, but highly and very successfully integrated in every dimension of its process.

IRD Duhallow is a "community-based integrated rural development company", owned by the local communities, located in northwestern County Cork, Ireland. It was organized in 1987 and has successfully delivered, among many other things, the EU's high-profile LEADER programme since 1991. The multi-community development company integrates a great variety of programmes and projects from the Irish government, community organizations, business groups, labour unions, individual entrepreneurs, heritage organizations, social service and advocacy organizations, the EU, local governments, and others. It collaborates with some 37 geographically based communities and over 60 issue-based community groups addressing issues relating to youth, women, small business, farming, the social economy, mental health, recreation and sports, and lone parents, to education, child care, energy, the elderly, culture, occupation training and skills development, employment search, digital skills, self-advocacy for the disabled, equity and social justice, environmental issues, mental health, after-schools services, and many others.

While economic diversification was its primary founding mission, in the challenging contexts of rural underdevelopment and restructuring, this endogenous area development organization (area 2,000 km^2) has grown to integrate a rich variety of economic, social, cultural, environmental, and other initiatives in a functional region, transcending local public administrative borders. Central to the organization's integrated approach to development is the building of local capacity through participatory governance, social mobilization, strategic communications, research and advocacy, and the conduct of a holistic approach to personal, group, community, and organization development. Representatives of this development organization are active in Irish rural development networks, Irish national development politics, and various EU forums. The approach to territorial development

here is fueled by a strong commitment to endogenous process, place-based development, and multi-level collaborative governance. Annual multi-year planning is an integral part of the area development process, including development management through systematic monitoring and evaluation.
(Walsh, 2017)
For more information see: www.irdduhallow.com.

8 Implications—theory, policy, and practice

This exploratory research was not expected to conclude with a "present/ absent" answer on new regionalism in the development policies and planning practices in these Canadian case studies. Even though there is considerable overlap across the five sub-concepts (see Chapter 3) that constitute new regionalism (e.g., place-based development, multi-level collaborative governance), it is not to be inferred from our findings that we can rely on one sub-concept, in this case integrated development, to suggest the same for all others (see Chapter 3 for some conditions on this claim).

Having said this, if the modest presence of an integrated approach to development policy and planning practice is in any way indicative of the overall development context in this field site, it does not suggest a robust presence of new regionalism. Does this call into question the universality of this mode of development policy and practice as suggested by much of the literature (e.g., Amin, 1999; Jessop, 1994; Scott, 2007; Storper, 1997)? The answer might be that this field research and analysis in itself does not negate the posited universal presence of new regionalism in post-Fordist reflexive capitalism. However, if our findings are linked to a broader assessment of the research project's overall findings across all five sub-concepts of new regionalism (Douglas, 2014a), the posited presence of this new approach to regional development in Canada is clearly in question.

Addressing a specific characteristic of new regionalism, one might look to evidence of what we have called multi-level processes, involving varying scales, in the development planning practice. This is occasionally evident in the Eastern Ontario, and indeed the Kootenays case studies. However, beyond the bureaucratic and related protocols of intergovernmental processes (e.g. county to province), the realities of overlapping multi-regional arrangements in both regions, and the presence of some extra-governmental organizations (e.g., the Trusts in BC), development planning practices exhibit limited evidence of these processes (see Chapter 5 for further information on multi-level collaborative governance).

So, the general conclusion here, with respect to a putative theory of new regionalism, is that one set of characteristics that would imply its presence is not evident. This serves to question the universality of this theoretical construct.

With respect to policy and practice, the modest and uneven evidence of an integrated approach to development should raise a number of concerns and issues for attention. Besides the axiomatic understanding that a development practice that takes more perspectives (e.g., social, environmental) into account in its scoping, analysis, design, and execution will be more efficacious than one that is more singular in its perspective, there must be a concern regarding the apparent shortfall in perceived inclusiveness of the process and its connecting with other levels of policy and practice. These characteristics would be regarded as deficiencies by most theoreticians and practitioners. The openness to seeing the economy as much more than the narrowly defined monetized and formal economy should be taken as something of a compensating encouragement. Also encouraging are the predispositions for multi-disciplinarity in development planning practice and an awareness of the complexity of the issues being dealt with. This was evident in both the Eastern Ontario and the Kootenays, BC regions. However, a further manifestation of the low level of integration in the policy and practice is the low level of perceived practices suggesting any explicit community development perspective.

The policy and practice fall far below the conventional political and professional rhetoric and aspirations relating to the pursuit of an integrated approach to rural and regional development. Even if the results of this field research are tempered by the results from other perspectives (e.g., place-based development), the empirical evidence presented in this chapter raises several serious matters for provincial policy-makers, municipal and other local government officials, professional practitioners, and the diverse NGO sector that variously attaches itself to these development agents.

9 Summary

This research set out to examine the evidence in Canadian regions of selected characteristics of what has become to be called new regionalism, over the last three decades of research and discourse. Rather than address the societal, institutional, and other characteristics that have been posited as markers of this new post-Fordist advanced capitalism (e.g., thick institutional milieu) the focus of the major research project from which this research emanates was on the local development policy and practice that might be associated with these new conditions. Five sub-concepts were identified (e.g., innovation and knowledge transfer) and the perspective that would see an integrated approach to development policy and planning was selected for this chapter. Through 15 indicators, the extensive field research in one particular case study region, Eastern Ontario, examined the evidence for an integrated approach to development policy and practice, and posed this against the other case study regions.

Whatever the normative case might be for a new regionalism approach to regional development, the conclusions from this analysis, with all qualifiers, suggest that there is little evidence of an integrated approach in perspectives and practice. There are some indications of such a perspective, but few. The evidence from this particular analysis accords with a more macro or general set of conclusions from the multi-region research project as a whole. The analysis and conclusions from this research pose a number of challenging questions for policy, practice, and research, and the associated claims of an integrated approach to rural, community, and regional development.

References

AESOP—Association of European Schools of Planning. (2012). 2012 Newsletter. Association of European Schools of Planning. Retrieved from www.aesop-planning.eu /newsletter/en_GB/archive/2012.

Allmendinger, P. (2017). *Planning Theory*. London: Palgrave.

Amin, A. (1999). An institutional perspective on regional economic development. *International Journal of Urban and Regional Research*, *23*(2), 365–378.

Argyris, C., & Schön, D. (1974). *Theory in Practice: Increasing Professional Effectiveness*. San Francisco, CA: Jossey-Bass Publishers.

Banfield, E. C. (1959). Ends and means in planning. *International Social Science Journal*, *XI*(3), 361–368.

Bhattacharyya, J. (2004). Theorizing community development. *Journal of the Community Development Society*, *34*(2), 5–34.

Brown, R. H. (1987). *Society as Text*. Chicago, IL: University of Chicago Press.

Brundtland, G. H. (1987). *Our Common Future*. Oxford: Oxford University Press.

Chekki, D. A. (Ed.). (1979). *Community Development: Theory And Method Of Planned Change*. New Delhi: Vikas Publishing House.

Cicin-Sain, B., & Knecht, R. W. (1998). *Integrated Coastal And Ocean Management: Concepts And Practices*. Washington, DC: Island Press.

Douglas, D. J. A. (1993). *Community Development: Observations And Lessons From Experience*. Guelph: University School of Rural Planning and Development, University of Guelph.

Douglas, D. J. A. (2006). The fiscal imbalance and rural municipalities. In *Building Prosperity From The Ground Up: Restoring Municipal Fiscal Imbalance* (88–94). Ottawa: Federation of Canadian Municipalities.

Douglas, D. J. A. (2010a). Theorizing rural planning and development. In Douglas, D. J. A. (Ed.), *Rural Planning and Development in Canada* (Chapter 11, 329–354). Toronto: Nelson.

Douglas, D. J. A. (2010b). Community development: A cornerstone of rural planning and development. In Douglas, D. J. A. (Ed.), *Rural Planning And Development In Canada* (Chapter 10, 281–327). Toronto: Nelson.

Douglas, D. J. A. (2010c). Introduction. In Douglas, D. J. A. (Ed.) *Rural Planning and Development in Canada* (2–9). Toronto: Nelson.

Douglas, D. J. A. (2014a) *"New regionalism" as the local development paradigm?: Cautionary evidence from some recent research in Canada*. Presentation to the OECD-LEED Conference, Stockholm. Retrieved from http://cdnregdev.ruralresilience.ca/?page_id=29

Douglas, D. J. A. (2014b). *"Integrated" in regional development discourse, policy and practice: Selected perspectives, candidate indicators, measures, research questions and critical reflection in the context of new regionalism*. Working Document CRD-1, for the project—*Canadian*

Regional Development: A Critical Review of Theory, Practice and Potentials, Guelph: University of Guelph.

Douglas, D. J. A. (2016). Power and politics in the changing structures of rural local government. In Shucksmith, M., & Brown, D. L. (Eds.), *Routledge International Handbook Of Rural Studies* (Chapter 50, 601–614). London: Routledge.

Douglas, D. J. A. (2018). Governance in rural contexts: Toward the formulation of a conceptual framework. *EchoGeo. Processus de gouvernance dans les territoires ruraux*. Special Edition. *43*. January, 1–16.

Ekins, P. (Ed.). (1986). *The Living Economy: A New Economics In The Making*. London: Routledge & Kegan Paul.

Ekins, P., & Max-Neef, M. (Eds.). (1992). *Real Life Economics: Understanding Wealth Creation*. London: Routledge.

EU. (1999). *European Spatial Development Perspective: Towards Balanced And Sustainable Development Of The Territory Of the EU*. Luxembourg: European Commission.

Faludi, A. (1984). *Planning Theory*. Oxford: Pergamon Press.

Faludi, A. (Ed.). (2008). *European Spatial Research And Planning*. Cambridge, MA: Lincoln Institute of Land Policy.

Friedmann, J. (1987). *Planning In The Public Domain: From Knowledge To Action*. Princeton, NJ: Princeton University Press.

Gittell, R., & Vidal, A. (1998). *Community Organizing: Building Social Capital as a Development Strategy*. Thousand Oaks, CA: Sage.

Government of Ireland. (2017). *Ireland 2040: Our Plan—National Planning Framework*. Dublin: Department of Housing, Planning, Community, and Local Government.

Healey, P. (2004). The treatment of space and place in the new strategic spatial planning in Europe. *International Journal of Urban and Regional Research*, *28*(1), 45–67.

Healey, P., McDougall, G., & Thomas, M. (Eds.). (1982). *Planning Theory: Prospects for the 1980s*. Oxford: Pergamon.

IUCN. (1980). *World Conservation Strategy: Living Resource Conservation For Sustainable Development*. New York: United Nations.

Jessop, B. (1994). Post-fordism and the state. In Amin, A. (Ed.) *Post-Fordism: A Reader* (Chapter 8, 251–279). Oxford: Blackwell.

Kaiser, E. J., Godschalk, D. R., & Chapin, Jr., F. S. (1995). *Urban Land Use Planning*. Urbana, IL and Chicago, IL: University of Illinois Press.

Kates, R. W., Parris, T. M., & Leiserowitz, A. A. (2005). What is sustainable development? Goals, indicators, values, and practice. *Environment: Science and Policy for Sustainable Development*, *47*(3), 8–21.

Markey, S., Breen, S., Vodden, K., & Daniels, J. (2015). Evidence of place: Becoming a region in rural Canada. *International Journal of Urban and Regional Research*, *39*(5), 874–891.

Mitchell, B. (1986). The evolution of integrated resource management. In Lang, R. (Ed.) *Integrated Approaches To Resource Planning And Management* (13–26). Calgary: University of Calgary Press.

Morgan, K. (1997). The learning region: Institutions, innovation and regional renewal. *Regional Studies*, *31*(3), 401–503.

Nozick, M. (1992). *No Place Like Home: Building Sustainable Communities*. Ottawa: Canadian Council on Social Development.

Ortiz-Guerrero, C. E. (2013). The new regionalism: Policy implications for rural regions. *Cuadernos de Desarrollo Rural*, *10*(70), 47–67.

Province of Ontario. (2011). *The Growth Plan For Northern Ontario*. Toronto: Ministry of Municipal Affairs and Housing, Province of Ontario.

Rennie, J. K., & Singh, N. C. (1996). *Participatory Research For Sustainable Livelihoods: A Guidebook For Field Projects*. Winnipeg: International Institute for Sustainable Development.

Roberts, H. (1979). *Community Development: Learning And Action*. Toronto: University of Toronto Press.

Scott, J. W. (2007). Smart growth as urban reform: A pragmatic "recoding" of the new regionalism. *Urban Studies, 44*(1), 15–35.

Scott, J. W. (Ed.) (2008). Introduction. In *De-coding new regionalism: Shifting socio-political contexts in Central Europe and Latin America* (Chapter 1, 4). Farnham, UK: Ashgate Publishing Limited.

Stoker, G. (1998). *Governance as Theory: Five Propositions*. Oxford: UNESCO, Blackwell.

Storper, M. (1997). *The Regional World: Territorial Development In A Global Economy*. New York: Guilford Press.

Tindal, C. R., & Tindal, S. (2009). *Local Government in Canada*. Toronto: Nelson.

Vodden, K., Douglas, D. J. A., Kelly, S., & Reimer, B. (2015) *Rhetoric versus reality: Examining new regionalism in Rural Canada*. Presentation to the Regional Studies Association Annual Conference, Piacenza, Italy. Retrieved from http://cdnregdev .ruralresilience.ca/?page_id=29.

Walsh, M. (2017). Strategies for building community resilience—The Duhallow experience. In Brinklow, L., & Gibson, R. (Eds.), *From Black Horses To White Steeds: Building Community Resilience* (Chapter 1, 33–61). Charlottetown, PEI: Island Studies Press, University of Prince Edward Island.

Welch, R. (2002). Legitimacy of rural local government in the new governance environment. *Journal of Rural Studies, 18*(4), 443–459.

8 Rural–urban interactions and interdependence

Bill Reimer, Joshua Barrett, Kelly Vodden, and Luc Bisson

1 Introduction[1]

The public media often represent rural and urban places as fundamentally in conflict. Urbanization and the resulting political tensions have exacerbated this view with challenges for resources and attention. This debate seldom reflects the fundamental interdependence of rural and urban places, however, and remains relatively uninformed regarding the empirical evidence demonstrating that interdependence.

Rural places provide the timber, food, minerals, and energy that serve as bases of urban growth (Alasia, 2004). Rural places also provide labour and markets, process urban pollution, refresh and restore urban populations, and maintain the heritage upon which much of our Canadian identity rests. Urban Canada provides the markets for rural goods, much of its technology, and most of its financial capital, along with a good deal of its media-based culture. Decisions and actions taken in one locale will often have implications for those in the other—whether directly or indirectly. To understand both locations, therefore, one must understand the interrelationships within which they exist.

Rural–urban interdependencies are implicated in many elements of new regionalism perspectives (Lichter & Brown, 2011; OECD, 2010; Tacoli, 2006). The focus on a region itself usually includes both low- and high-density locations: rural- and urban-like settlements and the relationships among them. Those who consider regions as useful units for economic development typically include both rural and urban areas within those regions—with the assumption that both are involved as their assets become part of the innovation systems driving success (Castle, Wu, & Weber, 2011; Partridge & Clark, 2008). This is reflected as well in political new regionalism as governance systems are imagined and described (OECD, 2013). Regional integration demands a consideration of rural–urban interdependencies. Metropolitan new regionalism reinforces this interdependence with both rural and urban settlement patterns being considered in transportation, service provision, land use, and other planning decisions. All of these approaches assume the integration of rural and urban places within regions as an important element of their frameworks.

New regionalism approaches also reinforce the importance of rural–urban interdependence between and among regions. The identification of network-based systems, subsidiary governance organization, and competitive advantage all imply a consideration of the ways in which a regional system in one location might be connected to those in others. This includes situations where relatively remote regions are connected to metropolitan centres. The new regionalism vision is one of considerable rural–urban interdependence both within and among regions.

There is, however, uneven elaboration of the nature of rural–urban interdependencies within new regionalism literature. In those cases where they are acknowledged, the focus tends to be on trade and exchanges—the movement of people, goods, or provision of services among and within regions (Reimer, 2013). Those focusing on political new regionalism add a discussion of the institutional structures of governance that bind locations when it comes to planning, regulations, service provision, and relative power (Halseth & Ryser, 2006). Conflicts over land and asset use in the rural–urban fringe provide foci of attention for environmental concerns but sharing of a common history or identity are less frequently considered as a basis for such interdependence or action. The first task in examining such interdependencies as represented in new regionalism, therefore, is an elaboration of their nature and manifestations.

This chapter provides a framework for considering rural–urban interdependence as it is reflected in the literature on new regionalism and an analysis of interview results within the *Canadian Regional Development* project. The results not only reinforce the importance of rural–urban interdependence as an important feature of new regionalism, but they identify more specific elements of this theme that are underdeveloped in both the theoretical literature and in practitioner sensibilities. Several implications from this analysis are included for researchers, policy-makers, practitioners, and citizens.

2 Rural–urban interdependence as a theme in new regionalism

2.1 Rural–urban interdependence

Interdependence means that "changes in one place affect the other"—a relatively abstract formulation but one that can be effectively applied to rural and urban places. Sources of interdependence can include a wide range of factors, including natural resources, labour, changes to population, heritage, markets, and finances, as well as environmental concerns such as air pollution, greenhouse gases, and water quality (External Advisory Committee on Cities and Communities, 2006; Reimer, 2005; Robinson et al., 2008). In Canada, and many other countries, rural provision of resources serves as a base for urban growth and urban areas provide markets, technology, financial capital, and manufactured goods—and policies and actions around these have implications for both rural and urban areas (Reimer et al., 2011)

In order to manage the range of possible factors, we consider the dynamics of rural–urban interdependence with respect to four spheres: exchanges, institutions, environment, and identity. All four of these spheres should be considered for a full accounting of this interdependence, but we expect that their relative saliency will vary from place to place and time to time. Our findings suggest that they do. These variations can also provide insights into local conditions that frame any regional development activities in those places.

Within academic literature there is a growing recognition of the importance of rural–urban interdependence, but discussions of conceptual frameworks for what this might mean and empirical studies documenting such interdependencies tend to rely on economic approaches (Buttel & Flinn, 1977; Irwin et al., 2009; Lichter & Brown, 2011; Partridge & Clark, 2008; Tandoh-Offin, 2010). Addressing the interdependencies between rural and urban regions, Bosworth and Venhorst (2018) and Hibbard, Senkyr, & Webb (2015) argue that traditional approaches to evaluating economies are no longer appropriate for today's rural regions: a different lens must be provided in analyzing regional and rural economies. An elaborated rural–urban interdependence framework offers such a lens.

Researchers have documented that a wide variety of dynamics and types of interactions connect rural and urban regions. Central Place Theory (Christaller & Baskin, 1966; Lösch, 1954), urban–rural fringe analysis (Beesley, 2010), and discussions of occasional counter-urbanization flows (Bryant, 2003) have all added elements to this material. In addition, studies regarding such diverse processes as commuting flows (Partridge, Ali, & Olfert, 2010), food systems (Cohen & Garrett, 2010; Lucy, 2008; Tacoli, 2006), and climate change (Irwin et al., 2009) all point to rural–urban interdependencies—yet, we require a better understanding of other linkages (Ozor, Enete, & Amaechina, 2016). This is especially the case since the role and interdependencies between rural and urban regions is ever changing (Lichter & Brown, 2011).

2.2 Trade and exchanges

Economic interdependence is the most common focus of attention when rural–urban relationships are discussed within the regional development literature. In most cases it is framed in terms of trade and exchanges, whether of goods, services, labour, or finances. These exchanges often occur in complex ways—involving chains of trade and diverse conditions. Sometimes it is direct as with farmers' markets or commuting (labour markets), but often it is indirect via other nations or complex intra-firm transactions within our commodity-dependent and increasingly globalized economy. In Canada, more than 90% of our positive balance of trade in goods and services is due to the export of rural products (agriculture, forestry, energy, minerals) (CANSIM, 2007)—goods that originate in rural regions but make their way to national and global markets through urban fabrication, assembly, transportation systems, financiers, and regulators (Reimer, 2013, p. 95). Labour is also increasingly mobile, with workers moving in complex ways within and between rural and urban regions (Halseth et al., 2010; Milbourne & Kitchen, 2014; Tacoli, 2006).

2.3 Institutions

Institutional interdependence is demonstrated in both formal and informal ways. Government policies, whether designed specifically for rural places or of a more general nature, will often reinforce the interdependence between rural and urban areas by virtue of their application. A medical policy favouring specialists and shared equipment will place different transportation and accommodation demands on rural people and on urban services and infrastructure. Transportation policy designed for high-density spaces is likely to isolate those where people are more widely distributed. In a similar manner, private and third-sector (not-for-profit organizations) institutions reflect this interdependence when, for example, corporate decisions dramatically alter rural land use, cash flow, and financing options for rural residents (e.g., the location of big-box stores); urban-based hunting or recreation groups transform wetlands and habitats; or when advocacy and advertising organizations redefine rural identities in strategic ways (Halfacre, 2007; Murdoch & Pratt, 1993; Shucksmith & Brown, 2016a).

2.4 Environment

Over the past 50 years the environmental sciences have demonstrated the ways in which our common environment binds us all in a multi-level system of interdependence (Buttel & Flinn, 1977). This can also be seen dramatically on a regional scale. The ecological footprint for the Toronto Census Metropolitan Area, for example, is 59 times the metro area's actual size (nearly one-third the size of Ontario) (Wilson & Anielski, 2005). This footprint rests largely on rural areas (through food, fibre, and water provision, pollution processing, and waste management). Agricultural runoff can destroy the favourite recreation areas of both urban and rural dwellers, urban air pollution threatens rural forests, uncontrolled resource exploitation can poison urban water supplies (O'Connor, 2002), and urban sprawl can undermine rural communities and despoil landscapes while contributing to the global warming that threatens us all. Of all the forms of interdependence, the environment has emerged as one of the most visible to the general public (Ontario Ministry of Municipal Affairs and Housing, 2002). The public concern with the quality of food, the purity of water, recreational benefits of natural assets, and local manifestations of climate change have been encouraged by the popular media, creating an opportunity for recognition that is often missing from the common interests reflected in trade, institutions, or identity. For that reason, our discussion of environmental interdependence serves as a basis for several strategic options for improving rural–urban relations.

2.5 Identity

Rural–urban interdependence based on identity is seldom discussed in the literature. Research from the 1997 to 2008 *New Rural Economy* project demonstrates, however, that it remains a powerful feature of rural–urban interdependence

(Reimer, 2006). As discussed in Chapter 6, people form attachments to places—attachments that deeply influence their perception, preferences, and choices. Social psychologists have also documented how this can easily become a central feature of how people view themselves and their personal and collective worth (Devine-Wright, 2009). In some of the more settled regions of the country (e.g., NL, NS, QC) rural markers of identity have become synonymous with provincial and sub-provincial identity as reflected in language, dialects, traditional industries, architecture, music, values, and other characteristics. Challenging or upsetting those identifications can lead to community and individual collapse—as illustrated most dramatically by the history of Indigenous peoples in Canada and the disregard of the association between identity and geographical places in colonial policies (Chandler & Lalonde, 1998). Visions of the rural by urban people or of the urban by rural people significantly condition our expectations when we plan, visit, or engage with each other across—or even within these regions. The bright lights of city life and the tranquility of rural places are both constructions that affect migration, expectations, and openness to others in ways that are not always beneficial. As we have found in the past, ignoring these aspects of interdependence can easily jeopardize the social cohesion of all Canadian society.

2.6 New regionalism

Rural–urban interdependence is a theme with a mixed relationship to new regionalism. New regionalism has primarily been examined with a bias to urban settings—in spite of the fact that most authors assume the urban-associated hinterlands to be part of the economic or political system. In general terms, Wheeler (2002) suggests there is a lack of understanding of the interdependence between rural and urban areas in the new regionalism literature. For example, much of the discussion focuses on the (perceived) power imbalance and conflict between rural and urban areas, and a hierarchical spatial order that privileges urbanized areas over rural counterparts in terms of public policy and institutional representation (Overbeek, 2009).

The differing demographic and spatial contexts of regions can also make the exploration of new regionalism insights difficult. For example, regions can vary from those where an urban centre dominates to those where the nearest urban centre is remote, and in each case the nature of their interdependence is different. In addition, this interdependence is reflected both within and among regions (Gallent, 2006; Tacoli, 1998).

In spite of these challenges, there is sufficient evidence to support critiques of urban-centric new regionalism to ensure that more rural areas within and among those regions are given scholarly and practitioner attention—particularly with respect to their contributions to and impacts on urban places (Ortiz-Guerrero, 2013; Markey et al., 2015). Table 8.1 identifies some of the key themes and related literature regarding these relationships.

Table 8.1 Rural–urban interdependence themes in the new regionalism literature

Theme	Cited in (not exhaustive)
Rural communities are valuable for their recreation and environmental assets	Breen, 2016; Hamin & Marcucci, 2008; Ortiz-Guerrero, 2013; Reimer, 2005
Rurally located resources provide a base for urban economic growth	Baxter et al., 2005; Hamin & Marcucci, 2008; Reimer et al., 2011, Tsukamoto, 2011
Four spheres of interdependence: economy, institution (policies, design), environment, identity	Hamin & Marcucci, 2008; Ortiz-Guerrero, 2013; Reimer, 2005; Reimer et al., 2011
Three types of R–U relations: Flows between, different territorial bounds, different functional relations	Bellini et al., 2012; Overbeek, 2009
Need for shift to emphasize interrelationships (governance) and functional interdependencies as opposed to the more conventional conflict that occurs	Breen, 2016; Devlin et al., 2015; External Advisory Committee on Cities and Communities, 2006; Wallis, 2002
Interdependencies are important to consider in planning (e.g., the R–U fringe areas)	Gallent, 2006; Vodden, 2015; Wallis, 2002; Wheeler, 2002

2.7 A matter of scale

The particular geographic or scalar resolution at which rural–urban interconnections are examined creates an additional dimension that must be considered in our analysis. For example, place-based development in relation to identity will look very different at the local scale relative to the national one. For better or worse, fragmented national identity remains a significant barrier to place-based development in Canada, whereas local density often plays a reinforcing role in such development. This suggests three key dimensions to consider when looking at rural–urban interdependence and its relationship to our project themes: the four mechanisms of interdependence, the five themes of new regionalism (see Chapter 3), and the level of scale at which they are considered. We will consider five levels of scale: community, regional, provincial, national, and international. These distinctions are selected since they all have institutional structures in place for decision-making and resource distribution.

3 Rural–urban interdependence as a theme in Canada

In Canada, the main driver for exploring rural–urban interdependence is the enormous influence that resource development policies and practices have on people's lives and the environment—from a macro-scale down to the local level. The pervasiveness of these connections has been extensively documented by Harold Innes' contributions to staples theory since the 1930s (Innis, 1995, 1999) and its associated metropolitan–hinterland thesis (Careless, 1979).

Unfortunately, city-regions and high-profile urban metropoles are often treated as "engines of growth" (Duranton, 2007; Jean, 1997). Savoie (2003) suggests Canada's regional development problem is now primarily urban–rural in nature, rather than regional or provincial. This debate seldom reflects the fundamental interdependence of rural and urban places, however, and remains relatively uninformed regarding the empirical evidence demonstrating that interdependence. As Tacoli (2006) points out, without recognition and attention to the linkages among rural and urban sectors and regions, researchers and policy-makers alike lack understanding of the contributions these linkages make to livelihoods, local economies, and social-cultural transformation, as well as the opportunities and challenges that they present.

4 Interview questions and indicators

To what extent and in what ways are issues of rural–urban interdependence reflected in regional development policy and practice in Canada? This was the research question posed as a part of the 2011 to 2015 *Canadian Regional Development* research initiative. To answer it, researchers conducted 102 key informant interviews with residents, government officials, business people, and community organizations within the project's case study regions (22 respondents in BC, 33 in ON, 19 in QC, and 28 in NL) to gain insights into rural–urban interactions and interdependence in policy and practice. These interviews covered each of the five research themes.

With respect to the rural–urban interdependence theme, questions focused on the nature of the organizations with which the interview participants were involved, the networks within which they worked, their interactions with people and groups in regional and external urban (or rural) areas, and, for rural interview participants, the relative control and involvement of urban people, groups, and policies in their activities—with some focused attention on those organizations and policies that related to both rural and urban areas in their region.

Our coding protocol was developed to capture specific types of interdependencies within each of the four spheres of interdependence as well as connections across various themes and scales (see Table 8.2). Concepts used to identify trade and exchange relationships include, but are not limited to, labour, finance, and trade. Institutional concepts include government, family, and corporations, with these relationships also analyzed by institutional scale. Environmental concepts can be identified through recreation or nature-based recreational amenities, or other shared interests, such as food, air, and water. Concepts that can reveal relationships based on identity include place attachment, families, religious, and cultural groups or affiliations. In all cases the coding protocol allowed for types of relationships to be identified within the data that were not previously anticipated (see "Other" category). Our data analysis from across regions and provinces allowed for comparison of perceptions and practices relating to rural–urban interdependence. This included analyses of the frequencies with which the presence of particular types of interactions and interdependencies arose within the data, which are presented below.

Table 8.2 Rural–urban relationships codes

Trade and exchanges	Institutional	Identity	Environment
People	Local–local	Place attachment	Energy
Jobs	Local–provincial	Language	Food
Goods	Local–federal	Religion	Water
Services	Local–international	Ethnicity	Air
Finances	Government	Family	Land use
Knowledge/experience	Private sector	Culture	Waste
Infrastructure	Third sector	Lifestyle	Recreation
Other	Family/culture	Employment/tasks	Climate
	Other	Political	Other
		Other	

Our data analysis from across regions and provinces allowed for comparison of perceptions and practices relating to rural–urban interdependence. This included an analysis of the frequency with which the presence of particular types of interactions and interdependencies arose within the data. Although common themes and questions were agreed upon by the project researchers, the style of engagement with interview participants and the recording of information was not consistent across all study regions—for reasons of logistics, capacity, and researcher preference. The greatest variation occurred between the Ontario interviews and the others. In the former, the researchers recorded summaries of the respondents' responses regarding each issue, whereas with the others, the questions and answers were recorded using audio equipment and transcribed for analysis. The coding process, therefore, relied on the summaries for Ontario but transcriptions for the others. This means that comparisons among BC, QC, and NL using frequency and standardized information can be made with more reliability than those including ON.

5 Findings

5.1 Recognizing rural–urban interdependence

In what ways are rural and urban places interdependent in Canada—as perceived by local leaders and regional development practitioners? In general, most of the interview participants mentioned all four of the types of interdependencies at least once.

If we consider the number of times that an interdependency issue was mentioned by the respondents (or interviewer summaries in the case of ON), we see that institutional issues were most common (54% of the 5,431 interdependence mentions in Table 8.3). This is likely to have been influenced by respondent selection since most participants were involved with public and third-sector regional development institutions as employees or volunteers. Trade was the second most commonly mentioned type of relationship (27%),

Table 8.3 Evidence of the presence of rural–urban types of interdependency from interview data (number of mentions)

Type	Kootenays BC (n=22)	Eastern ON (n=33)	Rimouski QC (n=19)	Kittiwake NL (n=28)	Total (n=102)
Institutions	M	M	M	M	M
Trade	L	L	L	L	L
Environment	L	L	L	L	L
Identity	L	L	L	L	L
Number of mentions	(1667)	(936)	(718)	(2110)	(5431)

L (Low) = 1% to 33% of the total interdependency mentions related to this type of interdependency; M (Medium) = 34% to 67% of the total interdependency mentions related to this type of interdependency; H (High) = 68% to 100% of the total interdependency mentions related to this type of interdependency.

followed by environment (11%), and identity (9%). This ordinal pattern is followed in all four regions (see Table 8.3).

5.2 Trade and exchanges

All interview participants mentioned some form of trade or exchange as a basis for rural–urban interdependencies but the type of exchange varied in some important ways.

Most interview participants identified the exchanges of knowledge and ideas as the most prevalent example of rural–urban exchange (95 out of the 102 interviews) (see Table 8.4). This included sharing experiences among regional development agencies often facilitated by annual conferences, for example, but also through personal relationships, the exchange of knowledge among post-secondary institutions through their instructors, and among businesses and organizations that provide work term opportunities, especially for youth (Reimer & Brett, 2013). When asked about institutional linkages, a respondent from the regional centre of one case study region referred to the use of external speakers as an important source of knowledge in the following manner:

> … we would bring in someone from a major department of government or a business … and we hold meetings around tables with the heads of Marine Atlantic and we invite representatives from the other Chambers to come in to make sure that everyone has their voice with them.
>
> [Business organization, NL]

Some representatives of rural organizations also viewed activities for visitors as a way to share knowledge about rural people, communities, and ways of life. Referring to their remote community's collaboration with urban-based

Table 8.4 Evidence of the presence of rural–urban trade by type of exchange from interview data

Exchange Type	Kootenays BC (n=22)	Eastern ON (n=33)	Rimouski QC (n=19)	Kittiwake NL (n=28)	Total (n=102)
Knowledge	H	H	H	H	H
Finance	H	M	H	H	H
Services	H	M	H	H	H
People	H	M	M	H	H
Goods	M	M	M	M	M
Infrastructure	L	N	N	L	L
Other/unspecified	L	L	L	L	L

N = no mention of the concept was made in the interviews being considered; L (Low) = 1% to 33% of the interviews indicated that the concept was present; M (Medium) = 34% to 67% of the interviews indicated the concept was present; H (High) = 68% to 100% of the interviews indicated the concept was present.

universities, the National Film Board, and urban artists, one of our respondents expressed it in the following way:

> … we think of it as engagement, so the way we use the house [a local inn and studio], for example, this is a cinema thing in partnership with the National Film Board of Canada and we don't play any kind of film but a specific collection to share certain knowledge.
>
> [Community organization, NL]

While knowledge was the most common type of exchange noted by interview participants, exchanges of finance and services were also common (85 and 84 respectively out of 102 interviews). One respondent from Newfoundland emphasized how rural consumers help to sustain businesses within regional service centres—in this case, the town of Gander: "Well Gander wouldn't exist without rural, there's no ifs, ands, or buts" [Business organization, NL]. Impacts of global flows of goods and services were also evident, as well as development responses to these changes. One interview participant from Québec, for example, explained in the following way the role that local agencies have played:

> I think we can provide a counterbalance to the global movements, that is to say, counterbalance the flow of concentration. Large commercial type chains like Walmart and the like have so many strong resources, but we are able to explain to the large food chains how important it is to introduce regional agricultural products for support to our economy.
>
> [Provincial organization, QC—author translation]

Technology has helped rural businesses access urban and global markets but also rural workers to access distant job opportunities, "because they have connectivity to work abroad".

[Regional government, ON]

Mobility and "exchange" of people was a common theme across the study regions (74 out of 102 interviews). In many cases, residents in rural communities must not only travel to urban centres to access goods and services but also to sustain their livelihoods.

There is no question that the rural areas are dependent upon the urban centers. There is no question. We have, the city of Trail in itself is the employment center for arguably the area and I would say Castlegar as well for the large part. There is a tremendous amount of labour force mobility between Castlegar and Trail ....

[Community organization, BC].

We should also mention that almost 70% of workers living in rural areas in these communities actively work within the city of Rimouski.

[Regional organization, QC—author translation]

While some rural residents commute to job centres far and near, others choose to migrate. Loss of youth to large cities, within or out of province, was another common theme within the study regions. This creates the need to attract young families and bring outside education and experience into communities that have experienced population losses. At the same time, some communities within the study regions experienced increased numbers of incoming visitors or property owners on a seasonal basis. The interviews reveal that mobility choices and their implications are strongly linked to identity, culture, attachment to place (discussed further below), and to historical employment patterns as a basis for rural–urban relationships.

The exchange of goods was quite frequently mentioned as a reflection of interdependence (60 out of 102 interviews). In some cases, this occurred within discussions about the disadvantages of rural as opposed to urban communities—or the competition between them:

If they are able to, people go to Alberta for their shopping because the tax is lower.

[Community organization, BC]

I can recall when I was young that we have inside the village four places where we could buy groceries, four places. And it was like that if we go back like 45 years. And there were four farms in our village where we had different products like eggs and others. And even in my farm we were going door-to-door to sell our eggs. And we also had a general store but now if you look in the village you have almost nothing … the price of food inside big grocery stores inside the city came down drastically. So, people were now going into the city to buy their food which was costing them less than if they were buying from us.

[Provincial organization, QC—author translation]

Most people go to urban centres for their significant grocery purchases.

[Municipal government, NL]

There was also recognition of the way in which exchanges of goods to urban places could be of benefit to rural ones.

… because the city is full of potential buyers and the rural communities produce products with not only themselves in mind, but also for city dwellers, so there should be way closer ties between the rural citizens and the citizens of the city.

[Regional organization, QC—author translation]

Exchanges or sharing of infrastructure was mentioned by only three interview participants of the 102 interviewed. This was noticeably different from the other types of exchange in spite of the fact that infrastructure like roads, railroads, power, communication, and pipelines are some of the most direct links connecting rural and urban places.

5.3 Institutionally-based interdependence

Institutional interdependencies are mentioned at least once by all interview participants although the type of institution showed some variation in relative frequency. Government and third-sector institutional interdependencies were mentioned at least once in the highest number of interviews (93 and 89 respectively out of 102 interviews) (see Table 8.5). Private sector and family issues were mentioned at least once (each) in 69 of the interviews. There was some variation in these figures across the provinces but the relative ranking of the institution type remained about the same. For example, the private sector was most often mentioned in BC and NL while family was mentioned relatively infrequently in Ontario. This is a case where the variation in interviews and coding may be responsible for such a difference, but it may also signal an occasion for additional analysis. A closer examination of each type of institutional interdependency follows.

5.4 Level of government

Rural and urban places are highly interdependent in terms of government policies, programs, and financing. Since this occurs via relations at a number

Table 8.5 Evidence of the presence of rural–urban interdependence by institution type from interview data

Characteristic	Kootenays BC (n=22)	Eastern ON (n=33)	Rimouski QC (n=19)	Kittiwake NL (n=28)	Total (n=102)
Government	H	H	H	H	H
Private	H	M	M	H	H
Third sector	H	H	H	H	H
Family	H	M	H	H	H
Other/unspecified	L	L	L	L	L

L (Low) = 1% to 33% of the interviews indicated that the concept was present; M (Medium) = 34% to 67% of the interviews indicated the concept was present; H (High) = 68% to 100% of the interviews indicated the concept was present.

Table 8.6 Evidence of the presence of rural–urban interdependence by level of government from interview data

Linkage Type	Kootenays BC (n=22)	Eastern ON (n=33)	Rimouski QC (n=19)	Kittiwake NL (n=28)	Total (n=102)
Local-local	H	H	H	H	H
Local-provincial	H	H	H	H	H
Local-federal	L	L	N	L	L
Local-international	M	M	L	M	M
Other/unspecified	L	L	L	L	L

N = no mention of the concept was made in the interviews being considered; L (Low) = 1% to 33% of the interviews indicated that the concept was present; M (Medium) = 34% to 67% of the interviews indicated the concept was present; H (High) = 68% to 100% of the interviews indicated the concept was present.

of different levels, we coded the responses with respect to their relative scale: local to local, local to provincial, local to federal, and local to international (see Table 8.6).

The most notable finding is the relatively low number of mentions regarding local–federal links (only 8 out of the 102 interviews). Even links of an international nature (43 out of 102) are more likely to be mentioned than those with the federal government or other national institutions, although several interview participants acknowledged that "the federal government is a major funder for initiatives" [Regional organization, NL]. This reflects findings from the *New Rural Economy* project that indicate rural communities tend to have only weak connections with federal agencies and policy-makers (Halseth & Ryser, 2006).

Interview participants mentioned local-to-local institutional relationships at least once in all of the interviews (but local–provincial rural–urban institutional relationships are also common—being mentioned at least once in 91 of the 102 interviews). Development activities at the regional level are often in response to provincial program initiatives designed by officials in urban headquarters. Provincial and (and to a far lesser extent) federal governments provide policy guidelines and regulations that enable and constrain regional initiatives, in part as important sources of finances for regional development.

One participant explains the influence of provincial (referred to in Québec as "national") policy in the following way:

> In the national policy on or around Québec this policy influences many organizations in the territory and the way that villages can ask for money within the rural areas of the territory. It is often from the top-down, which is something that could be from the bottom-up in my view.
>
> [Community organization, Québec—author translation]

> Well, if you look at the rural policy in Québec the answer is "yes" and if you look at agriculture policies, of course they influenced the development of agriculture at a regional level. It is certain.
>
> [Municipal government, QC—author translation]

Interview participants in BC expressed the need for more appropriate policy for rural communities. Institutional interdependencies sometimes result in rural–urban tensions and a feeling that the contributions of rural resources to urban economies are not adequately recognized.

> I think that government policy is not overly supportive of [little pockets of communities], I think there is more of an urban bias to a lot of the government policy that we see around economic development or community development.
>
> [Regional organization, BC]

> It is common for most rural areas to feel that the tendency at senior levels of government is to focus on more urban areas as opposed to the more favorable rural policies and recognize … that the overall wealth, specifically as it pertains to resource management or natural resources, … lie[s] within the rural areas not the urban.
>
> [Regional organization, BC]

Rural–urban tensions also exist between larger and smaller local governments within regions (local–local relationships). Communities with larger or wealthier populations are often seen as having greater access to taxation revenues, for example, which can in turn lead to debates about which organizations or government departments should be responsible for the costs of regional services (see Case Study 8.1). In some cases, the larger populations of the regional centres are used to justify their having greater representation or decision-making power on regional boards, like with the MRCs in Québec. One of our interview participants, for example, informed us that "With its demographic weight, the city [Rimouski] controls 85% of the budget of the MRC. So since the city has a right to veto the MRC and the city decides to say no, then the decision is no—it's over" [Community organization, QC—author translation]. In other cases, distances between communities make it difficult for local governments to collaborate on a regional basis.

> The dissatisfaction, because of the geographic division, is substantial. We cancelled meetings; it increases the cost of everything that we do. It does not make a whole lot of sense from very many angles.
>
> [Regional organization, BC]

Case Study 8.1 The MRC of Rimouski-Neigette: managing a large urban centre in a rural region

The regional county municipality (Municipalities Regionale de Comte— MRC) of Rimouski-Neigette is located about 300 km east of Québec City. It is bordered by the river to the north, the New Brunswick border to the south, the MCR La Mitis to the east, and the MRC of the Basques to the west. It is composed of one unorganized territory and nine municipalities (see Chapter 4, Map 4.4).

The MRC Council for Rimouski-Neigette is composed of the nine mayors of the municipalities within the region and one representative from the municipality of Saint-Anaclet-de-Lessard. The extra representative was added since the mayor of that municipality was elected as Prefect of the Council. The MRCs have two different sets of responsibilities. The first, land use planning, is imposed by the provincial government. This includes plans for the water management of the rivers within the MRC boundaries, the preparation of municipal evaluation rolls, the administration of non-organized territories inside the MRC, the establishment of a waste management plan, and a fire protection plan. The plans are reviewed by the provincial government to ensure they conform to provincial regulations and revised every five years.

The MRC can also establish its own set of responsibilities to facilitate regional and local development. These are optional for each municipality since they can ask to be withdrawn from any such contracts so long as they provide a resolution from their council. These optional contracts can include investment funds for private sector start-ups (see www.mamot.gouv.qc.ca /amenagement-du-territoire/guide-la-prise-de-decision-en-urbanisme /acteurs-et-processus/mrc/).

The Rimouski-Neigette MRC has taken on most of these responsibilities in an active manner, working with its constituent municipalities to share services, maintain its agricultural zone, support sustainable development objectives, and build opportunities for recreation, culture, and heritage (see www.mrcrimouskineigette.qc.ca/wp-content/uploads/2017/03/Fonds-de-d%C3%A9veloppement-des-territoires-Priorit%C3%A9s-dintervention-2017-2018.pdf).

With the agreement of the Québec government, the MRC also has established the Société de promotion de Rimouski (SOPER) to provide services for entrepreneurship and entrepreneurs. This responsibility is shared with a federal institution, the Société d'aide au développement des collectivités (SADC), which operates in the rural areas of the MRC. The agreement includes a rural development fund that is managed by SOPER.

These activities have not been without their challenges. One of the most pervasive has been the uneven population distribution between the city of Rimouski and the other municipalities in the MRC. In 2016, the city of Rimouski contained about 86% (48,664) of the MRC population of 56,650. The eight other municipalities and unorganized territory in the MRC had a combined population of 7,986. According to provincial regulations, this means that the city of Rimouski holds veto power on the Council since it comprises more than 50% of the population in the MRC.

Interview participants indicated that this imbalance had created tensions between the urban centre of Rimouski and the surrounding villages, but that it was diminished to some extent by more recent initiatives. This is reflected in the following quotes from our local interviews (our translation).

> The city of Rimouski, when considering its size, is capable of paying for all services and also capable of sharing with people who are living in the surrounding rural communities. We have a recreation agreement with the city of Rimouski regarding an arena, pool, or other infrastructure that we could not have in [our village]. If a young person from our village wants to play a sport in Rimouski, he will pay the same price as a young person from Rimouski … For example, it only costs a dollar for my sons to be members of the Rimouski Municipal Library whereas previously it cost $100 when we did not have an agreement.
>
> [Municipal government 1, QC—author translation]

I think one of the problems is not with the elected representative of the city, but with the citizens of Rimouski. For us, Rimouski is very close, while the rural territories (especially the remote villages like ours) are very very far and misunderstood by the citizens of Rimouski. Additionally, we feel that they are not aware of what happens in our village, while the opposite is not the case.

[Municipal government 2, QC—author translation]

I think that the situation in terms of the relationship between the MRC and the city of Rimouski was not good at all because over time the city of Rimouski was not comfortable with that thinking, so over the years it created an atmosphere of real confrontation which is hard to change.

[Municipal government 3, QC—author translation]

For now, I can say that the conflicts are resolved without lights and cameras. Exactly the opposite of what has happened before where the mayor decided to resolve everything publicly and through the media. Now we have a mayor and a municipal administration that is willing to settle issues without all the public attention.

[Municipal government 4, QC—author translation]

Our interview participants also pointed to the different conditions and approaches to decision-making that exist within the more formal bureaucracies of the MRCs and the smaller settlements in the region. This is reflected in the following quote:

I have to admit that for some people and some elected to the MRC, there is no understanding at all of how here in [small village] we can have close relationships between elected officials and municipal administration. Here, it is common for us to have meetings between elected officials and the municipal government at my home in an informal setting—and for many of the elected in other rural communities, they can't understand how that's done.

[Municipal government 1, QC—author translation]

At present, these tensions are managed by informal means (Reimer et al., 2008). Over the last few years, for example, the mayor of Rimouski has been reluctant to use the veto power since he considers it unfair to the smaller municipalities. This informal arrangement has sustained relatively congenial relationships on the Council although there is some public concern expressed regarding the perceived lack of sensitivity to the rural municipalities and regions. It also relies on the personal sentiments of the Rimouski mayor, leaving long term consistency uncertain. As indicated in one of the quotes above, this concern is tempered by the many services that the city provides to the surrounding communities.

5.5 Private sector

Private sector institutions were implicated in rural–urban relationships in both positive and negative ways (see Table 8.5). The following quotations illustrate how urban centres both draw consumer dollars out of rural communities and provide markets as well as financial and other supports to rural businesses:

> It is about an hour's drive to Walmart from Grand Forks, and people would still rather go there than buy local.
>
> [Municipal government, BC]

> Yes, we collaborate with every organization in the territory to help start new businesses and we collaborate in all the ways that we can. For example, by helping with the analysis of the business plan and meeting with the entrepreneurs to analyze the risk-taking of every organization around the table to make sure that the entrepreneur has the best services for him to start his businesses. The way we make decisions among ourselves, I mean all the organizations around the table, is by consensus.
>
> [Regional organization, QC—author translation]

> There is a public private partnership with the town of Gander to provide Destination Gander, which represents opportunities for tourism in the area.
>
> [Regional organization, NL]

> One small example of collaborations between the rural and the urban is the Local Food Economy Study which was done. This has led to a program where the rural farmers come to the city to personally sell their food to the city residents.
>
> [Regional organization, ON]

5.6 Third sector

Third-sector institutional links were often mentioned with respect to public and private sector involvement (see Table 8.5). Each of these sectors plays a significant role in regional development as sources of financial capital, labour, knowledge, services, and, in the case of regional non-profit organizations, as facilitators of rural–urban relationships. One respondent identified the important role of Community Futures Development Corporations (CFDC) that exist in two of the four provinces (ON and BC), for example:

> There are all sorts of rural–urban partnerships. The CFDCs have an important role to play here. The public respect for the Board Members of the CFDC was an important element here in facilitating bridges between rural and urban interests. It was suggested that the EODP's skills training initiatives were an important factor in reducing rural and urban differences.
>
> [Regional organization, BC]

Non-government regional development organizations such as CFDCs can help to bring a range of institutional representatives together. Organizational representatives from BC explained this in the following ways:

> We have also been involved with the Aboriginal BEST [Aboriginal Business and Entrepreneurship Skills Training] training program … And on our board, we also have somebody from the First Nations. And we also have somebody from the Métis community as directors on our board. So we can link in there.
>
> [Regional organization, BC]

> When you have 60 or 65 community leaders that are all focusing on either smaller areas or greater areas of the whole, these types of projects and activities are bound to come up over the course of time. And then they just gather steam within the organization. And we have been fortunate enough where the local governments, even the province for that matter and our private enterprise, private sector partners in the community have also bought into this as well.
>
> [Regional organization, BC]

5.7 Family

The role of family relationships was mentioned in 70 of the 102 interviews. All of the provincial interview participants reflected this level, except for Ontario (see Table 8.5). Migration, for example, creates family ties between rural and urban communities.

> I know for example that the Stroud family claims to be the original European settler in Glovertown … my point is there are fairly significant connections with St. John's as I suppose there are with all towns in Newfoundland. Now there's that little townie-outport friction, that's changed, most people don't pay any attention to it but you still won't get many people from Glovertown who are very positive about St. John's.
>
> [Municipal government, NL]

Several interview participants explained that family ties can also be a barrier to rural–urban mobility or collaboration within or among regions.

> Many people who were born and raised in communities have started family businesses. As such, it is difficult for them to move elsewhere.
>
> [Municipal government, BC]

> ... in several other villages you find families' lines and considerable confrontation and conflicts amongst them. And this greatly affects the participation of citizens because once you have one family participating in a social activity, you can bet that all the other families in conflict with that one will not participate.
>
> [Municipal government, QC—author translation]

Another respondent identified several difficulties that families face when one or both parents work and their children's school is located in a different community from where they live.

5.8 Multiple institutional interdependence

An in-depth reading of the transcripts from our interviews provides some more nuanced impressions regarding the institutional contexts in which each region operates. Although our four field site regions involve all institutional sector types in their regional development relationships, rural–urban related interactions are described as more formal in the Kootenays and more informal in the Kittiwake/Gander-New-Wes-Valley than in other case study regions. In the Kootenays, the governance system is led by municipal and regional district governments, together with regional organizations (as indicated in the quotes above), with strong market and bureaucratic-based relationships and capacity relative to other regions (Reimer et al., 2008). Kootenay interview participants emphasized the role of the private sector and government agencies in fostering and managing rural–urban relationships. The Columbia Basin Trust (CBT) also has a significant funding base and dominant influence. The CBT provides programs, initiatives, and financial investments within the Columbia Basin to help enhance the socioeconomic status of residents and communities within the region (see https://ourtrust.org/).

In the Kittiwake/Gander-New-Wes-Valley region in NL, municipal governments and others seem to work more through third-sector groups than in other regions. Participants described strong capacities in associative (based on organizing and participating around common interest) and communal (based on respect for family, ethnic, or other identity-based loyalties) relationships in the region, but a weaker presence of market and bureaucratic (rational/legal) relationships, although the latter are enhanced via associative relationships (Reimer et al., 2008). Regional development practitioners and community leaders tend to gain influence by using connections and networks to reach decision-makers (e.g., for lobbying)—possibly a reflection of relatively weak formal regional governance institutions. Meetings regarding regional concerns relevant to both urban and rural/small towns tend to focus on recreation, infrastructure, and economic development issues.

Eastern and Northern Ontario provide other examples of multi-institutional collaborations that contribute to the management of rural–urban interests. Eastern Ontario has very active CFDCs across the region, an active CFDC apex-organization, considerable rural–urban interactions via educational organizations (e.g., Trent and Queen's universities, Loyalist College, Sir Sandford Fleming College), the trans-regional presence of Parks Canada and the Trent-Severn Canal system, multiple mentions of local foods systems as rural–urban connectors, and the urban-based cottage associations as powerful rural forces (see Case Study 8.2).

Case Study 8.2 Rural–urban engagement in Northern Ontario

At the height of the forestry crisis in the mid-2000s, the Northwestern Ontario Municipal Association (NOMA) chose to target provincial decision-makers by getting support from mayors and Members of Provincial Parliament (MPPs) in nearly 200 southern Ontario communities. This included a letter campaign to cities like Mississauga, the City of Toronto, Oakville, and Burlington: cities that would be affected by a decline in the forest industry. The letter stated that: "The Forestry Industry in Ontario is in crisis and we need your help; otherwise we will all lose!"

This campaign was designed to put pressure on the provincial government by positioning the forest sector as an **Ontario** industry versus a **regional** one. As the NOMA president explained, "The more people—like southern mayors and MPPs from southern Ontario—who are aware of it and bring it to the attention to the premier and members of cabinet, the more likely we can get a hearing" (Fort Francis Times, 2005). One key informant spoke about this "tactic" to find "Southern allies" in detail:

> One of the tactics we used was we … went through the industry across Ontario that had a relationship to wood and we … found out the dollar value of their part of the pie. So companies in Mississauga, companies in Toronto, actually multiple companies, we were able to quantify how much value there was from a stick of wood in Northern Ontario that went through their place of business and then we communicated that to every Member of the Legislature riding by riding and as well municipalities. We

> got Hazel McCallion on side, we got the then Mayor of Oshawa on side, we got David Miller the Mayor on side, all of them helping to advocate for us because we recognized earlier on that even as Northern Ontario we're down to 10 seats okay? So we're still a small piece of the political pie at Queen's Park. So we needed some bigger clout. So we went and found some allies. And that's what we've had to do in Northwestern Ontario and in Northern Ontario for years. Find Southern allies. So we were able to quantify for all of those folks what the challenges in the forestry industry would mean to their community. [From Hall, 2012]

In response, the provincial government appointed the former president of Lakehead University in Northwestern Ontario as the Northwestern Ontario Economic Facilitator and introduced a number of initiatives for the forestry sector. The report recommended a development strategy with long-term structural impacts for Northern Ontario.

In 2012, the provincial government decision to divest the Ontario Northland Transportation Commission (ONTC) to manage provincial transportation also sparked a regionalism crisis in Northeastern Ontario. Municipal, business, and labour interests joined together under the moniker of the Northern Communities Working Group to demand a "New Deal for Ontario Northland" or nd4on. This group consisted of the mayors from North Bay, Timmins, Cochrane, Englehart, Iroquois Falls, Kapuskasing, and Black River-Matheson along with broader municipal support from the North Eastern Ontario Municipal Association (NEOMA) and the Federation of Northern Ontario Municipalities (FONOM). It also included the North Bay and District Chamber of Commerce and the Ontario Northland General Chairpersons Association, which represents the interests of unionized employees at Ontario Northland.

In addition to the traditional approach of using television and print media to bring attention to their cause, this group launched a social media strategy including a website and a web-based postcard campaign to garner support. They also partnered with the Northern Regional Publishing Group of Sun Media to include advertisements and window inserts in eleven newspapers across Northern Ontario (ND4ON, 2012a). The North Bay District Chamber of Commerce took out a full-page ad in the Ottawa Sun to "inform residents of Premier McGuinty's home town that selling off Ontario Northland, a public entity, isn't sitting well with businesses in the region" (ND4ON, 2012b: online). Like their counterparts in Northwestern Ontario, this Working Group transcended territorial boundaries to initiate support in more populous political ridings.

The Working Group also paid particular attention to the language surrounding the provincial decision to divest ONTC. The McGuinty Liberal government had referred to the transfer of government money to ONTC as a **subsidy**. However, similar transfers to government transportation agencies, like Metrolinx in the Greater Toronto Area, were identified as **investments**. This is reflective of the general view surrounding regional development: interventions in Northern Ontario are seen as **subsidies** or **handouts** while interventions in Southern Ontario are seen as **investments**.

These crises in Northern Ontario have, thus, generated a defense of traditional industries and rural economic development through rural–urban alliances. Their aim was to improve the provincial response to the forestry crisis and divestiture of regional assets by transcending regional boundaries and recasting the crisis as a provincial rather than a regional issue.

(Modified from: Hall, 2012)

Institutional relations affect other kinds of relationships. Financial exchanges, for example, are a critical component of relationships between local and senior governments.

> The other challenge of course is that everything we do we're dependent —so dependent—on government to help us out with the financial resources so and that's where we've been arguing and debating with government about a new financial arrangement, a fiscal framework to give towns more, a more sustainable source of income.
>
> [Municipal government, NL]

5.9 Environment

Table 8.7 identifies the specific topics mentioned in those interviews where environment-related comments with respect to rural–urban relations were made at least once. The most frequently referenced examples of environment-related relationships are associated with tourism and recreation (61 out of 102 interviews). Tourism is a large component of rural and regional economies. Visitors from urban centres are drawn by natural amenities based in rural areas such as "iceberg alley" in Kittiwake, NL, the Trent-Severn Canal system in Eastern Ontario, the rivers, lakes, and forests of Rimouski, or the

Table 8.7 Evidence of the environmental factor in rural–urban relationships from interview data

Topic	Kootenays BC (n=22)	Eastern ON (n=33)	Rimouski QC (n=19)	Kittiwake NL (n=28)	Total (n=102)
Recreation	M	M	M	H	M
Water	M	L	M	L	M
Waste	M	L	L	M	L
Land	M	L	M	L	L
Energy	M	L	L	L	L
Food	L	L	L	L	L
Air	L	N	N	L	L
Climate	L	N	N	N	L
Other/unspecified	M	L	L	L	L

N = no mention of the concept was made in the interviews being considered; L (Low) = 1% to 33% of the interviews indicated that the concept was present; M (Medium) = 34% to 67% of the interviews indicated the concept was present; H (High) = 68% to 100% of the interviews indicated the concept was present.

mountains and streams of the Kootenays. National parks and biosphere reserves also provide recreational opportunities to a wide range of communities across their regions, provinces, and even the country. The larger towns and cities in these regions offer a range of cultural and leisure activities for visitors and residents that supplement these natural assets. Further, communities often share the costs and use of recreational infrastructure, such as trail systems that cross through several communities or recreational complexes.

It was noted that people often treated natural environments as respites from their day-to-day activities. As such, many entities and organizations have capitalized on these locations for tourism strategies. Other aspects of the environment, such as extraction of natural resources and water quality, were also mentioned in the interviews, but were associated more often with other domains (e.g., commuting flows related to natural resources development or institutional relationships related to water management).

Watersheds and drinking water supplies provide a basis for regional efforts in all four provinces. The Columbia Basin Trust's Water Smart program in BC is one of several examples provided where water-related expertise is shared across a region—in this case to assist with water conservation efforts. In BC and NL, communities hire regional water operators and have established regional water systems (Breen & Minnes, 2014). A watershed committee in the lower St. Lawrence River, QC offers specific programs to reduce the ecological footprint of human activities and claims that they "have the highest standards in terms of environmental protection in the agricultural world" [Provincial government, QC—author translation]. In ON, shared concerns regarding the water condition of the Great Lakes, other lakes, wetlands, and groundwater bring players together but also create conflicts, as one interview participant explains:

> Rural municipalities and their constituents are very concerned with the additional costs of complying with the Ministry's standards under the Clean Water Act. The people of the town of Lindsay do not want to pay for the rural areas' well systems and the rural populations have resentment that they have to pay for Lindsay's sewage system.
>
> [Provincial government, ON]

Difficulties such as human resource challenges with regional water systems (e.g., training, technical knowledge), and the need for improved communication among communities when establishing policies to manage water systems were noted. Amalgamation was a controversial topic throughout the regions studied. Some interview participants referred to municipal and environmental protection amalgamation experiences as a barrier to regional efforts of all kinds while others suggested that after amalgamation, tackling issues with water and sewer seems much more feasible [Municipal government, NL].

In BC, interview participants cited cases of watershed plans created through partnerships among municipalities and the provincial government. However, formal control over the management of water resources by provinces has created difficulties. BC interview participants point to concerns about lack of consultation on water policy, while recognizing it is more effective to lobby the government as a group than just a single municipality. ON interview participants point to water quality disasters such as Walkerton, when provincial austerity measures contributed to seven deaths and 2,300 people falling ill in May 2000 (O'Connor, 2002).

Energy and climate change issues were less likely to be mentioned in our interviews (23 and once respectively out of 102 interviews), although they have the potential for considerable rural–urban collaboration. The Kootenays has taken a leadership role in this regard and was the only region where relationships related to climate change were discussed. Cranbrook, in the Kootenays, hosted a large bioenergy conference, for example, and communities within the region are working together to try and address climate change.

> Communities have minimal time to deal with climate change issues. As a result, some organizations have hired specifically climate change advisors that go into communities and provide consultations, building relationships, and hold symposiums … Climate change needs to be managed on a regional level. Many regions work together on housing issues—why not climate?
>
> [Regional organization, BC]

Food access and quality issues were mentioned in only 17 of the 102 interviews. However, they have stimulated many rural–urban initiatives—especially in Ontario and Québec. The Québec Rural Pact has supported local food and urban agriculture initiatives, and city–rural festivals (Jean & Reimer, 2015). Regional agriculture agencies also help to transfer knowledge, goods, and services across the agriculture sector. The Eastern Ontario region has also used local food movements as a vehicle for rural and urban integration. At the same time, regional interview participants called for more provincial policy and related supports to put local goods on the market. As one of our regional development interview participants said: "If I would write a policy for regions I would write it to help producers in regions put our products on the market. That is where I would put the money to help regions right now" [Regional organization, QC —author translation]. In BC, the Kootenay Lake Partnership works with government and non-government partners to promote agriculture and a number of agencies are working towards establishing an agricultural plan for the region (see www.kootenaylakepartnership.com/).

5.10 Identity

Although identity related to rural–urban relations was one of the least mentioned topics in our interviews (only 9% of the 5,431 mentions as discussed regarding Table 8.3), 92 of the 102 interview participants mentioned it at least once. A closer examination of the details of those mentions shows it is closely related to the more dominant themes of place attachment, types of employment, and culture (see Table 8.8).

Several interview participants indicated that they hold a strong sense of place-identity: using it as a justification for travelling for work instead of

Table 8.8 Evidence of the presence of rural–urban identity from the interview data

Identity Type	Kootenays BC (n=22)	Eastern ON (n=33)	Rimouski QC (n=19)	Kittiwake NL (n=28)	Total (n=102)
Place	H	M	H	H	H
Employment/tasks	M	M	M	M	M
Culture	H	M	L	M	M
Political	L	L	L	L	L
Family	N	L	L	L	L
Language	N	L	N	N	L
Ethnicity	L	L	N	N	L
Lifestyle	L	N	N	L	L
Religion	L	L	N	N	L
Other/unspecified	L	N	N	L	L

N = no mention of the concept was made in the interviews being considered; L (Low) = 1% to 33% of the interviews indicated that the concept was present; M (Medium) = 34% to 67% of the interviews indicated the concept was present; H (High) = 68% to 100% of the interviews indicated the concept was present.

relocating. It was also used as a rationale for moving back to a region after years of living elsewhere.

> A lot of people like it here. I lived away for many, many years and I was drawn back. I was looking for a job to come back, it wasn't the job per se, I wanted to come back to the area. There are many people like me, a lot of people just within this organization are people that went away and came because they want to live here.
>
> [Regional organization, BC]

> A lot of our people have had to be transient. They travel to Ontario, Alberta, and wherever all over as we say as Newfoundlanders say all over God's creation to work and to make a living and yet they keep coming back to retire and they come home they come on a regular basis to their community and so I think there's a good sense of a strong sense of community pride and attachment to their community and to their extended families.
>
> [Municipal government, NL]

> Yes, there has been a significant awareness of and attention to "amenity migration", as more and more ex-urban people come to rural and smaller communities for the amenities that they can access, on a daily basis. This is bringing highly qualified, highly skilled, often well connected, articulate, sometimes wealthy, and active new residents to particular parts of rural Ontario.
>
> [Regional organization, ON]

These place-based attachments and identities are closely tied to employment and, in many cases, attachments to natural surroundings and related recreational opportunities. Tensions and conflicts have arisen as urban residents move to rural areas, often facilitated by access to internet-based communications technologies. Such tensions are often due to different perspectives regarding rural assets and activities and the kinds of services that might be reasonably expected in rural areas with limited tax bases.

Historical rivalries linked to community identities and a "heritage of independence from urban dominance" [Regional organiztion ON] create further barriers to urban-rural collaboration.

> In my village certainly, the citizens have a very strong sense of belonging to the village. I can tell you that any merger with Rimouski will never pass there. It is like an old village because even though you have some new families that have been going there for many years, you still have four or five very strong families inside the village that transfer to themselves houses, land, etc.
>
> [Regional business, QC—author translation]

Each community has its own distinct culture.

[Municipal government, NL]

Interview participants suggest that a cultural change is needed to move from a dominant focus on competition to collaboration between rural and urban communities. Interview participants explained that language also influences rural–urban relations in Eastern Ontario:

> The language divide is very evident for this part of Ontario. People are separated in clusters by language and do not work together ... Sometimes festivals in neighbouring towns collaborate, but many times they do not because of the anglophone vs. francophone rivalry.

[Regional business organization, ON]

6 Reflections and future directions

These results are encouraging in a number of ways. First, because they support the value of the framework proposing the four spheres of rural–urban inter-dependence. The interview responses provide useful information regarding the nature of rural–urban interdependence and they suggest that the four domains reflect quite different mechanisms through which this interdependence operates. By viewing this interdependence with respect to (at least) four spheres, it avoids the tendency to limit the focus to trade and exchanges, identifies key gaps in our analysis, and encourages new directions to advance our understanding of rural–urban relationships. Trade and exchanges, for example, seem to be important bases for interdependence within the private sector, with economic objectives serving as points of reference. As we have seen in the interview responses, this interdependence can have positive or negative outcomes for rural places (e.g. new markets for rural products or replacement of local services for urban ones, and economic leakage). Institutional interdependence, on the other hand, pre-dominates in discussions about the public sector. These discussions are most often about the ways in which general policies and programs restrict local options for action either by misrepresenting the local conditions or by imposing require-ments on local action for which capacity is inadequate. Our research also pro-vides examples where more productive, collaborative relationships among institutions support rural and regional development (e.g., the Québec rural policy and the multiple collaborations in Eastern Ontario).

Second, our findings further demonstrate the ways in which these relation-ship types are interconnected (see also Chapter 7). The movement of people, for example, bridges several of the four domains—sometimes being treated as a labour exchange issue, sometimes as an issue of institutional servicing (e.g., for those employed in regional services), or as an interdependency driven by place identity. The importance of identity and the environment for rural–urban relationships receive relatively little attention, however, and the potential of demographic shifts for these domains are seldom discussed, although the implications are obvious (e.g., the loss of local knowledge and identity through death and out-migration of the elderly; conflicts in the perception of nature and environment through the in-migration of urbanites) (Shucksmith & Brown, 2016b, Part I: Demographic Change).

Third, the framework appears to be sensitive to important variations in these four domains of interdependence. Among this sample, the predominance of institutional types of interdependence is clear, with trade issues second, and environment and identity relatively low in expressed saliency. This pattern is replicated across the four provinces and case study regions in each that were considered—raising questions about the source of this consistency. Is it the result of the methodology employed (e.g., the sample selected, the questions, or coding procedure) or the nature of the regions and/or the rural–urban interdependencies themselves? The question warrants further investigation through the application and development of the framework in other regions to allow for further comparison.

Finally, the framework and analysis hint at some important policy implications. The relatively low saliency of environment and identity-based interdependence, for example, suggest that these are under-recognized as important bases of rural–urban interdependence or represented in antagonistic ways. The contrast of rural and urban places and people that are often found within the urban fringe, for example, often focus on the differences and conflicts over land use rather than the ways in which these challenges confirm their interdependence. It may also be that the impacts of urban policies on rural environments are indirect and therefore largely invisible. Urban-focused policies and plans for an oil-based economy, all-climate and all-season food production, and inadequately processed pollution, for example, all have important environmental impacts on rural (and ultimately urban) regions. Without recognition of this interdependence, we are unlikely to develop the social and economic mechanisms to control their negative impacts, build on common interests, and appropriately distribute the costs and benefits.

The recognition of rural–urban interdependence becomes even more problematic with respect to identity issues. Perhaps the most important example can be found in the case of Indigenous peoples, where our insensitivity to the relationship between identity, community, health, culture, and well-being (Chandler & Lalonde, 1998) has created significant concerns for all Canadians. In more general terms, rural and urban place-based identity is often considered an antiquated issue in the relatively high-mobility context of contemporary Canada, but its manifestation in social action, social cohesion, and product branding suggests it remains an important consideration for policy and analysis. As we explore new frameworks for rural and urban interdependence, finding the place of shared, complementary, and cohesive identities will become an important objective (Bhattacharyya et al., 2004; Douglas, 2010).

These results are suggestive but preliminary. Although we have data from a wide range of places and people, they reflect the usual challenges of sampling, analysis, and interpretation found in mixed methods approaches. First, these data provide information regarding the interview participants' perception of the issues discussed—which will bear an indirect relationship to more objective measures we might use. They remain, however, useful when considering the conceptual context for policy development and action related to the issues of rural–urban interdependence. Second, they reflect the particular interview participants selected for this sample. We contacted people who are knowledgeable about their regions and are key players in it as well as those who represent a wide range of regional stake-holders, but the representativeness can always be improved by including a broader spectrum of participants (see Chapter 7). Finally, methodological differences across the provinces and provincial research teams and/or the structured coding framework used as a basis for our quantitative analysis have undoubtedly influenced our results.

In general, this research reinforces the importance of rural–urban inter-dependence, highlights opportunities, challenges, and tensions experienced within rural–urban relationships, and adds to our understanding of these rela-tionships and interdependencies by providing a framework that is more expansive and structured than the usual research approaches addressing this topic. It suggests that looking beyond the exchanges and movement of goods and people will yield important insights on the complex ways in which the fates of rural and urban people are shared. It also directs policy-makers to pay attention to the ways in which policies and programs in one location have implications for those in others—while providing specific examples of the mechanisms and domains through which those interdependencies arise. The results reinforce the results of Chapter 7 and call for more collaborative and integrated policy and program development across rural and urban domains to recognize these interdependencies. We also hope it provides sufficient inspiration for researchers to investigate and elaborate these mechanisms so that our policies better match the conditions in which they are applied.

Note

1 This section is an excerpt from the project's Rural Urban primer, found on the project's website: http://cdnregdev.ruralresilience.ca.

References

Alasia, A. (2004). Mapping the socio-economic diversity of rural Canada. *Rural and Small Town Canada Analysis Bulletin, 5*(2), Retrieved from http://nre.concordia.ca/__ftp2004/StatCan_BULLETINS/vol5_e/21-006-XIE2003002.pdf.

Baxter, D., Berlin, R., & Ramlo, A. (2005). *Regions & Resources: The Foundations of Brit-ish Columbia's Economic Base.* The Urban Futures Institute report 62. Urban Futures

Institute: Vancouver, BC, Retrieved from www.donorth.co/appurtenancy/pdfs/bax ter_bc_economy.pdf Accessed 2018-12-23.

Beesley, K. B. (2010). *The Rural–urban Fringe in Canada: Conflict and Controversy*. Brandon, MB: Rural Development Institute, Brandon University.

Bellini, N., Danson, M., & Halkier, H. (2012). *Regional Development Agencies: The Next Generation? Networking, Knowledge and Regional Politics*. Routledge.

Bhattacharyya, D., Jayal, N. G., Pai, S., & Mohapatra, B. N. (eds) (2004). *Interrogating Social Capital: The Indian Experience*. New Delhi: Sage Publications.

Bosworth, G., & Venhorst, V. (2018). Economic linkages between urban and rural regions—What's in it for the rural? *Regional Studies, 52*(8), 1075–1085. doi:10.1080/00343404.2017.1339868.

Breen, S., & Minnes, S. (2014). *A regional approach to drinking water management: NL-BC comparative water systems study* [Unpublished report]. Corner Brook, NL: Grenfell Campus, Memorial University of Newfoundland.

Breen, S. (2016). From staples theory to new regionalism: Managing drinking water for regional resilience in rural British Columbia. PhD Dissertation. Simon Fraser University.

Bryant, C. (2003). *Where Are They Going? A Look at Canadian Rural in-Migration between 1991 and 1996*. Montréal: Concordia University.

Buttel, F. H., & Flinn, W. L. (1977). The interdependence of rural and urban environmental problems in advanced capitalist societies: Models of linkage. *Sociologia Ruralis, 17*(2), 255–281. doi:10.1111/j.1467-9523.1977.tb00870.x.

CANSIM. (2007). International merchandise trade by commodity, chained 2007 dollars. quarterly (12-10-0004-01).

Careless, J. M. S. (1979). Metropolis and region: The interplay between city and region in Canadian history before 1914. *Urban History Review, 3*(78), 99–118. doi:10.7202/1019408ar.

Castle, E. N., Wu, J., & Weber, B. A. (2011). Place orientation and rural–urban interdependence. *Applied Economic Perspectives and Policy, 33*(2), 179–204. doi:10.1093/aepp/ppr009.

Chandler, M. J., & Lalonde, C. (1998). Cultural continuity as a hedge against suicide in Canada's first nations. *Transcultural Psychiatry, 35*(2), 191–219. doi:10.1177/136346159803500202.

Christaller, W., & Baskin, C. W. (1966). *Central Places in Southern Germany*. Englewood Cliffs, NJ: Prentice-Hall.

Cohen, M. J., & Garrett, J. L. (2010). The food price crisis and urban food (in)security. *Environment and Urbanization, 22*(2), 467–482. doi:10.1177/0956247810380375.

Devine-Wright, P. (2009). Rethinking NIMBYism: The role of place attachment and place identity in explaining place-protective action. *Journal of Community & Applied Social Psychology, 19*(6), 426–441. doi: 10.1002/casp.1004.

Devlin, J., Vinodrai, T., Parker, P., Clarke, A., Scott, S., Bruce, B., Lipcsei, R., Deska, R., Collins, D., Bangura, T., & Sanders, K. (2015). Evaluating regional economic development initiatives: Policy backgrounder. *Report for the Ontario Ministry of Agriculture, Food and Rural Affairs*, 2.

Douglas, D. (Ed.). (2010). *Rural Planning and Development in Canada*, Toronto: Nelson Education Ltd.

Duranton, G. (2007). Urban evolutions: The fast, the slow, and the still. *The American Economic Review, 97*(1), 197–221.

External Advisory Committee on Cities and Communities. (2006). *From Restless Communities to Resilient Places: Building a Stronger Future for All Canadians.* Ottawa: Infrastructure Canada.

Fort Francis Times. (2005). Forestry stakeholders band together to lobby government. Wednesday, July 13, 2005. Retrieved from www.fftimes.com/news/district/forestry-stakeholders-band-together-lobby-government Accessed 2018-08-03.

Gallent, N. (2006). The rural–urban fringe: A new priority for planning policy? *Planning Practice and Research, 21*(3), 383–393. doi:10.1080/02697450601090872.

Halfacre, K. (2007). Trial by space for "radical rural": Introducing alternative localities, representations and lives. *Journal of Rural Studies, 23*(2), 125–141.

Hall, H. (2012). Stuck between a rock and a hard place: The politics of regional development initiatives in Northern Ontario. PhD Thesis, Dept. of Geography, Queen's University, Kingston, Ontario, 272–277. Retrieved from http://hdl.handle.net/1974/7391.

Halseth, G., Markey, S., Reimer, B., & Manson, D. (2010). Introduction: The next rural economies. In G. Halseth, S. Markey, & D. Bruce (Eds.), *The Next Rural Economies: Constructing Rural Place in a Global Economy* (1–16). Oxfordshire, UK: CABI International. Retrieved from http://billreimer.ca/research/files/HalsethChapter1Pre-publication02.pdf.]

Halseth, G., & Ryser, L. (2006). Trends in service delivery: Examples from rural and small town Canada, 1998 to 2005. *Journal of Rural and Community Development, 1*(2), 69–90.

Hamin, H. M., & Marcucci, D. J. (2008). Ad hoc rural regionalism. *Journal of Rural Studies, 24*, 467–477.

Hibbard, M., Senkyr, L., & Webb, M. (2015). Multifunctional rural regional development: Evidence from the John Day Watershed in Oregon. *Journal of Planning Education and Research, 35*(1), 51–62. doi:10.1177/0739456X14560572.

Innis, H. A. (1995). *Staples, Markets, and Cultural Change: Selected Essays of Harold A. Innis.* Montréal: McGill-Queens University Press.

Innis, H. A. (1999). *The Fur Trade in Canada: An Introduction to Canadian Economic History.* Toronto: University of Toronto Press. Originally published in 1933.

Irwin, E. G., Bell, K. P., Bockstael, N. E., Newburn, D. A., Partridge, M. D., & Wu, J. (2009). The economics of urban-rural space. *Annual Review of Resource Economics, 1*(1), 435–459. doi:10.1146/annurev.resource.050708.144253.

Jean, B. (1997). Territoires d'avenir. Pour une sociologie de la ruralité. Québec: Presses de l'Université du Québec.

Jean, B., & Reimer, B. (2015). Québec's approach to rural development. A successful rural policy under budgetary pressure. Presented at the Water-Food-Energy-Climate Nexus: An Emerging Challenge for Rural Policy, Memphis, TN: RPLC. Retrieved from www.rupri.org/wp-content/uploads/2015/06/JeanReimerOECDQuébecRuralPolicyMemphis2015v06.pptx.

Lichter, D. T., & Brown, D. L. (2011). Rural America in an urban society: Changing spatial and social boundaries. *Annual Review of Sociology, 37*, 565–592. doi:10.1146/annurev-soc-081309-150208.

Lösch, A. (1954). *The Economics of Location* (2nd Revised edition). New Haven, CT: Yale University Press.

Lucy, J. (2008). The city in the country: Growing alternative food networks in Metropolitan areas. *Journal of Rural Studies, 24*(3), 231–244. doi:10.1016/j.jrurstud.2007.10.002.

Markey, S., Breen, S.-P., Vodden, K., & Daniels, J. (2015). Evidence of place: Becoming a region in rural Canada. *International Journal of Urban and Regional Research, 39*(5), 874–891. https://doi.org/10.1111/1468-2427.12298.

Milbourne, P., & Kitchen, L. (2014). Rural mobilities: Connecting movement and fixity in rural places. *Journal of Rural Studies, 34,* 326–336. doi:10.1016/j.jrurstud.2014.01.004.

Murdoch, J., & Pratt, A. C. (1993). Rural studies: Modernism, postmodernism and the "post-rural". *Journal of Rural Studies, 9*(4), 411–427. doi:10.1016/0743-0167(93) 90053-M.

ND4ON. 2012a. Northern Communities Working Group and Northern Regional Publishing Group of Sun Media partner for ONTC. Press Release, May 15, 2012. Retrieved from http://web.archive.org/web/20130308042531/ http://nd4on.ca :80/ Accessed 2018-08-03.

ND4ON. 2012b. Letter to McGuinty: Meet with Us in the North. Press Release, June 1, 2012. Retrieved from http://web.archive.org/web/20130308042531/ http://nd4on.ca:80/ Accessed 2018-08-03.

O'Connor, H. D. R. (2002). *Report of the Walkerton Inquiry: The Events of May 2000 and Related Issues.* Toronto: The Queen's Printer for Ontario. Retrieved from www.attorneygeneral.jus.gov.on.ca/english/about/pubs/walkerton/.

OECD. (2010). Trends, perspectives and policies for rural Canada. In *OECD Rural Policy Reviews* (41–116). Organisation for Economic Co-operation and Development. Retrieved from www.oecd-ilibrary.org/content/chapter/9789264082151-4-en.

OECD. (2013). *Rural–Urban Partnerships.* Paris: Organisation for Economic Co-operation and Development. Retrieved from www.oecd-ilibrary.org/content/book/ 9789264204812-en.

Ontario Ministry of Municipal Affairs and Housing. (2002). *Oak Ridges Moraine Conservation Plan.* Toronto, ON: Ontario Ministry of Municipal Affairs and Housing (1–73). Retrieved from www.mah.gov.on.ca/Page1707.aspx.

Ortiz-Guerrero, C. (2013). The new regionalism. Policy implications for rural regions. *Cuadernos de Desarrollo Rural, 10*(70), 47–67.

Overbeek, G. (2009). Opportunities for rural–urban relationships to enhance the rural landscape. *Journal of Environmental Policy & Planning, 11*(1), 61–68. doi:10.1080/ 15239080902775058.

Ozor, N., Enete, A., & Amaechina, E. (2016). Drivers of rural–urban interdependence and their contributions to vulnerability in food systems in Nigeria—A framework. *Climate and Development, 8*(1), 83–94. doi:10.1080/17565529.2014.998605.

Partridge, M. D., Ali, K., & Olfert, M. R. (2010). Rural-to-urban commuting: Three degrees of integration. *Growth and Change, 41*(2), 303–335. doi:10.1111/j.1468-2257.2010.00528.x.

Partridge, M. D., & Clark, J. (2008). *Our Joint Future: Rural–urban Interdependence in 21st Century Ohio* (White Paper Prepared for the Brookings Institution). C. William Swank Chair in Rural—Urban Policy, Ohio State University: Brookings Institution. Retrieved from http://www.academia.edu/2895162/Our_Joint_Future_Rural-Urban_Interdependence_in_21_st_Century_Ohio

Reimer, B. (2005). A Rural Perspective on Linkages Among Communities. *Prepared for Building, Connecting and Sharing Knowledge: A Dialogue on Linkages Between Communities.* Ottawa: Infrastructure Canada.

Reimer, B. (2006). The rural context of community development in Canada. *Journal of Rural & Community Development, 1*(2), 155–175.

Reimer, B. (2013). Rural–urban interdependence: Understanding our common interests. In J. R. Parkins & M. Reed (Eds.), *Social Transformation in Rural Canada: Community, Cultures, and Collective Action* (91–109). Vancouver, BC: UBC Press.

Reimer, B., & Bollman, R. D. (2010). Understanding rural Canada: Implications for rural development policy and rural planning policy. In D. J. A. Douglas (Ed.), *Rural Planning and Development in Canada* (10–52). Toronto: Nelson Education. Retrieved from www.nelsonbrain.com/shop/content/douglas00812_0176500812_02.01_chapter01.pdf.

Reimer, B., & Brett, M. (2013). Scientific knowledge and rural policy: A long-distant relationship. *Sociologia Ruralis, 53*(3), 272–290. doi:10.1111/soru.12014.

Reimer, B. (2011). Social exclusion through lack of access to social support in rural areas. In G. Fréchet, D. Gauvreau, & J. Poirer (Eds.), *Social Statistics, Poverty and Social Exclusion: perspectives Québecoises, Canadiennes et internationals* (152–160). Montréal: Les Presses de l'Université de Montréal

Reimer, B., Lyons, T., Ferguson, N., & Polanco, G. (2008). Social capital as social relations: The contribution of normative structures. *The Sociological Review, 56*(2), 256–274. doi:10.1111/j.1467-954X.2008.00787.x.

Robinson, J., Berkhout, T., Burch, S., Davis, E. J., Dusyk, N., & Shaw, A. (2008). *Infrastructure & Communities: The Path to Sustainable Communities*. Victoria: Pacific Institute for Climate Solutions.

Savoie, D. (2003). *Reviewing Canada's Regional Development Efforts*. St. John's: Royal Commission on Renewing and Strengthening Our Place in Canada (147–183). Retrieved from http://www.gov.nl.ca/publicat/royalcomm/research/savoie.pdf.

Shucksmith, M., & Brown, D. L. (2016a). Framing rural studies in the global North. In *Routledge International Handbook of Rural Studies* (1–26). London: Routledge.

Shucksmith, M., & Brown, D. L. (2016b). *Routledge International Handbook of Rural Studies*. London: Routledge. Retrieved from www.oecd-ilibrary.org/content/book/9789264204812-en

Tacoli, C. (1998). Rural-Urban Interactions: a guide to the literature. *Environment and Urbanization, 10*(1), 147–166.

Tacoli, C. (Ed.). (2006). *The Earthscan Reader in Rural–Urban Linkages*. London and Sterling, VA: Routledge.

Tandoh-Offin, P. (2010). The evolving rural and urban interdependence: Opportunities and challenges for community economic development. *Journal of Geography and Regional Planning, 3*(12), 339–345.

Tsukamoto, T. (2011). Devolution, new regionalism and economic revitalization in Japan: Emerging urban political economy and politics of scale in Osaka-Kansai. *Cities, 28*(4), 281–289.

Wallis, A. (2002).The new regionalism: Inventing governance structures for the early twenty-first century. Retrieved from /www.miregions.org/Strengthening%20the%20Role/The%20New%20Regionalism%20Paper%20by%20Wallis%20at%20CUD.pdf

Wheeler, S. (2002). The new regionalism: Key characteristics of an emerging movement. *Journal of the American Planning Association, 68*(3), 267–278.

Wilson, J., & Anielski, M. (2005). *Ecological Footprints of Canadian Municipalities and Regions* (Report for the Federation of Canadian Municipalities) (1–61). Edmonton, AB: Anielski Management Inc. Retrieved from http://anielski.com/wp-content/documents/EFA%20Report%20FINAL%20Feb%202.pdf]

9 Learning, knowledge flows, and innovation in Canadian regions

Heather M. Hall and Kelly Vodden

1 Introduction

Over the last two decades, the topic of innovation has captured the attention of policy-makers and researchers across Canada and internationally (see for example, Expert Panel on Federal Support to Research and Development, 2012; Conference Board of Canada, 2016; European Commission, Joint Research Centre, 2016; Wolfe & Gertler, 2016). Innovation is seen as the catalyst for jobs and economic growth as well as the solution to pressing economic, social, and environmental challenges. As described in Chapter 3, one of the central themes of new regionalism is learning, knowledge flows, and innovation, which are seen as vital components in the "new" knowledge-intensive economy and are considered critical to fostering resilience and development in dynamic, changing regions (Ward & Jonas, 2004; Hettne, 2005; Rainnie & Grobbelaar, 2005; Carter & Vodden, 2017). This recognition has led to a focus on understanding how innovation can be advanced and supported. As a result, policy-makers have focused on creating the tools and programs needed to foster innovation and entrepreneurship, while researchers have concentrated on understanding the underlying dynamics that are occurring within regions (e.g., Wolfe & Gertler, 2016) and the "geography of innovation" (e.g., Shearmur et al., 2016).

This literature on innovation has offered a number of important insights. Perhaps one of the most significant arguments is the understanding that innovation is a social process (Wolfe, 2009), which includes interaction and learning between a wide variety of stakeholders, from individual entrepreneurs and firms to institutions like government agencies, universities, colleges, and innovation centres. Emerging from this literature was the "rediscovery of the region" (Storper, 1997) as the ideal setting for learning and innovation to occur. Put simply, place or geography matters. As Martin (2010, p. 20) argues "innovation is indeed often a highly localized phenomenon, dependent on place-specific factors and conditions" that include the "economic, social, cultural, and institutional conditions inherited from the previous industrial and technological histories of a locality".

The purpose of this chapter is to explore this theme of new regionalism in Canadian regions, particularly in rural regions, which have largely been ignored in the innovation literature. In doing so, we respond to Isaksen and Karlsen's (2016, p. 277) call for "more empirically based, theoretical reflections about the specifics of innovation activity in the peripheries" to ensure "industrial and innovation policies ... are based on sound knowledge of such regions and do not routinely build on theories that reflect experiences from well-known, dynamic core regions". The remainder of this chapter is divided into four major sections. In the first section, we describe the key arguments emerging from the literature on innovation, learning, and regional development. We also apply a rural lens to capture insights for rural regions. In the next section, we outline policy and academic thinking on innovation and regional development in Canada. This is followed by a discussion of innovation in Canadian regions, using empirical evidence from our case study regions in British Columbia, Ontario, Québec, and Newfoundland and Labrador. Finally, we reflect on a number of important lessons that emerge regarding learning, knowledge flows, and innovation, and provide areas for future policy and research discussions. Further reflections on our findings related to learning and knowledge flows within Canadian regional development networks are offered in Chapter 10.

2 Innovation, learning, and regional development

One of the most cited definitions of innovation is from the Oslo Manual, which defines innovation as "the implementation of a new or significantly improved product (good or service), or process, a new marketing method, or a new organizational method in business practices, workplace organization or external relations" (OECD, 2005, p. 46). A more recent definition acknowledges that innovation "goes far beyond R&D" and "beyond the confines of research labs to users, suppliers and consumers everywhere – in government, business and non-profit organizations ..." (OECD, 2015, para 1). This more holistic perspective on innovation can include new or improved ways of organizing and/or sharing ideas within or between organizations as well as new or improved strategies or approaches to address policy challenges or build on opportunities (Markey et al., 2012).

While much of the new regionalism literature has focused on the economic dimensions of innovation, others have explored the important role of learning and innovation in social, environmental, and policy outcomes (Peterson et al., 2007; Shaw et al., 2012; Neumeier, 2012). For example, in discussing the role of regional bodies and multi-level collaborative governance in natural resource management in Australia, Lockwood et al. (2009) emphasize the importance and potential of regional approaches in community learning and incorporating new knowledge and learning into decision-making and adaptation to both threats and opportunities. Just as rapid changes are occurring within the "new economy" (e.g., Storper, 1997), social–ecological changes within a region often also require an ability to learn, innovate, and adapt (Vodden et al., 2013).

Over the last several decades, a number of territorial innovation models have emerged from the new regionalism literature (Hall & Walsh, 2013). These include industrial districts (Becattini, 1990), clusters (Porter, 1990), innovative milieus (see Proulx, 1992; Coffey & Bailly, 1996), learning regions (Florida, 1995; Morgan, 1997), triple helix/quadruple helix (Leydesdorff, 2012), and regional innovation systems (Cooke, 1992; Cooke & Morgan, 1998). There are several common links between these models. First is the importance of the "region" (Shearmur et al., 2016). For example, Storper (1997) argued that the region is the "nexus of untraded interdependencies" that "take the form of conventions, informal rules and habits that coordinate economic actors under conditions of uncertainty" and constitute region-specific assets that help firms and institutions develop a capacity for learning and adaptation, and to grow and generate wealth (Amin, 1999; MacKinnon et al., 2002; Cumbers et al., 2003).

Cooke and Morgan (1998, Morgan, 1997) emphasize the importance of knowledge and learning, arguing that "knowledge is the most strategic resource and learning the most important process" (Cooke & Morgan, 1998, p. 17). But how can this resource be utilized in the interest of regional development? Innovation research suggests that a set of linked actors, firms, and institutions within the region regularly communicating and interacting is both a result of and a precondition for, learning and innovation (Malmberg & Maskell, 1997; Vodden et al., 2013). Tacit knowledge or the knowledge that typically derives from "being there" (Gertler, 1995) has become particularly important versus codified knowledge that can easily be transferred (Polanyi, 1962; Storper, 1995; MacKinnon et al., 2002). This tacit knowledge is sticky or place-based, providing significant advantages for some regions. Nauwelaers (2011) explains that firms and organizations need to be constantly learning from within and open to outside sources of knowledge to prevent lock-in. In this sense, Bathelt et al. (2004) suggest innovation is fostered by "local buzz and global pipelines". As Asheim et al. (2007) explain, buzz includes "rumours, impressions, recommendations, trade folklore, and strategic information" (p. 660), while global pipelines take into account information and knowledge flows across different regions (Bathelt et al., 2004; Wolfe & Gertler, 2004). Bristow (2010) suggests that resilient regions rely on strong inter and intra-regional networks for information sharing and learning when dealing with economic or environmental shocks, while Lockwood et al. (2009) call for "establishing all governance bodies as learning organisations" (p. 184).

The literature on territorial innovation also emphasizes the importance of institutions, including both "hard" institutions and "soft institutions" (i.e., social and cultural factors) that play a role in regional development (Amin & Thrift, 1994, 1995; Harrison, 2006). They suggest four main characteristics of "institutional thickness": 1) a strong institutional presence (institutional arrangements between an array of actors); 2) a high level of interaction between these institutions to encourage networking, cooperation, and exchanges; 3) the presence of well-defined structures of coalition building and collective representation; and 4) inclusivity and collective mobilization, or in essence a common sense of purpose on a widely held agenda or regional development project (Amin & Thrift, 1994, p. 14; see also Martin, 2000; Goodwin et al., 2002).

Finally, one of the most important arguments emerging from this literature is the understanding that innovation is a social process (Wolfe, 2009). This perspective questions the notion of the lone inventor and the linear process of innovation (Amara et al., 2003; Sternberg, 2009; Johnson, 2011; Nauwelaers, 2011). Innovation is viewed as a messy process that often involves interaction between the various economic actors or innovation stakeholders (e.g., firms, customers, postsecondary institutions, government agencies). This interaction can lead to collective learning, to the creation and use of new knowledge, and, ultimately, innovation (Vodden et al., 2013).

These insights have been translated into a number of approaches for policy and practice (OECD, 2011; Cooke, 2013; Bradford & Bramwell, 2016; Shearmur et al., 2016; Uyarra & Flanagan, 2016). General approaches are place-neutral or "spatially blind", meaning they ignore geographic differences. In contrast, place-based approaches recognize the importance of geographical context for innovation and economic development. The current EU focus on smart specialization (Foray, 2015; European Commission, 2016), which is creating regionally specific strategies, is an example of this approach. Innovation policies can also be systems based, focused on enhancing the functioning of the innovation system through initiatives like business networks, associations, or networking events, and facilitating external linkages. Finally, they can be actor–based, focusing on support for entrepreneurs through incubators and/or skills training, for example (policy categories adapted from Isaksen et al., 2016, 2017).

Before turning to a discussion of what these arguments and insights mean for rural economies, it is worth noting a number of criticisms associated with this theme of new regionalism. In particular, there are a number of issues with how these ideas gets translated into policy. For example, these ideas are often reduced to a simple formula where economic development and innovation will result from having the right institutions (or mix of institutions) in place. As Doloreux and Melançon (2008) show in their study of rural Québec, simply investing in better knowledge infrastructure will not automatically translate into innovation. Similarly, this literature often downplays the role of external forces shaping regional development, including macroeconomic trends and state policies (Coe et al., 2004; Uyarra, 2007; Moulaert & Mehmood, 2010). It also places much of the burden of regional development on regional actors to "pull themselves up by their bootstraps" and often absolves state actors of their responsibility to act (Keating, 1997; Jones, 2004; Hudson, 2005; Morgan, 2006; Pike & Tomaney, 2009). In reality, many of the policy levers that are important to regional development outcomes are beyond the control of regional actors and rest with provincial/national decision-makers or other stakeholders (Jones, 2001; Hudson, 2006, 2007; Uyarra, 2007; Vodden et al., 2013).

2.1 *Applying a rural lens to innovation & regional development*

One of the biggest challenges associated with innovation studies and policy from a rural development perspective is the extensive focus on large-city regions as the obvious spaces where innovation thrives, which as Polèse et al. (2002) argue, "can blind us to the innovations occurring outside these regions" (p. 133). Rural and peripheral regions are not typically cited in case studies on innovation, with innovations that are occurring tending to be overlooked. Perhaps more concerning, these regions are often discounted as economic failures and "inauspicious" spaces for innovation (Johnstone & Haddow, 2003; Virkkala, 2007; Hall & Donald, 2009). Traditional measures of innovation also tend to be inappropriate for evaluating rural regions. For example, patents numbers (and other indicators based on a "new to world" innovation concept) ignore new to region or new to firm innovations and are, therefore, insufficient when used alone (Hall & Walsh, 2013; Vodden et al., 2013). In addition, data are often not available at smaller and disaggregated levels of geography (Slaper et al., 2011; Hall & Walsh, 2013).

Fortunately, there is a small but growing body of literature focused on understanding innovation in rural and peripheral regions. For example, Isaksen and Karlsen (2010) explain how rural innovation is typically focused on "doing-using-interacting" (DUI) versus "science, technology, innovation" (STI). In the DUI model, innovation is often more incremental in nature and might occur through in-house problem-solving by an individual or a group of workers or from addressing, for example, specific supplier, customer, or client group needs. This stands in contrast to STI or more radical innovation that often occurs within large corporate R&D departments, research intensive small- and medium-sized enterprises, and postsecondary institutions or other research centres (Isaksen & Karlsen, 2010).

With regards to institutional challenges, Tödtling and Trippl (2005) suggest three particular issues: 1) thinness or low levels of clustering and a weak prevalence of institutions; 2) lock-in; and 3) fragmentation or a lack of interaction between institutional stakeholders. Rural regions can be impacted by any of these scenarios, but they are particularly susceptible to institutional thinness, while older industrial regions are typically more prone to lock-in. Related to this, traditional theories of innovation and economic development have emphasized the importance of agglomeration economies or the benefits of geographic proximity. This is a significant challenge in rural regions. However, recent research suggests networks in rural regions can act as a "surrogate for agglomeration" and support the transfer of entrepreneurial knowledge (Copus et al., 2011; Hall et al., 2014). These networks can be enhanced, for example, by building on existing external trade and transportation routes to create expanded connections and opportunities (Carter & Vodden, 2017).

3 Innovation and regional development in Canada

Over the last decade, a significant amount of media, policy, and research attention has been paid to Canada's so-called "innovation problem". Recent media headlines include "STEM skills alone won't solve Canada's Innovation Problem" (Kominko, 2017), and "how to fix Canada's innovation conundrum" (Sulzenko, 2016). Likewise, a 2009 report by the Council of Canadian Academies focused on "why Canada falls short" with regards to innovation and business strategy, while the Conference Board of Canada asked, "who dimmed the lights?" on Canada's declining global competitiveness rankings (Conference Board of Canada, 2012). A number of factors have been cited to explain Canada's innovation challenge, including a commercialization gap, limited spending on business research and development, a high degree of risk aversion, inadequate government procurement of advanced research, limited collaborative relationships between industry and universities, and a lack of alignment between provincial and federal economic development and innovation policies (Council of Canadian Academies, 2009; Bibbee, 2012; Conference Board of Canada, 2012, 2013; Expert Panel on Federal Support to Research and Development, 2012).

Innovation policy in Canada has largely been synonymous with science and technology policy (for an overview see Doern et al., 2016). However, Hawkins (2012, p. 4) warns that this approach is problematic because "very few of Canada's innovators are actually technology producers". Instead, Canada's most economically significant industries are tied to the natural resources and services sectors. Perhaps more importantly, Hawkins (2012) argues that "our resource industries are also among our most economically significant knowledge industries" (p. 4). Yet as Hall and Donald (2009) argue, the resource sectors are often ignored and perceived as "dirty, dangerous, and dying" (p. 20). Hawkins further argues that policy-makers need to understand innovation from a uniquely Canadian perspective that recognizes our unique industrial history and composition, and that our primary concern should be adding "high levels of value in all of our key positional industries" (Hawkins, 2012, p. 19). This argument is based on the observation that when we export unprocessed or semi-processed products, we also export most of the opportunities to innovate and create sustainable employment and business spin-offs.

Ironically, Canada has never had a strong regional innovation policy focus despite its long history of regional development policies and programs (see Chapter 2). Regional development institutions, like the Atlantic Canada Opportunities Agency (ACOA), have focused on supporting innovation and entrepreneurship through funding for research and development as well as business growth and expansion. However, there has never been a coherent regional innovation strategy that understands regional competitive advantages and focuses on investing in priorities to advance them. Instead, programs often reflect political priorities rather than regional realities (Hall, 2012, 2017).

Likewise, provincial governments have pursued various programs in economic development and innovation across the country, as illustrated by the case studies and results discussed later in this chapter. This changing programming landscape has led to various, often shifting programs and policies in support of learning and innovation. For example, in 2011 the BC Social Innovation Council was formed to provide recommendations to enhance social innovation in the province. In addition, the BC Innovation Council was established as a provincial crown agency to lead efforts to advance innovation and commercialization in BC, which includes a number of regional innovation councils (e.g., KAST (Kootenay Association for Science & Technology)) across the province (White et al., 2014b). In Ontario, the provincial government has a fairly extensive collection of programs and policies to support innovation and entrepreneurship (e.g., Ontario Centres of Excellence (OCE), the Regional Innovation Centres (RICs), and the Ontario Network of Entrepreneurs (ONE)). The RICs, for example, are located throughout the province and provide business advisory services to entrepreneurs across Ontario, including business incubation services. However, these programs are more likely to be accessed by entrepreneurs within the urban centres where the RICs are located and their programs often do not reflect the needs or realities of rural communities. Many provincial regional programs also lack uniformity in terms of their capacity, which creates an uneven programming landscape (see Vinodrai & Hall, 2018).

While much of the academic attention on innovation in Canada has focused on cities (Wolfe, 2009; Wolfe & Gertler, 2016), there is a small body of literature focused on understanding innovation in rural and northern regions across the country. For example, Doloreux and others have done extensive work in rural Québec on regional innovation systems in La Pocatière, within the Bas-Saint-Laurent administrative and economic region, and on the marine science and technology industry in the coastal region of Québec (Doloreux & Shearmur, 2006; Doloreux et al., 2007, 2016; Doloreux & Dionne, 2008; Doloreux & Melançon, 2009; Doloreux & Shearmur, 2009; Melançon & Doloreux, 2013). This work emphasizes the important role of public institutions as well as other innovation support organizations in encouraging firm-level innovation in rural communities. These institutions also help build and improve the regional knowledge infrastructure by being a conduit between research and industry.

Similarly, Hall and colleagues have examined firm-level innovation and innovation support across Northern Ontario. For example, Hall and Donald (2009) highlight a number of innovative social enterprises and firms in mining, healthcare, and forestry. Their work also underscores the importance of government support as a "lifeline" for rural and northern entrepreneurs who often face spatial biases when trying to secure financing from banks and/or other investors. However, they also note a number of "peripheral realities" that impact entrepreneurship, economic development, and innovation. These include remoteness, infrastructure constraints, the cost of transportation, and youth out-migration. More recently, Hall (2017) discusses the mining innovation system in Greater Sudbury. Despite its success, she cautions that much of the innovation is focused on extraction versus value-added development. In addition, very little of the resource wealth that is extracted is reinvested back into the region in a transparent way to advance economic development, fueling what Markey et al. (2012) describe as the "resource-bank approach to development". We describe our own findings related to learning, knowledge flows, and innovation within Canadian, primarily rural, settings further below.

4 Examining learning and innovation in Canadian regional development

4.1 Our approach

In our study, we were interested in identifying examples of innovation and openness to creativity, as well as the supports available for learning and innovation. We also examined the challenges to learning and innovation experienced by various regional development actors, including business, government, and non-government representatives. This inquiry sought to find evidence of challenges noted in previous studies while also remaining open to other possible challenges that may be unique to the Canadian and more specific case study contexts.

While taking into account the challenges associated with defining and assessing innovation, particularly in rural regions, this project considered traditional measurements of innovation (e.g., patents, applications for funding) and innovation capacity (e.g., urban proximity and productivity levels) as well as the perspectives of regional development actors on innovation and learning in their communities and regions, to provide a more complete story of innovation in each case (see also Vodden et al., 2013). Indicators explored within our interviews are illustrated in Table 9.1 and Table 9.2 to 9.4 below. Additional indicators related to knowledge sharing and learning are discussed in Chapter 10. We gathered data from secondary sources such as OECD patent databases, Statistics Canada, provincial road-distance data, and reports on funding programs and applications, as well as through semi-structured interviews, as described in Chapter 4.

For an overview of the indicator data gathered for each case study region see http://cdnregdev.ruralresilience.ca.

Two related research and knowledge mobilization efforts provided additional insights. First, the Canadian Regional Development (CRD) NL research team undertook the *Advancing Innovation in Newfoundland and Labrador* project in 2013–14 in collaboration with the Leslie Harris Centre of Regional Policy and Development and the Navigate Entrepreneurship Centre (Grenfell Campus) at Memorial University. The project sought to synthesize, share, and ground-truth knowledge related to innovation, particularly at the firm level, and ways it can be fostered with key innovation stakeholders to support economic development. Project deliverables included: a knowledge synthesis report, a series of workshops, and workshop reports and firm-level innovation case studies from NL (see Case Study 9.1). A final report summarized the key findings and provided recommendations for policy and practice (Hall et al., 2014). A project website (http://innovationnl.ca) was established to support knowledge exchange and host these and other innovation-related research results in the province.

In April 2017, CRD team members and Kootenays regional partner Selkirk College organized a session titled "Place, technology, and the future of rural

Table 9.1 A description of innovation indicators

Indicators	Justification/Sources
Innovation Capacity Indicators	
Availability of postsecondary institutions	Increased knowledge and experience generated in postsecondary institutions (The Center for Innovation Studies, 2005; Rose et al., 2009; Slaper et al., 2011).
Levels of postsecondary education	Education influences the quality of innovation within a given region (The Center for Innovation Studies, 2005; Rose et al., 2009; Slaper et al., 2011).
Training	The provision of training programs for employees may be correlated to an organization's innovation; quantity and quality of training opportunities should also be considered (OECD, 2005; The Center of Innovation Studies, 2005; Rose et al., 2009).
Access to information technology and communications infrastructure	Martinus (2012) states that maintenance of various forms of infrastructure is fundamental to networking, producing, and innovating. Providing technological support systems, including information technology and communications infrastructure, will allow actors to function more efficiently.
Urban proximity	Slaper et al. (2011) state that the distance an actor is from an urban area will determine ability to innovate.
Access to financing for innovation initiatives	The availability of programs and the ability of firms to apply for such programs influences support for innovative endeavors (The Advisory Committee on Measuring Innovation in the 21st Century, 2008).
Productivity; regional personal income per capita	Innovation will likely increase with productivity and subsequently induce increased wealth (The Center of Innovation Studies, 2005; Advisory Committee on Measuring Innovation in the 21st Century, 2008; Andrew et al., 2009; Rose et al., 2009).
Innovation Indicators	
Applications for innovation support	The Advisory Committee on Measuring Innovation in the 21st Century (2008) asserts that the number of applications directed towards funding agencies is illustrative of innovation efforts.
Technology use	The level and use of technology can indicate the level of innovation in an area (OECD, 2005; OECD, 2010; Davies, 2010; Slaper et al., 2011).
Patents	Introducing new products and services into a region complies with traditional notions of innovation and patents provide a related indicator (The Center for Innovation Studies, 2005; Rose et al., 2009; Davies, 2010; Slaper et al., 2011).

Source: Vodden et al. (2013)

Table 9.2 Evidence of the presence of innovation and openness to creativity from interview data

Example type	BC (n=22)	ON (n=33)	QC (n=19)	NL (n=28)[2]	Total (n=102)
New programs, strategies, plans, products or services	H	M	H	L	M
Culture/openness to change	M	M	M	M	M
Self-employment	L	N	N	L	L
Social enterprise	L	N	N	L	L

N = no mention of the concept was made in the interviews being considered; L (Low) = 1% to 33% of the interviews indicated that the concept was present; M (Medium) = 34% to 67% of the interviews indicated the concept was present; H (High) = 68% to 100% of the interviews indicated the concept was present.

communities" at the annual convention of the Association of Kootenay Boundary Municipalities. Participants discussed results of the CRD project as well as other research and experiences, including recent developments since fieldwork completion, related to the role of technologies in creating smarter, leaner communities and more efficient and effective local governments in rural regions. Technology was discussed by many interview participants in the Kootenays case study region as both an example and a form of support for innovation – including the adoption of technology to support and advance economic development, as well as attract and retain a technology-focused workforce (see Case Study 9.3).

In this chapter, we will focus particularly on examples of innovation, the innovation supports available, and the challenges to innovation in our study regions.[1] Findings related to resources for learning (see Table 9.3) as well as additional indicators of reflection, knowledge sharing, and challenges to knowledge sharing and learning are discussed further in Chapter 10. We explore these topics in the concluding chapter to this book as we reflect upon one of the core questions of this research – how knowledge and lessons learned about regional development are, and might be more effectively, shared within and across Canadian regions.

4.2 Examples of innovation

Research participants in all regions provided local examples of innovation and openness to creativity, with over half sharing examples of new programs, strategies, plans, programs and/or services (see Table 9.2). There was considerable regional variation, however, with BC and QC respondents providing high (H) levels and NL providing relatively few examples (L). Since many key informants for this project were representatives from support institutions like government agencies or NGOs, examples often focused on new or improved plans, programs, and services within their organizations. For example, in the Kootenays, key informants discussed the development of the Beetle Action Committees to deal with the outbreak of Mountain Pine Beetles in the region (see White et al., 2014b). The Town of St. Anthony on the Northern Peninsula, NL invested in a new energy efficient arena, including a system to use waste energy generated from maintaining the ice to heat water for showers and other parts of the building (White et al., 2014a).[2] The provincial department responsible for innovation in NL discussed changes in delivery of their programs to make them more accessible to rural areas. In Ontario, key informants discussed new sustainability plans along with other programs to revitalize commercial space and promote entrepreneurship (see White et al., 2014c).

For example, St. Anthony Basin Resources Incorporated (SABRI) is a social enterprise on the Northern Peninsula NL, which started a commercial mussel operation and cold storage facility where profits are reinvested back into the community (see Case Study 9.1). Another example is the Shorefast Foundation on Fogo Island in the Kittiwake region. This social enterprise was established in 2006 by Zita Cobb, a former resident of the island who went away and became a finance executive in a number of tech industries. To confront youth out-migration and limited employment opportunities on the island, Cobb invested over $10 million, combined with $5 million each from federal and provincial governments, to create an international destination for the arts and tourism (McKeough, 2010). As part of this effort, the luxurious Fogo Island Inn was constructed, complete with blankets and furniture made locally and available for purchase. Local textile workers were paired with international designers to produce innovative designs and products (Fogo Island Shop, 2017). Perhaps more importantly, locals are part of the process − bringing people on tours and educating them about the history of the island (Rajasekaran, 2015). A micro-lending program has been created for local entrepreneurs (Shorefast, 2017). In addition to the efforts of the Shorefast Foundation, a number of small-scale manufacturing firms in the Kittiwake region are investing in new technologies to advance their businesses and support their local communities (see Hall & White, 2013a; White & Hall, 2013a, 2013b, 2013c).

Case Study 9.1 St. Anthony Basin Resources Incorporated (SABRI), Northern Peninsula, Newfoundland and Labrador

St. Anthony Basin Resources Incorporated (SABRI) is located in St. Anthony on the Great Northern Peninsula (NL). This not-for-profit social enterprise was created in 1997 with a mission to administer a 3000-metric tonne allocation of Northern Shrimp on behalf of the communities from Big Brook to Goose Cove, in a manner resulting in expansion of the region's economic base and improved employment opportunities in harmony with a rural setting and lifestyle.

(SABRI, 2017, para 1)

Their management board consists of 15 volunteers including five fisherpersons, four fish plant employees, four community representatives, and two representatives from regional development committees.

Since 1997, SABRI has led several notable initiatives in the region including an oral history project, a mussel-farming project, and a cold storage facility. The oral history initiative started in 2008 and was funded through a partnership with Service Canada. A researcher was hired to conduct research and document stories with cultural and historical significance to the region. This included stories about life in the region, traditional foods/remedies, labour practices, and stories specific to the individual communities. These stories and photos are available on the SABRI website, and they provide a rich history of the region that is accessible to the public with the goal of increasing interest and ultimately tourism in the region, while helping to preserve the region's cultural heritage.

Another SABRI-led initiative is a mussel-farming project, which began in 2000. After conducting research into the mussel-farming industry, SABRI acquired their first license in 2002 and two additional licenses in 2003. The farm provides employment for three seasonal workers and an aquaculture specialist. It also provides a unique setting for training and education. For example, since 2008 SABRI has employed students from the College of the North Atlantic (CNA), providing invaluable experience and engaging youth in a regional industry. The project sought to support primary and secondary processing of mussels in the region.

A third initiative includes the construction of a cold-storage facility in the region. This $7.5 million project was led and financed through SABRI using a $3 million interest-free loan from ACOA. The construction phase provided employment for 25 to 30 people while operating the facility employs approximately 30 people. The cold-storage facility is the first of its kind in the region and has become a major destination for many vessels making trans-Atlantic voyages.

SABRI also has an annual budget for community development. These funds have been used to upgrade trails, develop trail guides, rest stops, and picnic areas, develop cruise docking facilities in L'Anse aux Meadows, install a Leif Erikson Statue in L'Anse aux Meadows, and invest in broadband infrastructure in St. Carols, Great Brehat, and St. Anthony Bight (SABRI, 2017).

Since their foundation, SABRI has partnered with a number of provincial and federal agencies. For example, ACOA and the Department of Innovation, Business, and Rural Development (IBRD) have partnered with SABRI on tourism initiatives that resulted in the expansion of infrastructure, marketing endeavors, and potential tourism destinations. As discussed above, SABRI actively partners with the provincial Department of Fisheries and Aquaculture and the federal Department of Fisheries and Oceans on marine-based initiatives. Another example is Service Canada, which has contributed to SABRI's projects by assisting in funding new employees and student experience programs. The SABRI experience illustrates that a key component of regional innovation is partnerships between government and firms/social enterprises. Government partners provide valuable financial resources but also knowledge from working on similar projects in other regions. A critical component in SABRI's innovative capacity is their emphasis on learning, including gaining insights on initiatives happening elsewhere. SABRI staff members attend workshops and seminars to enhance their skill-sets and introduce new knowledge into their operations. They also reflect on previous initiatives to self-evaluate their performance and improve their operations in the future.

Adapted from White and Hall (2013d)

4.3 Support for learning and innovation

All regions had access to programs and/or initiatives offered by various levels of government, NGOs, and/or postsecondary institutions to support innovation, learning, and economic development, although interview results suggest room for enhancement (see Table 9.3). The most commonly discussed type of support was cross-sector knowledge partnerships. With regard to knowledge infrastructure, three of the regions (Kittiwake, Northern Peninsula, and the Kootenays) are institutionally thin with access to one or two community college campuses and limited training facilities. Nevertheless, interview participants in all regions (albeit most prevalent in Eastern Ontario) recounted examples of knowledge partnerships that had mobilized available, and often external, resources to foster learning and/or innovation through collaborations between industry, NGO, government, and/or postsecondary sectors.

Table 9.3 Evidence of the presence of innovation supports from the interview data

Support type	BC (n=22)	ON (n=33)	QC (n=19)	NL (n=28)	Total (n=102)
Sources of support					
Public sector	L	L	N	L	L
NGO	N	N	N	L	L
Private sector	N	L	N	L	L
Knowledge infrastructure					
New technologies	M	L	L	L	L
Postsecondary institutions	L	M	L	L	L
Technology centres	N	L	N	N	L
Knowledge partners					
(Inter)governmental knowledge partners	M	L	L	L	L
NGO knowledge partners	L	L	N	M	L
Business knowledge partners	L	N	L	N	L
Cross-sector knowledge partners	M	H	L	M	M
Resources for learning					
Human resources	M	L	M	L	L
Support for individual learning	M	L	L	L	L
Entrepreneurship training	N	L	–	M	L
Support – other					
Support for local actors	M	M	M	M	M
Support for high risk financing	L	L	M	L	L

N = no mention of the concept was made in the interviews being considered; L (Low) = 1% to 33% of the interviews indicated that the concept was present; M (Medium) = 34% to 67% of the interviews indicated the concept was present; H (High) = 68% to 100% of the interviews indicated the concept was present.

Colleges play a vital role in training and education and are increasingly contributing to R&D efforts in the case study regions. In addition, one key informant noted in the Kootenays that the "… college is a big generator of the economy" [Municipal government, BC]. In Eastern Ontario, a number of key informants discussed the importance of having access to the five universities and four colleges in the region. Several organizations had worked directly with one or more postsecondary institutions and engaged with them for research and insights on policies and/or programs. Two particular examples cited were the Monieson Centre at Queen's University, which previously had a strong rural business focus, and Trent University's DNA regional innovation cluster, a strategic alliance of local public and private sector partners seeking to advance research and applications in DNA, forensic, and life sciences (Trent University, 2004). The Innovation Cluster – Peterborough and the Kawarthas – has recently worked closely with Trent University to launch the Trent Makerspace in 2017, a clean-tech space for innovation research and development (Peterborough Examiner, 2017).

Related to this, we were interested in whom key informants collaborated with and the nature of these collaborations in learning and innovation efforts (e.g., was knowledge generation and/or transfer a significant reason for collaboration). In addition to postsecondary institutions, some key informants discussed intergovernmental partnerships between municipalities or various levels of government on common initiatives (e.g., the Community Future (CF) program). One unique initiative in the Kittiwake region of NL is the Central Continuous Improvement Network led by the Association of Canadian Manufacturers and Exporters (CME). Through this network, CME facilitates networking between a group of manufacturing companies in the region (e.g., company tours) and provides one-on-one training (e.g., LEAN manufacturing). CME also shares insights on funding opportunities and suggests connections to researchers who can provide assistance with R&D challenges. Business owners/managers also share lessons and discuss common constraints.

In British Columbia, there are a number of support institutions and programs including the Kootenay Rockies Innovation Council (KRIC) and the Kootenay Association for Science and Technology (KAST) (see Case Study 9.2), as well as the Columbia Basin Trust (CBT). The CBT was created in 1995 after citizens lobbied the provincial government for a fair share of the benefits related to the Canada-US Columbia River Treaty. To improve the social, economic, and environmental well-being of the region, the CBT offers funding in a number of areas including climate change, youth, housing, workforce development, and community development (Columbia Basin Trust, 2017). One example of a CBT funded initiative is the Rural Development Institute (RDI) at Selkirk College, profiled in Chapter 6. The RDI and the Regional Innovation Chair in Rural Economic Development are contributing applied research on numerous pressing social, environmental, and economic issues in the region (see Rural Development Institute, 2017).

Case Study 9.2 Kootenay Association for Science & Technology (KAST), British Columbia

The Kootenay Association for Science & Technology (KAST) was created in 1998 and is supported by the British Columbia Innovation Council and the Southern Interior Development Initiative Trust (SIDIT). They have also received project support from the Columbia Basin Trust, Western Economic Diversification, the National Research Council's Industrial Research Assistance Program (NRC-IRAP), and the Discovery Foundation. Its goal is to foster science, technology, innovation, and entrepreneurship to encourage economic diversity and competitiveness in the West Kootenay region. KAST is governed by a board of directors consisting of representatives from both the private and public sectors, while day-to-day operations are managed by an executive director and several staff members (KAST, 2017).

They currently focus on three areas: economic development; tech culture and communities; and technology businesses. For economic development, KAST recently created the MIDAS Fabrication Lab, which is focused on developing and diversifying the metallurgical expertise in the region. It offers support for commercialization and digital fabrication training for companies, entrepreneurs, and students. In tech culture and communities, KAST has partnered with Startup Canada to offer StartUP Nelson to build a culture of entrepreneurship in the community. They also host "ladies learning code" workshops and a podcast series called "you can do that here!" which celebrates entrepreneurs in the region. With regards to technology businesses, KAST offers several programs including HERE – High value Expertise in a Rural Environment program, which provides professional services and expertise in technology-related start-ups to clients in the Venture Acceleration Program.

(KAST, 2017; MIDAS, 2017)

Key informants in the case study regions also indicated that there is support for local businesses, which helps grow and facilitate entrepreneurship and economic development. One common initiative to support local businesses across each of the case study regions is the Community Futures (CF) program, which was implemented in 1986 by the federal government (see Fuller et al., 2010 for an overview and comparison to LEADER). It has since evolved to include 268 non-profit offices[3] across the country that provide small business support services for entrepreneurs and support for community development in rural communities. This includes business loans, training, and other tools to support business growth and development and support for community-based projects (Community Futures, 2017). Each CF includes staff and a volunteer board of directors, which usually includes business owners from the region and other community leaders. While all CFs provide business loans to support entrepreneurs, the Prince Edward/Lennox and Addington Community Futures Development Corporation (CFDC) in Eastern Ontario is combining their efforts with an angel investment partnership as part of a five-year pilot project (see Case Study 9.3). Across Canada, the CFs have played a vital (and consistent) role in supporting rural innovation and addressing access to capital as one of the key challenges to innovation identified in our research (see Table 9.4).

Table 9.4 Evidence of the presence of innovation challenges from interview data

Type of challenge	BC (n=22)	ON (n=33)	QC (n=19)	NL (n=28)	Total (n=102)
Access to capital	H	M	M	M	M
Demographics	M	L	M	M	M
Policy conflicts	M	L	M	M	M
Trust issues	M	L	M	L	M
Human resources	M	L	M	M	M
Leadership	L	L	L	L	L

L (Low) = 1% to 33% of the interviews indicated that the concept was present; M (Medium) = 34% to 67% of the interviews indicated the concept was present; H (High) = 68% to 100% of the interviews indicated the concept was present.

Case Study 9.3 First Stone Venture Partnership and the Prince Edward County Innovation Centre, Ontario

In 2011, a former hotel in Picton, Ontario was transformed into the Prince Edward County Innovation Centre (PECIC) (County Live, 2011). Developed by Conrad Guziewicz, a former executive in a number of computer companies in Silicon Valley, with funding from the federal government, PECIC offers 25 offices to nurture tech start-ups in a rural region consisting of 25,000 people better known for its renaissance as a wine-growing region (Immen, 2012). Shortly after establishing PECIC, Guziewicz and several other PEC private investors created a venture partnership called First Stone Ventures Partnership. The goal of First Stone is "technology-based innovation in rural communities", which includes tech-based ideas built from more traditional industries like agriculture or the fisheries. These investors contributed $5 million to fund new entrepreneurial endeavours. This investment was matched by the federal government through the Prince Edward–Lennox & Addington Community Futures Development Corporation (PELA CFDC) to create the Upper Canada Equity Fund, a five-year pilot private–public co-investment partnership.

This private–public co-investment model is a unique approach in Canada to support innovation and entrepreneurship for several reasons. First, the fund is administered by a Community Futures organization that has matching private funding and where decisions are co-managed with private investors. The fund itself is focused on offering patient capital versus the typical venture capital focused on company sale and exit for a quick return on investment. This is directly related to the goal of the fund which is to build "sustainable companies to boost economic diversity in rural Ontario" (PELA CFDC, 2014). Finally, the PELA CFDC is retaining equity, which is not commonly used by CFs. In theory, the CFDC could profit from their investment if the start-ups are successful.

Interested entrepreneurs are encouraged to apply and after a vetting process they are invited to pitch their ideas to investors from First Stone and representatives from PELA. If successful, entrepreneurs receive funding and a spot in the innovation centre where they can access training, networking opportunities, corporate partnerships, and a wide variety of services (e.g., IT, finance, legal) (FSVP, 2017). Since its inception, Upper Canada Equity Fund has invested in 11 companies.

4.4 Challenges to innovation

Despite these examples of innovation and innovation support opportunities available in each region, key informants discussed a number of challenges for innovation and learning. The most cited impediment, noted by more than half of interview participants, was access to capital (Table 9.4). As one key informant in the Kootenays explained: "there is no capital ... that's our biggest challenge" [Regional government, BC], while another in the Northern Peninsula argued:

> we need money, we need investment money, we need easier access to it, we need people to work with us on our ideas from start to finish, and if something is different try not to can it, try to support different ideas.
>
> (White et al., 2014a, p. 22)

At the same time, as noted in the previous section there are a number of government programs available that support innovative activities, and in NL government representatives indicated that people are not applying to their programs (Hall et al., 2014). This malalignment is caused by several issues. One is a disconnect between the goals and objectives of the programs and the needs of entrepreneurs or other stakeholders. A second factor cited was the time-intensive nature of the applications and a lack of supports available in rural regions to guide applicants through the process. For example, key informants in Eastern Ontario discussed how the province-wide programs are typically delivered in a centralized manner with no staff on the ground in a particular region to offer assistance. Eastern Ontario participants also noted a tendency to rely on sources of funding external to their communities and sub-regions. Finally, there was a general consensus that many of the innovation programs are focused on urban (versus rural) regions and entrepreneurs, both in their design and delivery.

The second most commonly cited type of challenge across the case study regions was demography. Many of the communities are experiencing population aging, youth out-migration, and population decline. As one key informant in Kittiwake explained, "we need people, we need younger people" [Community organization, NL]. These demographic trends are often related to limited employment and educational opportunities in the case study regions with young people moving away to access other employment or educational prospects. There was a general sentiment in Ontario and the Kootenays, in particular, that these regions were becoming older, more conservative, and insular in their ideals. In trying to explain the importance of learning and new ideas, one key informant in NL noted: "we used to say the best thing for Newfoundland is put everybody aboard a boat or a plane for a couple of years and bring them all back and see what happens" [Business owner, NL]. However, in one workshop, a participant highlighted that "our problem is the boat keeps coming back empty" (Hall & White, 2013b). This leads to a lack of social and business entrepreneurs involved in efforts to encourage innovation. As noted earlier in this chapter, being open to and capable of learning and generating and trying new ideas is seen as important for innovation. Yet demographic trends in each of the case study regions were cited as significant challenges for being open to new ideas and learning about opportunities from elsewhere.

There was also a general consensus across the regions that there is a lack of support for rural development and innovation efforts by senior levels (i.e., provincial and federal) of government. In Eastern Ontario, one key informant even suggested that there is an anti-rural approach within provincial and federal governments, which are focused on winning votes in the more populous regions. In the Kootenays, another key informant indicated: "there is no official policy around rural development either federally or provincially. And so, we are screwed, right?" [Regional economic development organization, BC]. This sentiment was echoed in both case study regions in NL, with key informants explaining: there is a "lack of government commitment to rural development" and "this is my impression; the Newfoundland government wants nothing to do with rural" (Hall & White, 2013a, p. 20). During the interviews, many prominent rural regional development agencies across the country had their funding reduced or eliminated, leading in some instances to the centralization of programs and the closure of many organizations (see Hall et al., 2017). Even in Québec, which has had an explicit rural policy for decades (see Chapter 2), one key informant noted:

> here we have gone from 20 to 12 only in my department, so the capacity of innovation has almost disappeared … so the capacity of innovation has been cut because innovation comes with the time to think, time that we don't have now because we only extinguish fires and nothing else.
>
> [Provincial government, Quebec]

This retreat from the rural impacts innovation in several ways. First, it eliminates programs and funding support in rural regions, which is already viewed as a significant barrier to innovation and entrepreneurship. It also breeds uncertainty for entrepreneurs, who are left to ask themselves why they should invest in a particular community if senior governments are withdrawing their support. This is often exacerbated by the demographic declines discussed above. Finally, these cuts have reduced or eliminated regional staff and institutions that were key partners in rural economic development.

Geographical proximity was also discussed in a number of the case study regions. In Newfoundland and the Kootenays, key informants discussed issues with distance. For example, in the Northern Peninsula one key informant explained "there are some disadvantages, like the distance from everything" [Business owner, NL]. These regions have a limited number of postsecondary institutions and the closest urban centres are located hundreds of kilometres away. Reliable and affordable transportation infrastructure is also a serious constraint. One entrepreneur in Newfoundland further explained that having access to markets, suppliers, and knowledge partners is vital, which proximity can facilitate but is not necessarily imperative to achieve. Instead, this individual argued, it is having access to individuals, institutions, and information communications technology (ICT) infrastructure that is essential. It is worth noting that many rural and northern communities across Canada, including many in our case study regions, lack access to broadband internet and cell coverage (FCM, 2017). It is extremely hard to be an innovator in the twenty-first century without access to affordable and reliable ICT. It is also hard to promote the importance of learning without providing the resources to facilitate it.

One final challenge cited in all the case study regions was a lack of collaboration and trust between various stakeholders. As noted earlier, all regions had access to institutions and organizations that support innovation. However, key informants discussed an "institutional messiness" or a lack of coordination especially between local/regional, provincial, and federal governments. This produces layers of policies and programs to support innovation and economic development, which in some instances duplicate efforts and in others contradict them. Perhaps more worrisome still is the lack of formal regional strategies to enhance innovation and interaction between stakeholders. In all the case study regions, key informants also discussed the tensions between community leaders over autonomy, largely due to fears of local government amalgamation or previous amalgamation attempts. This often leads to competition between individual communities versus a more regional approach. Personality conflicts between individuals were also cited, as one key informant from Québec explained: "I think that innovation is possible but for that we have to be able to sit together and talk to each other without killing each other. As for the openness of that innovation, it's always a question of individuals" [Provincial government, Quebec].

5 Reflections and future directions

There are a number of important lessons that emerge from our case study regions regarding innovation, particularly as it manifests in Canada's rural regions. First, and quite simply, innovation is occurring in these regions. While most of the innovation is incremental and focused on new ways of doing, using, and interacting, we also see new approaches to confronting rural decline (e.g., Fogo Island, SABRI, First Stone). In these examples, several ingredients contributed to their success. These include bold thinking, often by community leaders, interaction and collaboration between the various levels of government and between private sector, government, community, and industry players, harnessing the importance of place, and – related to this – recognizing the assets that can be harnessed, including the landscape and the people who call a place home. In addition, these examples were driven through a coordinated and concerted plan to enhance local development.

Second, as previous research suggests (Doloreux & Dionne, 2008; Hall & Donald, 2009), innovation support organizations play a vital role in promoting entrepreneurship, business and community development, interaction, and learning in rural regions. However, the public policy retreat from the rural and lack of attention paid to rural regions within an increasingly urban landscape is undermining these efforts and there is a need for significantly expanded supports for local learning and innovation efforts. As Oughton et al. (2002) argue, there is a comparatively greater need for public spending on innovation in so-called lagging regions – not less (p. 98). Complicating matters more, these regions also have a lower capacity for absorbing innovation funding. As a result, significantly more attention is required in rural regions to increase capacity and advance innovation in these regions, and in the country as a whole.

Two new initiatives that emerged in 2017, which illustrate efforts to foster innovation in Canada's rural regions, continue to emerge and evolve. Metal Tech Alley is an initiative being led by the Lower Columbia Initiatives Corporation (LCIC) – an economic development partnership between the Columbia Basin Trust and the Cities of Rossland and Trail, the Villages of Warfield, Montrose, and Fruitvale, and electoral areas A and B of the Regional District of Kootenay Boundary. This region is home to Teck's fully integrated zinc and lead smelting and refining complex. Using the expertise of this global resource company as a base, Metal Tech Alley is focused on promoting digital fabrication and advanced materials and metallurgy; industrial recycling and the circular economy; and the industrial internet of things and big data technology. By focusing on their competitive advantage in metallurgy and combining this industrial strength with emerging technologies, Metal Tech Alley is focusing on competitive advantages to guide economic development (Metal Tech Alley, 2017).

Likewise, in 2016 the provincial government in Newfoundland and Labrador announced a regional innovation systems pilot initiative in five regions – including aerospace and defence projects in Gander and surrounding areas (Kittiwake Region) and fisheries and tourism projects in southern Labrador and the Great Northern Peninsula. The provincial government has created advisory boards in each region to guide this process, which is focused on using smart specialization to identify priorities and enhancing collaboration amongst innovation stakeholders. The initiative has been informed by the research discussed in this chapter, and members of the research team are assisting in various ways with the pilots.

Notes

1 This chapter is also based on findings and research from the *Advancing Innovation in Newfoundland* project (Hall & Walsh, 2013; Hall et al., 2014) and the *Social Dynamics of Economic Performance in City-Regions Newfoundland and Labrador Component* (e.g. Greenwood & Hall, 2016).
2 The NL case study region is Kittiwake region, however as discussed in Chapter 4 additional research with a focus on the themes of innovation and governance was also undertaken in the Northern Peninsula region of NL.
3 In Western Canada, offices are called Community Futures (CFs); in Ontario, they are called Community Futures Development Corporations (CFDCs); and in Atlantic Canada, they are known as Community Business Development Corporations (CBDCs). We use CF for consistency.

References

Advisory Committee on Measuring Innovation in the 21st Century Economy. (2008). *Innovation measurement: Tracking the state of innovation in the American economy*. Washington: Report submitted to the Secretary of Commerce.

Amara, N., Landry, R., & Lamari, M. (2003). Social capital, innovation, territory and public policy. *Canadian Journal of Regional Science, 26*(1), 87–120.

Amin, A. (1999). An institutionalist perspective on regional economic development. *International Journal of Urban and Regional Research, 23*(2), 365–378.

Amin, A., & Thrift, N. (1994). Living in the global. In Amin, A. & Thrift, N. (Eds.) *Globalization, institutions, and regional development in Europe* (1–22). Oxford: Oxford University Press.

Amin, A., & Thrift, N. (1995). Institutional issues for the European regions: from markets and plans to socioeconomics and powers of association. *Economy and Society, 24*(1), 41–66.

Andrew, J., Haanaes, K., Michael, D.C., Sirkin, H.L., & Taylor, A. (2009). *Measuring innovation 2009: The need for action*. Boston: Report submitted to the Boston Consulting Group Senior Management Survey.

Asheim, B., Coenen, L., & Vang, J. (2007). Face-to-face, buzz, and knowledge bases: sociospatial implications for learning, innovation, and innovation policy. *Environment and Planning C: Government and Policy, 25*(5), 655–670.

Bathelt, H., Malmberg, A., & Maskell, P. (2004). Clusters and knowledge: local buzz, global pipelines and the process of knowledge creation. *Progress in Human Geography, 28*(1), 31–56.

Becattini, G. (1990). The Marshallian industrial district as a socio-economic notion. In P. Pyke, G. Becattini, & W. Sengenberger (Eds.), *Industrial districts and inter-firm co-operation in Italy* (37–51). Geneva: International Institute for Labour Studies (ILO).

Bibbee, A. (2012). *Unleashing business innovation in Canada*. OECD Economics Department Working Papers, No. 997. Paris: OECD Publishing.

Bradford, N., & Bramwell, A. (2016). Regional economic development: institutions, innovation and policy. In Shearmur, R., Carrincazeaux, C., & Doloreux, D. (Eds.) *Handbook on the geographies of innovation* (292–308). Northampton: Edward Elgar.

Bristow, B. (2010). Resilient regions: re-"place"ing regional competitiveness. *Cambridge Journal of Regions, Economy and Society, 3*, 153–167.

Carter, K., & Vodden, K. (2017). Applicability of territorial innovation models to declining resource-based regions: lessons from the Northern Peninsula of Newfoundland. *The Journal of Rural and Community Development, 12*(2/3), 74–92.

The Center for Innovation Studies (2005). *Alberta innovation scorecard*. Calgary: The Center for Innovation Studies

Coe, N., Hess, M., Yeung, H., Dicken, P., & Henderson, J. (2004). Globalizing regional development: a global production networks perspective. *Transactions of the Institute of British Geographers, 29*, 468–484.

Coffey, W., & Bailly, A. (1996). Economic restructuring: a conceptual framework. In A. Bailly & W. Lever (Eds.) *The spatial impact of economic changes in Europe* (13–39). Avebury, Aldershot, Hants.

Columbia Basin Trust. (2017). *About us*. Available at: https://ourtrust.org/about/our-story/.

Community Futures. (2017). *About community futures*. Available at: https://communityfuturescanada.ca.

Conference Board of Canada. (2012). *Who dimmed the lights? Canada's declining global competitiveness ranking. Briefing September*. Ottawa: Conference Board of Canada.

Conference Board of Canada. (2013). *The state of firm-level innovation in Canada*. Ottawa: Conference Board of Canada.

Conference Board of Canada. (2016). How Canada performs. Available at: www.conferenceboard.ca/hcp/provincial/innovation.aspx

Cooke, P. (1992). Regional innovation systems: competitive regulation in the new Europe. *Geoforum, 23*(3), 365–382.

Cooke, P. (Ed.). (2013). *Re-framing regional development: evolution, innovation and transition*. London: Routledge.

Cooke, P., & Morgan, K. (1998). *The associational economy: firms, regions, and innovation*. Oxford: Oxford University Press.

Copus, A., Dubois, A., Hedström, M., Kairyte, E., Stastna, M., Potočnik Slavič, I., & Wellbrock, W. (2011). WP1: global engagement and local embeddedness of rural businesses, summary of research findings. In *DERREG – development Europe's rural regions in the era of globalization*. Aberystwyth: Aberystwyth University.

Council of Canadian Academies. (2009). *Innovation and business strategy: why canadian falls short*. The Expert Panel on Business Innovation. Ottawa: Council of Canadian Academies.

County Live. (2011). Picton motel transformed into $1.25 million innovation centre. *County Live*, November 16. Available at: www.countylive.ca/picton-motel-transformed-into-1-25-million-innovation-centre/.

Cumbers, A. MacKinnon, D., & McMaster, R. (2003). Institutions, power and space assessing the limits to institutionalism in economic geography. *European Urban and Regional Studies, 10*(4), 325–342.

Davies, S. (2010). *Innovative sectors in peripheral rural areas: Workshop on innovation in remote and peripheral areas*. European Policies Research Centre, 1–13.

Doern, G.B., Phillips, P.W., & Castle, D. (2016). *Canadian science, technology, and innovation policy: the innovation economy and society nexus.* Montreal & Kingston: McGill-Queen's Press-MQUP.

Doloreux, D., & Dionne, S. (2008). Is regional innovation system development possible in peripheral regions? Some evidence from the case of La Pocatière, Canada. *Entrepreneurship & Regional Development: An International Journal, 20*(3), 259–283.

Doloreux, D., Dionne, S., & Jean, B. (2007). The evolution of an innovation system in a rural area: the case of La Pocatiere, Québec. *International Journal of Urban and Regional Research, 31*(1), 146–167.

Doloreux, D., & Melançon, Y. (2008). On the dynamics of innovation in Québec's Coastal Maritime Industry. *Technovation, 28*(4), 231–243.

Doloreux, D., & Melançon, Y. (2009). Innovation-support organizations in the marine science and technology industry: the case of Québec's coastal region in Canada. *Marine Policy, 33*(1), 90–100.

Doloreux, D., & Shearmur, R. (2006). Regional development in sparsely populated areas: the case of Québec's missing maritime cluster. *Canadian Journal of Regional Science, 29*(2), 195–220.

Doloreux, D., & Shearmur, R. (2009). Maritime clusters in diverse regional contexts: the case of Canada. *Marine Policy, 33*(3), 520–527.

Doloreux, D., Shearmur, R., & Figueiredo, D. (2016). Québec coastal maritime cluster: its impact on regional economic development, 2001–2011. *Marine Policy, 71,* 201–209.

European Commission, Joint Research Centre. (2016). FAQs of RIS3. Available at: http://s3platform.jrc.ec.europa.eu/faqs-on-ris3.

Expert Panel on Federal Support to Research and Development. (2012). *Innovation Canada: a call to action.* Ottawa: Government of Canada.

FCM. (2017). Rural broadband. Available at: https://fcm.ca/home/issues/rural/rural-broadband.htm.

Florida, R. (1995). Toward the learning region. *Futures, 27*(5), 527–536.

Fogo Island Shop. (2017). About Fogo Island Shop. Available at: https://fogoislandshop.ca/pages/about-fogo-island-shop.

Foray, D. (2015). *Smart specialization: opportunities and challenges for regional innovation policy.* London: Routledge.

FSVP. 2017. About first stone venture partners. Available at: http://fsvp.ca/about/about-first-stone/.

Fuller, A., Larsson, L., & Pletsch, C. (2010). *Insights from comparing the community futures program in Ontario with leader in Sweden.* Ottawa: Prepared for Industry Canada/FedNor.

Gertler, M.S. (1995). "Being there": proximity, organization, and culture in the development and adoption of advanced manufacturing technologies. *Economic Geography, 71*(1), 1–26.

Goodwin, M., Jones, M., Jones, R., Pett, K., & Simpson, G. (2002). Devolution and economic governance in the UK: uneven geographies, uneven capacities? *Local Economy, 17*(3), 200–215.

Government of NL. (2017). The way forward: business innovation agenda. Available at: www.nlinnovationagenda.ca/pdf/business_innovation_agenda.pdf.

Greenwood, R., & Hall, H.M. (2016). The social dynamics of economic performance in St. John's: A metropolis on the margins. In Wolfe, D. A. and Gertler, M. S. (Eds.)

Growing urban economies: Innovation, creativity, and governance in Canadian city-regions (363–388). Toronto: University of Toronto Press.

Hall, H.M. (2012). *Stuck between a rock and a hard place: the politics of regional development initiatives in Northern Ontario*. PhD Dissertation, Department of Geography. Ontario: Kingston.

Hall, H.M. (2014). *Piñatas, pacifiers and the politics of regional development incentives: insights from Northern Ontario* at the Regional Studies Association, European Conference, Izmir, Turkey: June 16.

Hall, H.M. (2017). Exploring innovation in Northern Canada with insights from greater sudbury. Submitted to the special issue on circumpolar innovation. *Northern Review*, *45*(3), 33–56.

Hall, H.M., & Donald, B. (2009). *Innovation and creativity on the periphery: challenges and opportunities in Northern Ontario*. Working Paper Series: Ontario in the Creative Age. REF. 2009-WPONT-002.

Hall, H.M., Vodden, K., & Greenwood, R. (2017). From dysfunctional to destitute: the governance of regional economic development in Newfoundland and Labrador. *International Planning Studies*, *22*(2), 49–67.

Hall, H.M., & Walsh, J. (2013). *Advancing innovation in Newfoundland and Labrador project knowledge synthesis*. St. John's: Harris Centre.

Hall, H.M., Walsh, J., Vodden, K., & Greenwood, R. (2014). *Challenges, opportunities, and strategies for advancing innovation in Newfoundland and Labrador*. Final Report of the Advancing Innovation in Newfoundland and Labrador Project. St. John's: Harris Centre.

Hall, H.M., & White, K. (2013a). *Advancing innovation in Newfoundland and Labrador project*. Kittiwake Innovation Workshop Report. St. John's: Harris Centre.

Hall, H.M., & White, K. (2013b). *Advancing innovation in Newfoundland and Labrador project*. Labrador Straits Workshop Report. St. John's: Harris Centre.

Harrison, J. (2006). Re-reading the new regionalism: a sympathetic critique. *Space and Polity*, *10*(1), 21–46.

Hawkins, R. (2012). *Looking at innovation from a uniquely Canadian perspective. The case for a new alliance of practice, policy and scholarship*. Discussion Paper, Innovation. Ottawa: Institute for Science, Society and Policy, University of Ottawa.

Hettne, B. (2005). Beyond the "new" regionalism. *New Political Economy*, *10*(4), 213.

Hudson, R. (2005). Region and place: devolved regional government and regional economic success? *Progress in Human Geography*, *29*(5), 618–625.

Hudson, R. (2006). Regional devolution and regional economic success: myths and illusions about power. *Geografiska Annaler: Series B, Human Geography*, *88*(2), 159–171.

Hudson, R. (2007). Region and place: rethinking regional development in the context of global and environmental change. *Progress in Human Geography*, *31*(6), 827–836.

Immen, W. (2012). Small Ontario county lures Silicon Valley startup. *Globe and Mail*, May 7. Available at: www.theglobeandmail.com/report-on-business/small-business /sb-money/small-ontario-county-lures-silicon-valley-startup/article4104772/.

Innovation Cluster – Peterborough and the Kawarthas hiring clean-tech innovation specialist. August 29, 2017. Available at: www.thepeterboroughexaminer.com/news-story/8172649-innovation-cluster-peterborough-and-the-kawarthas-hiring-clean -tech-innovation-specialist/.

Isaksen, A., & Karlsen, J. (2010). Different modes of innovation and the challenge of connecting universities and industry: case studies of two regional industries in Norway. *European Planning Studies, 18*(12), 1993–2008.

Isaksen, A., & Karlsen, J. (2016). Innovation in peripheral regions. In Shearmur, R., Carrincazeau, C., & Doloreaux, D. (Eds.) *Handbook on the geographies of innovation* (277–285). Cheltenham: Edward Elgar Publishing.

Isaksen, A., Normann, R.H., & Spilling, O.R. (2017). Do general innovation policy tools fit all? Analysis of the regional impact of the Norwegian Skattefunn scheme. *Journal of Innovation and Entrepreneurship, 6*(1), 6.

Isaksen, A., Tödtling, F., & Trippl, M. (2016). Innovation policies for regional structural change: combining actor-based and system-based strategies.

Johnson, S. (2011). *Where good ideas come from.* New York: Riverhead Trade.

Johnstone, H., & Haddow, R. (2003). Industrial decline and high technology renewal in Cape Breton: exploring the limits of the possible. In Wolfe, D.A. (Ed.) *Clusters old and new: the transition to a knowledge economic in Canada's regions* (187–212). Montreal & Kingston: McGill-Queen's University Press.

Jones, M. (2001). The rise of the regional state in economic governance: "partnerships for prosperity" or new scales of state power? *Environment and Planning A, 33*(7), 1185–1211.

Jones, M. (2004). Social justice and the region: grassroots regional movements and the "English question". *Space and Polity, 8*(2), 157–189.

KAST. (2017). About. Available at: http://kast.com/contact-about/.

Keating, M. (1997). The invention of regions: political restructuring and territorial government in Western Europe. *Environment and Planning C: Government and Policy, 15* (4), 383–398.

Kominko, S. (2017). STEM skills alone won't solve Canada's innovation problem. *Huffington Post,* July 21. Available at: www.huffingtonpost.ca/sofiya-kominko/stem-skills -alone-wont-solve-canadas-innovation-problem_a_23040307/.

Leydesdorff, L. (2012). The triple helix, quadruple helix, … , and an N-tuple of helices: explanatory models for analyzing the knowledge-based economy? *Journal of the Knowledge Economy, 3*(1), 25–35.

Lockwood, M., Davidson, J., Curtis, A., Stratford, E., & Griffith, R. (2009). Multi-level environmental governance: lessons from Australian natural resource management. *Australian Geographer, 40*(2), 169–186.

MacKinnon, D., Cumbers, A., & Chapman, K. (2002). Learning, innovation and regional development: a critical appraisal of recent debates. *Progress in Human Geography, 26*(3), 293–311.

Malmberg, A., & Maskell, P. (1997). Proximity, institutions and learning: towards an explanation of regional specialization and industry agglomeration. *European Planning Studies, 5*(1), 25–41.

Markey, S., Halseth, G., & Manson, D. (2012). *Investing in place: economic renewal in Northern British Columbia.* Vancouver: UBC Press.

Martin, R. (2000). Institutional approaches in economic geography. In T.J. Barnes & E. Sheppard (Eds.), *A companion to economic geography* (77–94). Oxford: Blackwell.

Martin, R. (2010). Roepke lecture in economic geography – rethinking regional path dependence: beyond lock-in to evolution. *Economic Geography, 86*(1), 1–27.

Martinus, K. (2012). City infrastructure supporting innovation. *International Journal of Knowledge-Based Development 3*(2): 126–156.

McKeough, T. (2010). How multimillionaire Zita Cobb plans to turn a tiny Canadian island into an arts Mecca. *Fast Company*, December 15. Available at: www.fastcompany.com/1702241/how-multimillionaire-zita-cobb-plans-turn-tiny-canadian-island-arts-mecca.

Melançon, Y., & Doloreux, D. (2013). Developing a knowledge infrastructure to foster regional innovation in the periphery: a study from Québec's coastal region in Canada. *Regional Studies, 47*(9), 1555–1572.

Metal Tech Alley. (2017). About us. Available at: http://metaltechalley.com/about/.

MIDAS. 2017. About. Available at: www.midaslab.ca/about-midas/.

Morgan, K. (1997). The learning region: institutions, innovation and regional renewal. *Regional Studies, 31*(5), 491–503.

Morgan, K. (2006). Devolution and development: territorial justice and the north-south divide. *Publius: The Journal of Federalism, 36*(1), 189–206.

Moulaert, F., & Mehmood, A. (2010). Analysing regional development and policy: a structuralist realist approach. *Regional Studies, 44*(1), 103–118.

Nauwelaers, C. (2011). Intermediaries in regional innovation systems: role and challenges for policy. In Cooke, P., with Asheim, B., Boschma, R., Martin, R., Schwartz, D., & Tödtling,F. (Eds.) *Handbook of regional innovation and growth* (467–481). Cheltenham: Edward Elgar.

Neumeier, S. (2012). Why do social innovations in rural development matter and should they be considered more seriously in rural development research? *Sociologia Ruralis, 52*(1): 48–69.

Slaper, T.F., Hart, N.R., Hall, T.J., & Thompson, M.F. (2011). The index of innovation: a new tool for regional analysis. *Economic Development Quarterly, 25*(36): 36–53.

OECD. (2005). *Oslo manual: guidelines for collecting and interpreting innovation data*. Paris: OECD Publishing.

OECD. (2010). Trends, perspectives and policies for rural Canada. In *OECD Rural Policy Reviews* (41–116). Paris: OECD Publishing. Available at: www.oecd-ilibrary.org/content/chapter/9789264082151-4-en.

OECD. (2011). *Reviews of regional innovation: regions and innovation policy*. Paris: OECD.

OECD. (2015). *Defining innovation*. Available at: www.oecd.org/site/innovationstrategy/defininginnovation.htm.

OECD. (2018). 2013 Patents statistics: patents by region. Available at: http://stats.oecd.org/Index.aspx?DatasetCode=PATS_REGION#.

Oughton, C., Landabaso, M., & Morgan, K. (2002). The regional innovation paradox: innovation policy and industrial policy. *Journal of Technology Transfer, 27*(1), 97–110.

PELA CFDC. (2014). Upper Canada Equity Fund. Available at: www.pelacfdc.ca/upper-canada-equity-fund.php.

Peterborough Examiner. (2017). Innovation cluster – Peterborough and the Kawarthas hiring clean-tech innovation specialist. August 29, 2017. Available at: www.thepeterboroughexaminer.com/news-story/8172649-innovation-cluster-peterborough-and-the-kawarthas-hiring-clean-tech-innovation-specialist/.

Peterson, A., McAlpine, C.A., Ward, D., & Rayner, S. (2007). New regionalism and nature conservation: lessons from South East Queensland, Australia. *Landscape and Urban Planning, 82*(3), 132–144.

Pike, A., & Tomaney, J. (2009). The state and uneven development: the governance of economic development in England in the post-devolution UK. *Cambridge Journal of Regions, Economy, and Society, 2*(1), 13–24.

Polanyi, M. (1962). *Personal knowledge: towards a post-critical philosophy.* London: Routledge and Keegan Paul.

Polèse, M., Shearmur, R., Desjardins, P.M., & Johnson, M. (2002). *The periphery in the knowledge economy: the spatial dynamics of the Canadian economy and the future of non-metropolitan regions in Québec and the Atlantic provinces.* Montreal and Moncton: Institut national de la recherche scientfiique and the Canadian Institute for Research on Regional Development.

Porter, M.E. (1990). *The competitive advantage of nations.* New York: Free Press.

Proulx. (1992). Innovative milieus and regional development. *Canadian Journal of Regional Science,* 15(2), 149–154.

Rainnie, A., & Grobbelaar, M. (Eds.). (2005). *New regionalism in Australia.* Burlington: Ashgate.

Rajasekaran, V. (2015). How startups are prototyping the future of business on Fogo Island. Available at: www.sigeneration.ca/startups-prototyping-future-business-fogo-island/.

Rose, S., Shipp, S., Lal, B., & Stone, A. (2009). *Frameworks for measuring innovation: Initial approaches.* Washington: Athena Alliance, Science and Technology Policy Institute.

Rural Development Institute. (2017). *About us.* Available at: www.cbrdi.ca/about-us/.

SABRI. (2017). Our mission. Available at: https://sabrinl.com.

Shaw, T.M., Grant, J.A., & Cornelissen, S. (2012). Introduction and overview: the study of new regionalism(s) at the start of the second decade of the twenty-first century. In Shaw,T.M., Grant, J.A., & Cornelissen,S. (Eds.) *The Ashgate research companion to regionalisms.* Abingdon: Routledge.

Shearmur, R., Carrincazeaux, C., & Doloreux, D. (Eds.). (2016). *Handbook on the geographies of innovation.* Northampton: Edward Elgar Publishing.

Shorefast. (2017). Our activities. Available at: https://shorefast.org/our-activities/.

Sternberg, R. (2009). Innovation. In Kitchin, R. & Thrift, N. (Eds.) *International encyclopedia of human geography,* volume 1 (481–490). Oxford: Elsevier.

Storper, M. (1995). The resurgence of regional economies, ten years later: the region as a nexus of untraded interdependencies. *European Urban and Regional Studies,* 2(3), 191–221.

Storper, M. (1997). *The regional world: territorial development in a global economy.* New York: Guilford Press.

Sulzenko, A. (2016). How to fix Canada's innovation conundrum. *Maclean's,* June 29. Available at: www.macleans.ca/economy/economicanalysis/how-to-fix-canadas-innovation-conundrum/.

Tödtling, F., & Trippl, F. (2005). One size fits all? Towards a differentiated regional innovation policy approach. *Research Policy, 34,* 1203–1219.

Trent University. (2004). Available at: www.trentu.ca/dnabuilding/dnabuilding.pdf.

Uyarra, E. (2007). Key dilemmas of regional innovation policies. *Innovation: The European Journal of Social Science Research,* 20(3), 243–261.

Uyarra, E., & Flanagan, K. (2016). Revisiting the role of policy in regional innovation systems. In Shearmur, R., Carrincazeaux, C., & Doloreux, D. (Eds.), *Handbook on the geographies of innovation* (309–321). Northampton: Edward Elgar.

Vinodrai, T., & Hall, H.M. (2018). *Innovation-led growth and economic development beyond the metropolis: a review of best practices.* Prepared for Federal Economic Development Agency for Southern Ontario (FedDev Ontario).

Virkkala, S. (2007). Innovation and networking in peripheral areas – a case study of emergence and change in rural manufacturing. *European Planning Studies, 15*(4), 511–529.

Vodden, K., Carter, K., & White, K. (2013). *A primer on innovation, learning and knowledge flows*. Prepared for Canadian Regional Development: A Critical Review of Theory Practice and Potentials.

Ward, K., & Jonas, A.E.G. (2004). Competitive city-regionalism as a politics of space: a critical reinterpretation of the new regionalism. *Environment and Planning A, 36*(12), 2119–2139.

White, K., Breen, S., & Vodden, K. (2014b). *Innovation report: Kootenay Region*. Canadian regional development: a critical review of theory practice and potentials. Available at: http://cdnregdev.ruralresilience.ca/wp-content/uploads/2014/12/Kootenay_Innovation-WP-CRD16r1.pdf.

White, K., Carter, K., & Vodden, K. (2014a). *Innovation report: Northern Peninsula Region*. Canadian Regional Development: A Critical Review of Theory Practice and Potentials. Available at: http://cdnregdev.ruralresilience.ca/wp-content/uploads/2013/03/Northern-Peninsula-Innovation-report_FINAL.pdf.

White, K., Douglas, D., Minnes, S., & Vodden, K. (2014c). *Innovation report: eastern Ontario region*. Canadian regional development: a critical review of theory practice and potentials. Available at: http://cdnregdev.ruralresilience.ca/wp-content/uploads/2013/03/Eastern-Ontario-innovation-report-FINAL.pdf

White, K., & Hall, H.M. (2013a). *New Wood Manufacturers Inc: adaptability and sustainability in dynamic production*. Canadian Regional Development Project: critical review of theory, practice and potentials and the advancing innovation in Newfoundland and Labrador project. Available at: http://ruralresilience.ca/wp-content/uploads/2013/10/New-Wood.pdf.

White, K., & Hall, H.M. (2013b). *Versatile Stone Inc: innovation in newfoundland's only cultured stone producer*. Canadian Regional Development Project: critical review of theory, practice and potentials and the advancing innovation in Newfoundland and Labrador project. Available at: http://ruralresilience.ca/wp-content/uploads/2013/10/Versatile.pdf.

White, K., & Hall, H.M. (2013c). *Chatman's Bakery: diversification and innovation in the family business*. Canadian Regional Development Project: critical review of theory, practice and potentials and the advancing innovation in Newfoundland and Labrador project. Available at: http://ruralresilience.ca/wp-content/uploads/2013/10/Chatmans.pdf.

White, K., & Hall, H.M. (2013d). *St. Anthony Basin Resources Incorporated (SABRI): expanding regional social and economic benefits*. Canadian Regional Development Project: critical review of theory, practice and potentials and the advancing innovation in Newfoundland and Labrador project. Available at: http://ruralresilience.ca/wp-content/uploads/2013/10/SABRI.pdf.

Wolfe, D.A. (2009). *21st century cities in Canada: the geography of innovation*. The 2009 CIBC Scholar-in-Residence Lecture. Ottawa: Conference Board of Canada.

Wolfe, D.A., & Gertler, M. (2004). Clusters from the inside and out: local dynamics and global linkages. *Urban Studies, 41*(4/5), 1071–1093.

Wolfe, D.A., & Gertler, M.S. (2016). *Growing urban economies: innovation, creativity, and governance in Canadian city-regions*. Toronto: University of Toronto Press.

10 Conclusions

Implications for policy and practice

Kelly Vodden, David J.A. Douglas, Sarah Minnes, Sean Markey, Bill Reimer, and Sarah-Patricia Breen

10.1 Objectives

This volume presents the results of more than five years of empirical and the-oretical analysis of changes in Canadian regional development, the potentials of new regionalist approaches for improving the well-being of Canadian communities and regions, as well as lessons that the Canadian experience may offer to comparable jurisdictions. Given the Canadian context, we have placed particular emphasis on development processes within rural regions. This focus is warranted because of the important role that rural communities play in Canadian society and economy. While rural municipalities represent a shrinking *proportion* of the total Canadian population, the *number* of people in rural areas has remained relatively steady for more than three decades. If we adopt a definition of "rural" that includes smaller towns of up to 10,000 residents and all areas outside of "urban" Census Metropolitan and Census Agglomeration areas,[1] nearly six million Canadians (approximately 17% of the population) live in rural contexts and occupy the majority of the country's 10 million square km landscape (Bollman, 2016; Statistics Canada, Census of Population, 2016). Their residents and leaders help to shape the country's economy and socio-cultural makeup. Rural Canada also produces food, energy, clean air and water, and other valuable natural resources that support rural and urban communities alike (Canadian Rural Revitalization Founda-tion, 2015).

Unfortunately, "rural has taken a 'back seat' in terms of policy develop-ment" (Canadian Rural Revitalization Foundation, 2015, p. 2). Rural Canada also remains comparatively under-researched, thereby contributing to significant policy gaps. These gaps in policy and understanding, combined with the play-out of relatively unfettered market forces, contribute to discrep-ancies in well-being that regional development programs and initiatives seek to address. Despite playing important roles in Canadian society, many rural communities and regions are experiencing hardships associated with depopula-tion and restructuring of traditional natural resource-based economies. They also tend to be disproportionately affected by government cutbacks and pro-gram downsizing, even as responsibilities for local governments are increased.

Rural resource regions are also facing these challenges with declines in the human and institutional resources that are necessary to overcome the traditional patterns of limited economic diversification and low value-added staples reliance.

While it is recognized that resilience is not a likely prospect or assured possibility for every rural community (Douglas, 2017), regional development has been recognized in Canada and elsewhere as a strategy for addressing the development challenges and opportunities facing rural Canada. Seeking to contribute to this effort, and drawing from new regionalist insights internationally, our research team sought to answer the following questions within this volume:

1) How has Canadian regional development evolved over the past two and a half decades (since the creation of existing federal regional development agencies)?
2) To what extent have Canadian regional development systems incorporated the ideas of new regionalism in their policy and practice?
3) What can we learn from Canadian contexts about the merits or flaws of new regionalism?
4) What innovations have been developed in Canadian regional development that can contribute to the broader body of regional development theory and practice nationally and internationally?
5) To what extent is regional development in Canada, particularly in four selected Canadian provinces and regions, characterized by knowledge transfers and shared learning, and what factors or mechanisms constrain and/or facilitate learning, knowledge flow, and collaboration within Canadian regional development networks?

In the following sections we summarize our findings on these questions, beginning with the evolution of regional development in Canada over recent decades (Question 1, addressed in Section 10.2.1). We then revisit our key conclusions regarding the applicability of new regionalist insights within the Canadian context as well as what lessons might be learned from the experiences we have examined for new regionalist scholarship (responding to Questions 2 and 3 in Section 10.2.2). We also restate some of the innovative initiatives and approaches to regional development that have been highlighted in this volume (Question 4, Section 10.2.3) and discuss the importance of connecting these stories and our findings more generally with the process of regional development learning in our study regions, provinces, the country and beyond. This leads us to our final research question and Section 10.2.4 where we reflect on the role of knowledge sharing and learning within regional development systems and how such learning might be more deliberately and effectively fostered and encouraged. We conclude with implications of this research for policy design and professional practice, as well as the research agenda for regional, and particularly rural regional development in Canada and beyond.

10.2 What we learned

10.2.1 The diverse, changing, contested Canadian regional development landscape

Until the 1990s, Canadian regional development interventions were largely focused on "equalizing" interprovincial disparities and negotiated federal-provincial arrangements (Hodge, Hall, & Robinson, 2016). This occurred through two initial policy eras: pre–World War II nation-building and post-war top-down state intervention. As described in Chapter 2, this was followed by a post-1980s recession era of restructuring. Regional development in Canada experienced a fundamental shift in the years that followed, characterized by an ongoing withdrawal of regional development policy, planning, and programming on the part of the federal government. At the same time, federal regional development agencies like Western Economic Diversification (WD) and the Atlantic Canada Opportunities Agency (ACOA), along with special agencies for Québec and Ontario, placed emphasis on business development. This meant that systematically prepared and contextually specific strategic plans promoting more general integration and holistic approaches to development became rare at both provincial and federal levels.

In those places where regional development efforts exist, they involve a diverse set of actors, with overlapping and multi-level roles and policy and programme approaches. Increasing attention has been paid to the scale of the sub-provincial region and the emergence of a variety of sub-provincial arrangements and structures such as economic development trusts, boards or authorities, and inter-municipal collaborations. It is argued that these structures are more accessible and responsive to local communities than provincial and federal agencies and are more affordable and effective at instigating change than single community efforts (Markey et al., 2005). This complexity reflects a new regionalist approach to institutional restructuring and a reliance on multi-level collaborative governance networks that include regions as "new state spaces" (Reimer & Markey, 2008; Douglas & O'Keeffe, 2009; Vodden, 2009). Our findings demonstrated that these spaces and their ongoing (re)construction and governance are deeply contested and socially constructed for specific objectives, including both bottom-up and top-down responses to shifting political economic fortunes.

Institutional legacies vary across the country and in turn influence policies and events, as evident in the relatively unique outcomes in Québec as compared to other provinces and regions. These changing provincial regional development approaches have been further challenged by the absence of a coherent vision and long-term strategic planning. Even the more robust Québec model, built upon a 160-year history, has been threatened with financial cuts since 2014 (Jean, 2015). In general, we are left with a highly variable institutional landscape across the country and over time with which to attempt innovations in the principles and practices associated with new regionalism.

10.2.2 New regionalism in the Canadian context

Regional development is complex. As Savoie (2017, p. 365) explains, "regional development is about economics, the working of political institutions, bureaucracy, the rural-urban structure, the people factor, and attitudes, and still more factors". These complexities are what makes the interdisciplinary and multi-faceted nature of new regionalism attractive. The research presented in this volume highlights the possible emergence and divergence of new regionalism in Canada. A key area where the project has contributed to our understanding is the disconnect between theories of new regionalism that emerged primarily from the European context and the reality across the Canadian landscape. There are some variations across and within regions and key themes, but in general, there is a significant gap between policy and practice, and the theory and rhetoric, of new regionalist ideas.

Our exploration of the five new regionalism themes led to some important discoveries. First, examples of regional collaboration and aspects of collaborative multi-level collaborative governance were present in all cases. Regional organizations have promoted a variety of multi-sector governance arrangements (often senior-government facilitated) on infrastructure, economic development, and other issues. In some regions there were also examples of considerable inter-local government collaboration. Together these initiatives suggest a foundation for regional governance. However, only occasionally are policies or programs co-constructed by both top-down and bottom-up participation. Those that include both often rely on single purpose, fragile organizations that lack significant capacity. Power and resources are seldom transferred from senior governments to match the new responsibilities transferred to the local or regional level. Multi-level collaborative governance can be hindered by institutional barriers and the lack of financial or human resources when increased responsibilities occur. Our research demonstrates that multi-level collaborative governance is critical in the new regionalism approach but that its application requires further consideration, highlighting both effective examples and limitations. Structural and policy barriers, among others, must be addressed if the collaborative governance ideal is to be implemented more widely (see also Chapter 5).

Overall our research suggests that, despite recognition of the importance of place, there are considerable barriers to achieving place-based regional development in rural Canada. At present, place-based development is at best an emergent phenomenon at the regional scale within our case study regions. We were particularly interested in the definition and expression of place-based identity as a mobilizing force for regionalism. In the case study regions, we observed a strong local sense of place and identity(ies), but generally these identities were not associated with official regions with boundaries designated by senior levels of government. In many cases, we are failing to leverage the power of place in our development approaches. There were also issues with the compatibility of old and new regionalist ideas of place and place-based development. Community leaders in rural regions interviewed in this project identify an array of assets that afford development opportunities (including identity), but strategic application of these assets is limited.

In linking sense of place with identity, we are searching for a catalytic response whereby identity and sense of place are transformed into commitment to regionalism – and regionalist action. Our findings suggest, however, that while identity plays a critical role in fostering regional development processes, it is either too weak or actively resisted within the case study regions to be a significant force for place-based regional development. Identities tend to lie largely at community and smaller, sub-regional levels. The gradient from community to small clusters of neighbouring communities and sub-regions, toward a larger co-constructed regional community of interest, toward an effective "critical mass", is challenging (Douglas, 1990; Freshwater, Simms, & Vodden, 2011). This can be a detriment without effective regional development structures and processes that recognize and build on the place identities that characterize these spaces. The multiplicity and complexity of overlapping public policy and organizational regions can further detract from a common sense of region and identity to foster new regionalist action. Better understanding of the reflexive relationship between identity and place-based development holds promise for more effective and inclusive regional development, as do the many regional development organizations working to harness place-based development (see also Chapter 6).

The concept of integrated development was often invoked as jargon by governments at all levels within the case study regions. However, as discussed in Chapter 7, highly integrated development policies and practices are rare in the case study regions. We found little evidence of an integrated approach in perception and practice. There is considerable dissonance between practitioners' appreciation of the complexity and interconnected nature of development issues and their policies and practices. Regional development aspirations are often subjucated, as Bristow (2010, p. 153) observes, "to the hegemonic discourse of competitiveness". There were limited illustrations provided, for instance, of balancing questions of economic growth and social equity, or adoption of an holistic perspective in practice. Examples do exist throughout the country, however, that indicate potential for the application of such a perspective (see Chapter 7 and below).

Our next core theme, rural–urban relations, shows that rural–urban relationships are weak, particularly for local–federal institutional relationships. Trade and exchanges dominate the types of relationships between private-sector rural and urban actors. This limits opportunities for the types of integrated relationships advanced by new regionalist proponents. Institutional interdependencies between rural and urban places continue to define relationships in public sectors, which may also be subject to traditional operational patterns that "silo" government interactions and further erode the type of integrated development required in rural regions. This includes addressing tensions regarding appropriate policy and programming within and between rural and urban regions (e.g., city regionalism) and conflicts related to issues such as land use and infrastructure (e.g., water, waste management, transportation systems). Finally, we found little focus on environment and identity-based interdependencies, which we anticipated to be more of an emergent theme within rural–urban relations. In general, our research reinforces the importance of rural–urban interdependence and highlights opportunities, challenges, and tensions experienced within rural–urban relationships that have received limited attention in regional development scholarship and practice (Chapter 8).

Lastly, we found many examples of local innovation in process and organization. A small number of high profile organizational and development process innovations are evident at the regional level (e.g., the Eastern Ontario Wardens Caucus). However, these kinds of innovations are often poorly recognized in Canada – including within the new regionalism literature, despite its focus on governance (confirming some of the challenges identified above regarding learning and knowledge transfer). Formal organizations and supports for learning and innovation are usually concentrated in major urban settings, and are technology focused, which may lack relevance in rural settings and be ill-matched with their knowledge, skills, and other assets. Regional actors in rural regions can and do, however, play an important role in learning and innovation across the country (see Chapter 9 and below for examples).

These core lessons indicate that regional development theory and practice, particularly as they relate to rural regions, remain underdeveloped. Overall, this volume stresses that new regionalist principles and practices are emergent at best in rural and small-town Canada. There are significant barriers to new approaches, including limited capacity, wavering policy interest, changing or absent visions of rural and regional development at the provincial level and shifting institutional boundaries, organizational structures, and levels of support, and the legacies associated with failed regional development attempts of the past. Some of these failed attempts include the sectoral focus of former federal government area-based policies, the business-focused policies of the current federal regional development agencies, and unpopular local government restructuring efforts (e.g., forced amalgamations) that have left citizens wary of regional initiatives and organizations. However, in cases where new regionalist practices are being used these principles have proven to be beneficial. It is our hope that the following sections on theory, policy, and practice may help to enhance new regionalism's emergent status, and that our reflections on future research directions will help to guide ideas for ongoing learning.

10.2.3 Innovations and sources of inspiration

Despite challenges and limitations in regional development policy and practice in Canada, several inspiring examples have been highlighted in this volume that demonstrate potential for learning and positive change. In the realm of governance, for example, cross sectoral, inter-local and multi-level government collaborations that provide a foundation for regional governance include the Eastern Ontario Wardens Caucus (see Chapter 4), Northern Peninsula Regional Collaboration Pilot Initiative, Newfoundland and Labrador (NL), and the Yukon Regional Round Table (Chapter 5). Local and regional development organizations across the country have been particularly important for harnessing place-based development, harnessing the power of place, and supporting collaboration within and beyond specific regions. An inspiring example of this was the story of the village of Cap-à-l'Aigle, Québec. By utilizing their specific geoclimatic, physical, and social place-based assets then collaborating with both regional and international networks they were able to both build their local capacity and attract market and investment opportunities from both the USA and Europe (Chapter 6).

Examples of more integrated, holistic approaches to development profiled in this research include the commitments of Ontario's *Places to Grow* legislation, the integration of environmental concerns into mainstream decision-making, planning, and development practices in the Kootenays, the Skidegate Comprehensive Community Plan in Haida Gwaii, British Columbia (BC), and the Integrated Resource Development Duhallow in rural Ireland (Chapter 7). Ontario's Frontenac Arch Biosphere Reserve provides yet another example – integrating planning measures related to the environment, culture, society, and the economy while breaking down sector-based barriers through a regional network of governance (Minnes, 2013).

A positive example of rural–urban relationships outlined in Chapter 8, was the Northwestern Ontario Municipal Association's enlisting of urban municipalities' support for lobbying the provincial government regarding the forestry sector. In this case, we saw the positioning of the forestry sector in Northwestern Ontario as a provincial industry rather than solely a regional one. Another example is Québec's city-rural festivals, organized by Solidarité Rurale du Québec with support under the *Rural Pacte*. Water and watershed management has been yet another area of innovation, including the Columbia Basin Trust's Water Smart program and the Kootenay Lake Partnership in BC, regional water operators in NL and BC, and watershed committees in the lower St. Lawrence River that are working to reduce the ecological footprint of human activities, including agriculture (Breen & Minnes, 2013, Chapter 8). Place-based development strategies in the Gander River region, NL, in part through watershed groups, have helped bring Mi'kmaw, settler, urban, and rural residents together to pursue common development and resource conservation aims (Daniels, 2014).

We also saw many innovations in areas such as local tourism, heritage, and food systems as well as the development of institutions that support innovation in rural regions. For example, Selkirk College's Columbia Basin Rural Development Institute & Applied Research and Innovation Centre, provide an important support for the Kootenay region in BC. In the same region, the Kootenay

Association for Science & Technology provides support for training, economic development, and technology businesses in the region. Other examples outlined included St. Anthony Basin Resources Incorporated on the Northern Peninsula, NL, and the Prince Edward County Innovation Centre in Eastern Ontario. These organizations serve important convening functions within their region and provide a wealth of regional research and information to assist with evidence-based decisions and regional development learning.

Additional case study vignettes and details on each of the innovations noted above are provided at http://cdnregdev.ruralresilience.ca. While these examples largely highlight innovations in regional development at local and regional levels, national organizations like the Canadian Rural Revitalization Foundation (CRRF) provide an important role in documenting and sharing stories of innovation through its State of Rural Canada initiative (see http://sorc.crrf.ca/mapping-rural-innovation/). Similarly, the Rural Policy Learning Commons, building on networks created by CRRF, has created a learning network that reaches across the country and internationally to enhance rural capacity, build relationships and inform rural research and policy (see http://rplc-capr.ca).

10.2.4 On regional development learning

As discussed in Chapters 3 and 9, through a new regionalist lens, knowledge flows and learning are considered to be critical processes for positive regional development outcomes. While building "human capital" through training and development of individuals engaged in regional development remains important, this work extends further to build capacity and collective learning within communities, institutions and extended regional development networks. Important opportunities for learning exist through the sharing of experiences within and across communities and regions. This learning allows for specific corrective actions but also for re-evaluation of governing policies, goals, "mental maps" and values (Argyris & Schön, 1974). Such learning and evaluation processes create capacities for self-organizing and adaptation that are critical in a complex and ever-changing world.

Despite the critical importance of these learning feedback mechanisms, Canadian federal and provincial regional development actors have been criticized for showing resistance to act on the results of collective learning and opportunities for innovation, while local actors are observed as underestimating the need to invest in knowledge transfer or translation and to develop learning processes – both individual and organizational (Savoie, 1992; Vodden, 2015). Within this context we explored factors that enable or constrain knowledge flows and what mechanisms have been or can be used to foster learning, adaptations, and innovations.

We found that most regional development organizations, whether at the local, provincial, or federal level, self-describe as learning organizations. Despite this proclamation, deliberate efforts to seek and share knowledge are described as modest and significant constraints exist to knowledge generation and sharing within Canadian regional development networks. Lockwood et al. (2009, p. 181) similarly acknowledge the difficulties encountered in multi-level collaborative governance in regional natural resource management in Australia and in shifting from a culture that values "control, comfort, and clarity over reflection and learning" to active adaptive management through "directed and experimental interventions" and "systematic self-reflection".

Evaluations of programs and policies can serve as important sources of learning and innovation. Through our research, we found that federal and provincial organizations often have both informal and formal evaluation processes in place; however, even within these agencies we saw limited evidence of efforts to formally monitor and link inputs and outputs, outcomes, and impacts (Chapter 7). Further, formalized evaluations tend to be a centralized function in governments. Unfortunately, this often creates barriers to the sharing of results even within the government system (e.g., to regional staff members). Further, there is limited evidence that results of such evaluations are shared widely among partners as a way to foster dialogue and improvements. Formal, government-led evaluations tend to be judgement rather than improvement focused and seldom question the goals and values that guide policies and programs. In an era where the purported ideal is "evidence-based policy", what is considered to be evidence by key decision-makers is shaped by prevailing social and policy norms (Reimer & Brett, 2013). For example, community and regional organizations are often formally evaluated by senior government funding partners, but under the assumption that local communities and organizations are responsible for their own development and, often, with emphasis on highly valued economic outcomes such as jobs and revenues. These narrow objectives, combined with limited resources and the need to defend an organization's existence in the face of cutbacks, limit the shared learning potential of such evaluation processes.

Community organizations and municipalities tend to rely on more informal, pragmatic processes of knowledge gathering and sharing. Avenues such as meetings and retreats are used to reflect on experiences and knowledge is sought through networking with peers as well as government representatives and clients, and through "learning by doing". This creates knowledge divides between these informal modes of knowledge construction and sharing amongst local practitioners and the more formal systems of evaluation, knowledge gathering, and sharing across jurisdictions or with other types of experts (e.g., academia) (Reimer & Brett, 2013).

In addition to a dearth of deliberate, organized processes for learning through self-evaluation and reflection, there is minimal cross-sectoral or inter-regional/inter-provincial transfer of knowledge. While some opportunities of this kind are made available through selected intergovernmental vehicles, academic and professional networks, rural development organizations (e.g., CRRF), and often *ad hoc* events, there is no dedicated national body charged with the assembly of this strategic information, its systematic management, and its active distribution. Efforts such as the European LEADER+

Programme, which promoted and institutionalized trans-regional and jurisdictional knowledge transfer, are largely absent in spite of Canada's great need for sharing lessons across our large landmass and dispersed population.

Limitations in both training and knowledge sharing are often linked to human and financial resource constraints. Reimer and Brett (2013) point out, for example, that funding cutbacks have reduced opportunities for face-to-face knowledge sharing and community and regional actors are often encouraged to seek their own information using the internet despite pockets of weak communications infrastructure and technical knowledge across the country, particularly in rural and remote locations.

Limited attention to creating opportunities for co-constructing and sharing knowledge related to regional development means lost opportunities for social learning and ultimately for the effectiveness of regional development efforts. Our hope is that, through this volume and other avenues used to share the results of the Canadian Regional Development project, we will contribute to this much needed learning process.

10.3 New regionalism and Canadian regional development reconsidered

10.3.1 *Implications for regional development policy*

Our review of current policy highlights the recent dismantling of much of Canada's previous regional development infrastructure and a retreat from rural regions, sometimes voiced as the "rural as residual" syndrome. One result has been the creation of growing divisions among rural and regional development planning, practice, and policy. Achieving the regional development policy ideals outlined in new regionalism requires policy and program support if they are to be adopted "in the field" at any significant scale. Such support for regional institutions and processes can lead to more efficient governance and provide incentives for regional cooperation. There is also a need for new mechanisms to deliver effective regional policy and programs in a way that moves away from a top-down, client-oriented approach to a highly collaborative, partnership driven model of co-construction (as identified above). Doing so offers the promise that we might move beyond the simplistic spatial model that has traditionally guided Canadian regional development policy toward more holistic and place-based regional development learning, knowledge-sharing, and innovation that has been observed elsewhere and documented by new regionalist scholars.

We suggest that regional policies must consider a variety of criteria, including the need to: thoughtfully consider and build on rural and urban inter-relationships, integrate other related policies and actors (in a place, or territorial manner), and improve federal/provincial/regional/local relationships for greater policy integration. Overall, there is a need for stronger and more robust regional planning. There is also need for more place-sensitive development metrics for evaluating policies and programs that consider the particular values and needs of the communities and regions in which they are implemented. These policies must consider and integrate multi-discipline/sector/perspective approaches, including those that acknowledge economies as more than a system of formal, monetized activities, and that allow flexibility for policy implementation to take advantage of local and regional idiosyncrasies.

Furthermore, policies for rural regions should be developed and refined *with* rural regions, not *for* them and with flexibility and consideration of context. For example, fiscal policy should be evaluated to allow communities greater flexibility in funding, such as allowing changing taxation structures to provide increased benefit for communities hosting corporations within their boundaries. This will aid in the adoption of more rural-appropriate, sensitive regional policies (known in the policy literature as adopting a "rural lens"). Co-constructed approaches are favoured over top-down governing, approaches that allow rural communities to have a voice and focus on local priorities while providing more deliberative democracy and capacity-building for regional development. These approaches also provide opportunities to build trust between senior-level decision-makers and communities. Resulting policies are more likely to be driven by goals of enhanced effectiveness and betterment of the community and region(s) than by pure political gain"

The greatest challenge for this approach is the limited capacities of many small and remote communities. Since most Canadian municipalities have been treated as service-delivery entities, there is a dearth of resources and experience in planning, longer term decision-making, community engagement, and training that is essential to effective bottom-up approaches. Developing this capacity will require some important shifts in the relationships among municipalities, regional organizations, and provincial governments.

Given the many powerful examples of regional development efforts that exist, led by organizations and their leaders often struggling for support, it is important to leverage and strengthen existing regionalist structures. More policy without more capacity just equals more ignored policies. These policy improvements can be made at all levels of government, federal through local.

10.3.1.1 Federal

Critical reflection on our analysis suggests a number of additional possibilities for enhanced federal involvement in Canadian regional development. While the importance of human, institutional, and social capacities for the effectiveness of regional institutions is widely recognized in Canada and elsewhere (see Beer & Lester, 2015 for similar observations in Australia), our findings suggest a need for enhanced support for individual and collective learning within regional development organizations. The federal government has direct access to models of rural and regional development policies, programs, projects, and practices across a variety of international contexts. This includes the LEED program of the OECD, the LEADER program of the EU, the

Interreg program of the EU, and many others that have a direct bearing on policies and practices across rural Canada. However, such examples are selectively and discontinuously accessed by academics, provincial agencies, rural development networks, and others. There is no systematic compilation of these potentially valuable experiences and lessons and no single conduit for territorial and provincial governments, rural development agencies, or others active in rural regional development to access such information.

The federal government can play a unique and supportive role in compiling and expediting the transfer of information on critical lessons, including lessons learned from the results of development monitoring and evaluations, valuable case studies, creative multi-community collaborations and innovations in products and processes, and other matters germane to regional development across Canada's provinces and territories. Through an observatory-type function, the federal government could provide an ongoing vehicle for accessing this changing roster of policies, programs, projects, and practices, thus facilitating access to those that might benefit. The EU provides this very important networking and transfer function for all its member states. The Canadian government could do likewise for its provinces and territories, and others active in regional development. This would be particularly valuable service for rural and remote communities and regions where access to in-person networking opportunities and research centres is typically limited.

Closely related to the important role of such communication is the need for adequate infrastructure. Ongoing public investments in rural broadband, for example, will continue to be critical in the joining up of rural communities to form functionally operational regions and access regional development knowledge from across the country and the world. The federal government can play a greater role in expediting this strategically important process.

The federal government as a convenor and facilitator of information and relationships serves a critical function that has been seriously hobbled by decades of neoliberal-inspired cuts and off-loading and that requires reinvestment to ensure these important roles are fulfilled. Much of the institutional infrastructure for these federal contributions has been dismantled over the last decade. Both the Interdepartmental Working Group on Rural and Remote Canada and the federal Rural Secretariat personnel and programs have disappeared in spite of their significant contribution to national dialogue and information exchange regarding research, policy, and practice (Hall & Gibson, 2016). This does not mean that key elements cannot be reactivated – with new insights from the experience and scholarly analysis of the old approaches.

It is clear that non-governmental groups serve important roles in bridging the relative lack of confidence between rural citizens and the federal government. New rural economy research by CRRF has demonstrated that rural people have the most confidence in their local organizations and political representatives, with provincial links being second, and federal ones being third

(Jean, 2014). This is also reflected in the sources to which local policy-makers and practitioners turn when making decisions (Reimer & Brett, 2013). It makes sense, therefore, that our federal and provincial organizations should concentrate on supporting local and regional organizations like these over creating new infrastructure for information flow and local capacity-building. It will take some initiative and courage on the part of federal institutions to relinquish some control over communication and research in this manner, but the benefits for building local capacity warrant the approach. A similar lesson applies to provincial governments.

In this vein, rather than establishing its own infrastructure for such communication and learning, we suggest that the federal government work with existing national and regional organizations facilitating research and knowledge mobilization across Canada. Regional research and learning centres like the Leslie Harris Centre of Regional Policy and Development at Memorial University, the *Chair en développement rurale de l'UQAR* in Rimouski, the School of Environmental Design and Rural Development at the University of Guelph, the Rural Development Institute at Brandon University, the Institute for Northern Studies at the University of Saskatchewan, Selkirk College in BC, Alberta Centre for Sustainable Rural Communities, University of Alberta and the Community Development Institute at the University of Northern British Columbia provide important liaison functions in addition to the information and research insights that have informed federal initiatives. They generally also have the advantage of high levels of local knowledge and citizen confidence that is so important to the knowledge mobilization process (Jean, 2014). Yet, like the community and regional organizations they work with, many of these centres struggle to continue operating and/or meet growing expectations in a time of fiscal restraint. The recently formed Rural Research Centres Network (http://rplc-capr.ca) is an attempt to strengthen their individual and collective efforts and develop responses to these threats and opportunities.

10.3.1.2 Provincial

An important function for provincial governments is to help build local capacity at sub-provincial levels (community and regional). Senior levels of government, both provincial and federal, must shift to seeing themselves as partners (a collaborative governance approach) rather than merely as overseers and/or funding agencies. This can be difficult to promote in the policy arena. There is a need to invest in regionalization and collaboration and update existing provincial policies such as municipalities acts to ensure that differences in municipalities are represented, while providing the foundation for regional governance. This should include treating municipalities as more than service-delivery organizations and seeing them as "community governments" (Douglas, 2005; Tindal & Tindal, 2009).

Policies must be relevant and long term, yet responsive to time-specific issues to maximize their impact. Furthermore, flexible yet consistent funding to communities is needed, allowing them to direct local social, economic, political, and environmental priorities. This includes recognition of and support for rural planning, learning, and innovation efforts that build on place-based assets, identities, and experiences. Our results suggest that greater attention might also be paid to supporting initiatives and new frameworks that recognize and build on rural–urban interdependencies within regions, including those relating to identity and the environment.

Consistent with the notion of multi-level collaborative governance suggested in this book, both federal and provincial agencies can be important partners working to encourage and resource rural communities to collaboratively design and constitute appropriate regional network organizations. These collaborations would identify a range of common development objectives, challenges, needed resources, and other matters. Such objectives could be used as a basis for co-designing rural regions that encompass communities committed to common development agendas for specific and more general longer-term development priorities (e.g., enterprise development, climate change). Membership and regional boundaries might fluctuate depending on the issues being addressed, but the spatial design of these collaborations, the pooling of resources, the co-design of appropriate governance mechanisms, and the setting of a common regional development agenda would serve to create a greater degree of "critical mass" to address issues of limited capacity and scale in rural communities across Canada. Encouraging and selectively resourcing these spatial collaborations would provide the basis for unique and timely partnerships among the provinces, territories, and the federal government along with local/regional actors.

10.3.1.3 *Local*

While senior levels of government require encouragement to think regionally, local actors often need to be willing to reach beyond their parochialisms and resistance to change in order to create local-level policies that have a larger regionalist vision. Rather than dwelling on past assumptions and, in some cases, inter-community rivalries or rigidly clinging to outdated local development strategies, new regionalist principles and practices offer significant potential to organize local planning while engaging productively and collaboratively with other communities in the regions. The local development innovations profiled above provide powerful examples.

Local actors must also be well-organized and vocal about their expectations, aspirations, and development visions when dealing with policy-makers. This involves fundamentally understanding and knowing their communities' expectations and priorities, in addition to gaining a solid understanding of the development options available. This will help to ensure that development plans and strategies are place-based and draw upon local identities, including established or emergent regional identities and conceptualizations of place.

While this understanding of local context is critical for community and regional development policy and practice, our research shows that communities in various parts of the country are experiencing similar issues. Learning from others to get ideas and see what works and hasn't worked is also key. Hearing and learning from fellow communities and community leaders is also a powerful way to learn, be inspired, and adopt an attitude of possibility associated with community and regional development approaches. This may involve new and innovative practices and technologies. It also involves using and understanding local and regional histories and institutional strengths to leverage and reimagine already existing regional assets and resources. It may also make sense to build upon existing governance structures, rather than creating new ones. Establishing contacts of an ongoing nature with researchers and other networks can also help local actors improve planning efforts, stay connected with up-to-date research, and/or employ these networks to advocate for new or enhanced resources.

10.3.1.4 Indigenous peoples

As discussed in Chapters 1 and 2, Canada continues to struggle to come to terms with its colonial history. The Truth and Reconciliation Commission of Canada and its calls to action toward reconciliation is a recent development in a climate of increasing recognition of Indigenous perspectives, rights, title, and systems of governance, as are the many related provincial and related federal court rulings and modern treaty and land claims negotiations in the country. These developments, while not without their own problems and critiques, have challenged the relative autonomy of provincial and regional agencies and organizations while also creating a basis for new regional governance relationships.

With considerable overlap in Indigenous territories and rural regions in Canada the evolving relationship between Indigenous and settler communities and governments is likely to be increasingly critical in the decades ahead. It is anticipated multi-level collaborative governance initiatives will increasingly involve Indigenous actors, with new collaborations with Indigenous communities, businesses, and organizations as part of regional development governance arrangements. To date such engagement has been limited in the case study regions. At the same time Indigenous-led planning and governance initiatives will continue to be important for Indigenous peoples' ongoing pursuit of self-determination within this complex national and regional governance terrain (Booth & Muir, 2011).

While our research only began to touch on the unique contributions, as well as rights and circumstances related to Indigenous community and regional development in Canada, our findings suggest the need for increased recognition of the unique contributions and leadership of Indigenous nations and organizations within rural regions and across Canada as well as the opportunities to enhance their capacity and access to and engagement with regional development processes. Strengthening rural regions in Canada warrants special attention from senior governments to invest in the institutional capacity of Indigenous nations, governments and organizations, the health, education, and training of Indigenous peoples, and initiatives that foster more respectful and mutually enabling relations between Indigenous and neighbouring settler communities. Case studies such as the Yukon Regional Round Table, Skidegate Comprehensive Community Plan in Haida Gwaii, BC and watershed governance efforts on the Gander River in NL and Kootenay Lake in BC demonstrate the potential of Indigenous-municipal-regional cooperation, including the opportunity to learn from and build upon Indigenous approaches to development that recognize relationships between identity, community, land, culture, health, economy, and well-being. Other opportunities to be explored include infrastructure sharing arrangements, settlement of outstanding treaty grievances to bring greater land use certainty, as well as regional resource development and conservation strategies that recognize and benefit from Indigenous knowledge and knowledge systems.

10.3.2 *Implications for development practice*

Despite our central argument that new regionalism is nascent across rural Canada, the research profiled in this volume provides inspiring examples of development initiatives and local leadership in each of our case study regions, demonstrating the benefits that can accrue from regional thinking and approaches. Profiling and sharing regional governance and development models can play important roles in fostering regional thinking and enhanced practice. Nothing builds support more than success, as was seen in Eastern Ontario with the food movement and innovations in alternative energy. Community and regional development practitioners must continue to share knowledge and information to continue learning from one another and to develop best practices of regional development across Canada. As we articulate above, learning networks are indeed critical and – importantly – underdeveloped in Canada.

There is a valuable role for academic researchers to play, who are increasingly asked to more effectively bridge the gap between theory and practice and translate their research in ways that can, and do, inform action. This implies the active exploration of how new and evolving regional development concepts might be applied in real life contexts. At the same time, exploring and sharing regional development scholarship and ideas, such as those embodied in new regionalism and related frameworks, can assist practitioners to undertake critical re-visiting of the ideological and theoretical claims of their practice through a conscious re-visiting of the connections (or lack thereof) between their current practice and these ideas. For example, there is a need for better integration of programs, initiatives, and data-sharing programs.

Further, local development practitioners can make a conscious choice and commitment to adopt a "regional" approach to their practice. There are benefits of acting regionally as a pathway to enhance community resilience and prosperity. The recognition of the need to collaborate regionally is clear, but so is the difficulty in building the relationships to get there. For example, in practice, there is uncertainty on how to partner with larger communities and cities on issues of interdependence (including those that are environment- or identity-based types of interdependencies, requiring further recognition and attention). Appropriate resources, identified by local actors, are integral for business and other forms of development within a region and should be developed according to each region's needs. As we conclude in Chapter 9, success in rural regional development will require community and business leaders in rural regions who are willing to think boldly, to engage in coordinated and concerted planning efforts that identify and harness local assets, and to collaborate across sectors and levels of government to create and implement such plans in a way that advances well-being and innovation on multiple scales.

10.3.3 Implications for theory and future research

The research presented in this volume suggests several areas for reflection when considering theory and research. First, there is the need for further consideration of the ways in which new regionalism applies within rural settings – a challenge for new regionalist scholars that this book begins to address. Development that occurs in rural areas affects urban development, and vice versa, yet these relationships receive limited attention within urban-centric discourses on ideas such as learning and innovation systems. This urban focus may contribute to the gap between theory and practice we observed in our rural research settings and raises questions about if and how the emergent theoretical understandings of new regionalism may be modified to better suit rural regions in Canada and elsewhere. Appropriate modifications rely on systematic and critical empirical analysis, which is often missing within the Canadian context.

Positioning old and new regionalism as dichotomous approaches is also problematic since these modes of regionalism should be seen as partly overlapping phenomena. Zimmerbauer and Paasi (2013), for example, show the value of this latter approach in their study of resistance to rural–urban mergers under municipal amalgamations in Finland. As Christopherson et al. (2010) suggest, we found that new regions offer many possibilities not only for the creation of new political identities but also for new and alternative development discourses to be forged. However, new regions that are formed without connection to old ones can be ineffective and even damage social, cultural, and political capital (as in the example of forced municipal amalgamations). Territorial and historic place affiliations are often deep-rooted and can lead to conflicts within new regions and their affiliated institutions, if not taken into consideration. We have observed, at the same time, that new place-based identities can evolve over time. Individuals can and do hold multiple place-based identities, at both community and regional scales, and just as regional boundaries shift, place-based identities can change as well.

Our work also illustrates an increase in the variability of government and governance standards as one of the consequences of the diverse and changing regional development institutional landscape associated with new regionalism. This represents a potential challenge with new regionalism that may lead to more uneven development across provincial and national space. Similarly, a focus on economic development in the application of new regionalist ideas tends to direct policy support and program funds towards "winning" regions and exacerbates – rather than addresses – disparities, an initial focus of Canadian regional development policy. As others have observed, the more holistic approach to new regionalism suggested in this volume is rare in practice and plagued with considerable challenges within an era of neoliberal agendas and restructuring (Peterson et al., 2010).

The regional perspective offers an interesting way to reconsider and rebundle regional assets (Reimer & Markey, 2008). However, the benefits of acting regionally need to be better communicated to rural Canadian regions. There needs to be bridging of research with policy and practice. Regional development policy in Canada provides very limited channels between systematic research and regional or local policy-makers, however. Enhancing support for these kinds of interactions would strengthen our theorization while also facilitating the sharing of promising practices and adoption of these ideas to enhance policy and practice.

While the scarcity and uneven evidence of new regionalism in the Canadian contexts examined here might be taken, at one extreme, as dismissive of the relevance of this construction, we are mindful of the foundational values which inform many new regionalism perspectives. These values include support for local democracy, subsidiarity, self-determination and self-reliance, transparent governance, the freedom of assembly, including multi-community collaboration, the supportive and legitimate role of an activist liberal democratic state, the imperative for integrated analysis, design and implementation for social, cultural, environmental, economic and political sustainability, the human values of distributive welfare and social justice, and several others that are more often than not implicitly evident if not explicitly enunciated in the new regionalism. Such values are likely to support continued efforts for the evaluation and advancement of new regionalist approaches in spite of limited evidence for its implementation.

It is clear that further research is required, particularly in terms of revisiting the role and relevance of new regionalism in policy and scholarly and professional practice. Many practitioners are dynamic and willing to experiment. We need research to determine which communities are innovative, why, and what benefits, costs, and opportunities are a result of innovation and new approaches. More community-based projects are also required to explore the obstacles to regional approaches, and how to overcome these obstacles. We must also understand the critical role and interplay between senior governments and regionalist efforts at the sub-provincial level. Innovation must not be a catch-phrase to mask off-loading or cutting needed resources and supportive policy. Where are the boundaries of responsibility? A multi-sectoral and multi-actor approach to governance must inform how this question is answered, chief among which is a re-envisioned role for government to enable the diverse array of non-government actors who are involved in rural regional governance. Further investigation is also needed related to the evolving role of Indigenous governments, governance, and relationships with Canadian regional development, working with research guidelines and protocols that reflect Indigenous culture, history, and values in the production of such knowledge (Wilson, 2008).

Highlighting success stories and learning from policies from other jurisdictions will continue to be important. Additional research is also needed to follow up in other rural places, as well as urban areas in Canada. Specifically, there is a need for further research in the English literature on the MRC model in Québec. Further research is needed to get to the depths of rural regional development processes, going well beyond the formal practitioners to include civil society and informal initiatives (e.g., the voluntary sector, NGOs, and multiple other informal issue-based groupings).

Specific research questions include:

- With whom do community leaders engage?
- How do they get their information?
- What is the relative importance and impact of the various information providers?
- What are the networks currently used by regional and local policy-makers when informing themselves for policy decisions?
- What are the methods by which these networks communicate?
- How do regional and local policy-makers view the value of systematic research?

We suggest that research incorporate a capacity-building component, seeking to provide informants and participants with a full understanding of what is meant by the concepts being explored (in this case those related to new regionalism). A mixed method approach, using provincial and regional surveys as well as more in-depth qualitative methods (e.g., the case studies employed in this research), may be helpful in getting a more general picture of the state of regionalism in Canada's provinces and regions. A regular, large national survey focusing on communities, institutions, and organizations would be a tremendous opportunity, although challenging to resource and implement. An incremental approach could be to focus on single provinces, building on the research outlined in this volume to improve the approach(es) and prepare a larger scale national research effort.

Given the complexity and sprawling nature of new regionalist ideas, we also suggest support for multiple research designs and methodologies that identify and address the "necessary" questions for the foundational answers, and avoid the surfeit of "sufficient" research questions that can overwhelm a research project. This will require further definition and characterization of new regionalism if it is to be used as an organizing concept given its different varieties.

More information on "becoming a region" remains a fascinating research topic – with serious practical implications concerning the bottom-up capacity of regions to lobby and plan for their own sustainability and viability. Much is still to be learned about rural governance as well, including how to provide the appropriate checks and balances during governance and policy development. Finally, more attention is needed regarding ways and means of fostering transformative connections and solidarity of innovative regions and rural communities across our vast country.

10.4 Concluding thoughts

In examining the presence and applicability of new regionalist ideas in the current Canadian context, we have sought to contribute a uniquely Canadian perspective to the new regionalism literature. We have also demonstrated a gap between espoused regional development theory and theory in use in Canada, a gap that is particularly apparent in rural regions. Despite their contributions to Canadian economy and society rural areas continue to be largely left out of regional development program and policy design processes, and out of new regionalist scholarship. The longstanding but pressing need to address the "regional disparity disease" noted in the preface to this volume by Dr. Donald Savoie, founder of the Canadian Institute for Research on Regional Development, continues to exist. As he further suggests, the challenges of declining rural areas remain acute. Regional collaboration, planning, and actions offer a key approach to addressing these challenges, thus the potential of new regionalism warrants attention. Change is needed, including new perspectives, new policies and programs, and new capacity to think and act regionally.

Public policy pertaining to regional development in the country retains the practice of fashionable rhetoric with respectable theoretical lineage, including the use of core new regionalist concepts, but with few manifestations in practice. We see only incremental and uneven changes across the country that can be compared to the tenets of new regionalism. In alignment with the multi-faceted issues that regional development seeks to address, our results call for many rather than a single regional development solution. We further recognize that incrementalism is likely the most productive approach to evolving regional development policy and practice. Innovative and inspiring examples throughout the country may provide the seeds required for such incremental change to grow. Yet the cycle of change continues to occur more rapidly and building the capacity to co-construct knowledge, and plan and act collaboratively on that knowledge, is increasingly challenging while at the same time critical.

Finally, our approach and findings emphasize that regional development includes not only economic development, but also social, cultural, and environmental practices. More value must be placed on these practices, and resources provided to increase development capacity in each of these areas and, perhaps more importantly, for efforts that recognize and build on the necessary interconnections between these various aspects of development. This book has provided examples of regional planning on a variety of issues and topics across Canada, drawing from new regionalist principles and ideas. Nonetheless, there remains much more to be done as regional disparities, challenges, and opportunities continue to evolve along with our knowledge of ways in which regional development and various related actors can play a shared role in addressing them.

Note

1 Statistics Canada uses municipalities as census subdivisions. Those that are not part of a Census Metropolitan Areas CMA or Census Agglomerations (CAs) are assigned to one of five metropolitan influence zones (MIZ) categories (strong, moderate, weak, no metropolitan influenced zones, and territories outside CAs), determined according to the percentage of employed labour force that commutes to work in the core(s) of any CMA or CA, which is often related to distance from a CMA or CA (Statistics Canada, 2016).

References

Argyris, C., & Schön, D. (1974). *Theory in practice: Increasing professional effectiveness.* San Francisco, CA: Jossey-Bass Publishers.

Beer, A. & Lester, L. (2015). Institutional thickness and institutional effectiveness: Developing regional indices for policy and practice in Australia. *Regional Studies, Regional Science*, 2(1), 205–228.

Bollman, R. (2016). *Rural demography update 2016.* Presentation to the Rural Ontario Institute, Guelph, ON. Retrieved June 12, 2018 from www.ruralontarioinstitute.ca/file.aspx?id=26acac18-6d6e-4fc5-8be6-c16d326305fe.

Booth, A. & Muir, B. (2011). Environmental and land use planning approaches of Indigenous groups in Canada: An overview. *Journal of Environmental Policy and Planning*, 13(4), 421–442.

Breen, S. & Minnes, S. (2013). Water and watershed management: A regional development perspective. CRD Report 7. Retrieved from http://cdnregdev.ruralresilience.ca/wp-content/uploads/2014/12/Water_Watershed_Management-WP-CRD7.pdf.

Bristow, B. (2010). Resilient regions: Re-"place"ing regional competitiveness. *Cambridge Journal of Regions, Economy and Society*, 3(1), 153–167.

Canadian Rural Revitalization Foundation. (2015). *State of rural Canada 2015.* Retrieved March 12, 2018 from http://sorc.crrf.ca

Christopherson, S., Michie, J. & Tyler, P. (2010). Regional resilience: theoretical and empirical perspectives. *Cambridge Journal of Regions, Economy and Society*, 3(1),3–10.

Daniels, J. (2014). *The river multiple: Exploring identity and place in resource politics on the Gander River* (Master's thesis). Memorial University, St. John's, NL. Retrieved from http://ruralresilience.ca/wp-content/uploads/2015/02/Daniels-THE-RIVER-MULTIPLE-Final.pdf.

Douglas, D. & O'Keeffe, B. (2009). Rural development and the regional construct: A comparative analysis of the Newfoundland and Labrador and Ireland Contexts. In G. Baldacchino, R. Greenwood, & L. Felt (Eds.), *Remote control: Governance lessons for and from small, insular, and remote regions* (Chapter 4). St. John's, NL: ISER Books, Memorial University of Newfoundland.

Douglas, D.J.A. (1990). Rural community development and sustainability. In M. E. Gertler & H.R. Baker (Eds.), *Sustainable rural communities in Canada* (66–72). Saskatoon: Canadian Agriculture and Rural Restructuring Group.

Douglas, D.J.A. (2005). The restructuring of local government in rural regions: A rural development perspective. *Journal of Rural Studies*, 21(2), 231–246.

Douglas, D.J.A. (2017). Community resilience: Critical reflections from the Canadian rural development perspective. In L. Brinklow & R. Gibson (Eds.), *From black horses to white steeds: Building community resilience* (10–30). Charlottetown, PEI: Island Studies Press.

Federation of Canadian Municipalities (FCM). (2018). *Rural challenges, national opportunity: Shaping the future of rural Canada*. Ottawa: Federation of Canadian Municipalities.

Freshwater, D., Simms, A., & Vodden, K. (2011). Defining regions for building economic development capacity in Newfoundland and Labrador. Retrieved from www .mun.ca/harriscentre/reports/research/2011/DefiningRegionsEDCWeb.pdf.

Hall, H. & Gibson, R. (2016). *Rural proofing in Canada: An examination of the Rural Secretariat and the Rural Lens*. Prepared for the Parliamentary Rural Areas Committee, Sweden (p. 22). Guelph, Ontario: Swedish Agency for Growth Policy Analysis.

Hodge, G., Hall, H., & Robinson, I. (2016). *Planning Canadian regions*. Second Edition. Vancouver: UBC Press.

Jean, B. (2014). The voluntary and business sectors are the partners of local governance most appreciated in rural area. NRE[2] Insights Flyer 13, New Rural Economy Project, Concordia University. Retrieved from http://nre.concordia.ca/__ftp2004/in_si tes_flyers/NRE2_InSites_13_-_Bruno_Jean_1_(ENGLISH).PDF.

Jean, B. (2015). Regional policy in Quebec with a special stress on MRC of Rimouski-Neigette. Presented at the Canadian Rural Revitalization Foundation's Annual Conference, Guelph, Ontario. Video recording retrieved from http://cdnreg dev.ruralresilience.ca

Lockwood, M., Davidson, J., Curtis, A., Stratford, E., & Griffith, R. (2009). Multilevel environmental governance: lessons from Australian natural resource management. *Australian Geographer*, 40(2), 169–186.

Markey, S., Pierce, J., Vodden, K., & Roseland, M. (2005). *Second growth: Community economic development in rural and small town British Columbia*. Vancouver: UBC Press.

Minnes, S. (2013). Frontenac Arch Biosphere: A regional sustainability initiative. Retrieved from http://cdnregdev.ruralresilience.ca/wp-content/uploads/2014/11/ Vignettes_Frontenac_Arch_Biosphere_Final_2Nov2014.pdf.

Peterson, A., Walker, M., Maher, M., Hoverman, S., & Eberhard, R. (2010). New regionalism and planning for water quality improvement in the Great Barrier Reef, Australia. *Geographical Research*, 48(3), 297–313.

Reimer, B. & Brett, M. (2013). Scientific knowledge and rural policy: A long-distant relationship. *Sociologia Ruralis*, 53(2), 272–290.

Reimer, B. & Markey, S. (2008). *Place-based policy: A rural perspective*. Montreal: Concordia University. Retrieved from http://billreimer.ca/research/files/ReimerMarkeyRuralPlaceBasedPolicySummaryPaper20081107.pdf.

Savoie, D. (1992). *Regional economic development: Canada's search for solutions*. Toronto: University of Toronto Press.

Savoie, D. (2017). *Looking for bootstraps: Economic development in the maritimes*. Halifax, NS: Nimbus Publishing Limited.

Statistics Canada. (2016). Census of population. Retrieved June 12, 2018 from www .12.statcan.gc.ca/census-recensement/index-eng.cfm.

Tindal, C.R. & Tindal, S. (2009). *Local government in Canada*. Toronto: Nelson.

Vodden, K. (2009). Experiments in collaborative governance on Canada's coasts: Challenges and opportunities in governance capacity. In L. Felt, R. Greenwood & G. Baldacchino (Eds.), *Remote control: Lessons in governance from small places* (Chapter 13, 259–279). St. John's, NL: Institute of Social and Economic Research.

Vodden, K. (2015). The promise and challenge of collaborative governance on Canada's coasts. *Canadian Geographer*, 59(2), 167–180. Retrieved from http://onlinelibrary .wiley.com/doi/10.1111/cag.12135/epdf.

Wilson, S. (2008). *Research is ceremony: Indigenous research methods*. Halifax, NS: Fernwood Publishing.

Zimmerbauer, K. & Paasi, A. (2013). When old and new regionalism collide: Deinstitutionalization of regions and resistance identity in municipality amalgamations. *Journal of Rural Studies*, 30, 31–40.

Index

For Product Safety Concerns and Information please contact our EU
representative GPSR@taylorandfrancis.com Taylor & Francis Verlag GmbH,
Kaufingerstraße 24, 80331 München, Germany

Printed and bound by CPI Group (UK) Ltd, Croydon, CR0 4YY

02/05/2025

01859334-0001